Following Kohlberg

REVISIONS
A Series of Books on Ethics

General Editors
Stanley Hauerwas and Alasdair MacIntyre

Donald R.C. Reed

Following Kohlberg

Liberalism and the Practice of
Democratic Community

University of Notre Dame Press

Notre Dame, Indiana

Manufactured in the United States of America

Library of Congress Cataloging-in-Publication Data

Reed, Donald R.C.
    Following Kohlberg : liberalism and the practice of democratic
community / Donald R.C. Reed.
        p.   cm. — (Revisions)
    Includes bibliographical references and index.
    ISBN 0–268–02851–6 (cloth : alk. paper)
    1. Ethics.   2. Kohlberg, Lawrence, 1927–   .   3. Political
ethics.   4. Moral development.   5. Liberalism.   6. Democracy.
I. Title.   II. Series.
BJ55.R44   1997
170'.92—dc21   97–21491
                                                                CIP

∞ The paper used in this publication meets the minimum requirements
of the American National Standard for Information Sciences—Perma-
nence of Paper for Printed Library Materials, ANSI Z39.48-1984.

Moral advance consists not in adapting individual natures to the fixed realities of a moral universe, but in constantly reconstructing and recreating the world as the individuals evolve.

George Herbert Mead
"The Philosophical Basis of Ethics," 1908

To

Charlotte Collins Reed
Rock Jones
Beka Miles

and to
the late M. Francis Christie,
our Socrates, our Jeremiah

Contents

Preface

This is a revisionist introduction to Lawrence Kohlberg's research program. I argue that Kohlberg's psychological theory of moral stages has been wrongly taken to be the central or only component of the Kohlbergian project. The stage theory has received the most attention, but we cannot understand that theory adequately except in the context of Kohlberg's work in the construction and practice of democratic community. If I am right, most moral philosophers and psychologists have missed something crucial in Kohlberg's project.

In the first two chapters I describe what I believe was a basic incoherence between the two most important components of Kohlberg's project. One component was the psychological model of stages of moral development that Kohlberg constructed in his dissertation (Kohlberg, 1958) and refined during the 1960s and 1970s. The other component was the model of democratic community that informed Kohlberg's educational interventions in prisons and schools in the 1970s and 1980s. I argue that the psychological model presupposed a construal of morality in significant respects at odds with the construal of morality presupposed by the model of democratic community. But because critics of Kohlberg's project have focused almost exclusively on the psychological model, they have failed to recognize the extent to which Kohlberg might have been able to meet their criticisms. So in the third and fourth chapters I describe the stage model and the revisions Kohlberg and his colleagues made as they reviewed their own data and responded to critics. Then in the fifth chapter I summarize the basic rationale Kohlberg offered for the construal of morality that informed his stage model prior to and independently of his empirical research, and in the sixth I review Kohlberg's argument that his conception of mature moral reasoning is shown empirically to be adequate both as an adaptive cognitive schema and as a conception of morality or justice more narrowly.

Drawing the contrast in further detail, in the seventh and eighth chapters I describe what Kohlberg called "just community." I argue that he was led through his educational interventions toward a more community-centered conception and practice of justice than was compatible with the conception of justice that framed the psychological stage model. Finally, in the ninth and tenth chapters I discuss the so-called Kohlberg-Gilligan debate, arguing that Gilligan was never quite as critical as commonly supposed and that Kohlberg, through the just community work, was drawn to a conception of justice which Gilligan's work helped inform. In the end, Kohlberg and Gilligan agreed far more than most have believed, and yet Kohlberg never quite resolved the deep tension between the construals of morality informing his psychological and educational models. For this reason he was not able to offer adequate responses to critics without doing injury to one or the other component of his work. In the just-community model, I will suggest, lies much unexamined promise of the Kohlbergian project.

I wish to express appreciation for the generous support of my research provided by the Faculty Development Organization and the Faculty Research Fund Board at Wittenberg University. I wish also to express gratitude to the president, provost, and board of directors of Wittenberg for the 1995–96 sabbatical leave during which I completed revisions of this book.

Many individuals have contributed to my reassessment of the Kohlbergian project. Discussions with these few have been of special importance to me: Lyn Brown, Owen Flanagan, Jim Fowler, Ann Higgins, Dan Lapsley, Tom Lickona, Alasdair MacIntyre, Clark Power, Mark Tappan, and Sheldon White.

Several colleagues, friends, and former teachers have sustained me during my long reflections before and during the project of this book. In addition to those to whom I dedicate this book, these include Karen Abel, Paula Barker, John Churchill, Philip College, Darrel Colson, Andrew Dell'Olio, Ash Gobar, Stanley Hauerwas, Erin Purdy Hogan, Jim Huffman, Steve Johnson, Mike Jones, Alasdair MacIntyre, Jay McDaniel, Mike Morgan, Charles Scott, Tim Sedgwick, Tom Taylor, Henry Teloh, and Bob Welker. The unfailing help of Margaret Debuty in the Philosophy Department at Wittenberg has made many tasks easier and all more pleasant. Assistance of a different and especially valuable type was provided by Alasdair MacIntyre and Stanley Hauerwas. As editors they have been patient and generous, and though they are not responsible for my argument they have certainly helped me make it more accessible and direct. John McCudden, my editor at the University of Notre Dame Press, offered many suggestions and valuable advice, making the text more readable. Manoh Doe, my research assistant, did most of the tedious work on the index and added many entries she saw would be helpful to readers.

My parents, Fred and Evelyn Reed, have been quite simply wonderful. There are no words. My wife, Charlotte, and my sons, Slocomb and Caldwell, not only help me put things into perspective but make every day meaningful and worthwhile.

ONE

Introduction to the Kohlbergian Project

Four Moral Dilemmas

Lawrence Kohlberg thought that in moral reasoning lie the indices of moral maturity. Because of this, he was interested in how people reason about morally difficult situations. He argued that all people are moral philosophers and should be so interpreted by social scientists studying morality. As a psychologist, he studied morality in a way that focused on the universal features of the moral reasoning of individuals. In American psychology in the mid-1950s, when Kohlberg began his research, this was either naively old-fashioned or an idea ahead of its time. The "cognitive revolution" was still some years off.

Kohlberg posed to his subjects the following scenario:

The Heinz Dilemma

In Europe, a woman was near death from a special kind of cancer. There was one drug that doctors thought might save her. It was a form of radium that a druggist in the same town had recently discovered. The drug was expensive to make, but the druggist was charging ten times what the drug cost him to make. He paid $400 for the radium and charged $4,000 for a small dose of the drug. The sick woman's husband, Heinz, went to everyone he knew to borrow the money and tried every legal means, but he could only get together about $2,000, which is half what it cost. He told the druggist that his wife was dying, and asked him to sell it cheaper or let him pay later. But the druggist said, "No, I discovered the drug and I'm going to make money from it." So, having tried every legal means, Heinz gets desperate and considers breaking into the man's store to steal the drug for his wife. (Kohlberg, 1984, p. 640)

Would it be permissible morally—even though illegal—for Heinz to steal the drug in these circumstances? If stealing *would* be morally permissible in this case, does Heinz have a compelling duty to steal the drug? Would he have such a duty if the dying woman were not his wife? And so on.

The Heinz Dilemma is the most widely discussed of the standard eight Kohlbergian dilemmas. Kohlberg used moral dilemmas for a specific purpose. He wanted to elicit the moral reasoning of the people he and his colleagues interviewed in their research. His idea was that we can locate a person's progress in moral development in the underlying rationales she or he gives for her or his moral judgments, that is, in her or his moral philosophy. Moral maturity is indicated by the basic structure of the reasons people give in support of their moral judgments.

The Kohlbergian dilemmas have been central to Kohlbergian research methodology and assessment. I will therefore use moral dilemmas in presenting Kohlberg's theory. I add now, in brief form, three other dilemmas of my own invention. I will return to these and the Heinz Dilemma during my discussion in this book. I call these three the Needy Children Dilemma, the Disposable Hook-Up Dilemma, and the Elderly Parent Dilemma.

The Needy Children Dilemma

Beverly and Stephen married while Beverly was still a student at the local university. This was six years ago when they were twenty-one. Stephen was working in a nearby factory, and with Beverly's part-time job and some scrimping, the two of them managed their expenses and are now working at paying off Beverly's student loans and saving for a down payment on a house. Beverly is office manager in an accountant's office in their town. They have two girls, five and one years of age, and a boy, age three. Stephen's and Beverly's parents are supportive and help when they can.

Stephen and Beverly are Roman Catholic and live in the United States. Stephen thinks they should not have any more children of their own. He wants them to adopt if they want more children. There are too many children already who are needy. It is irresponsible, Stephen thinks, for them to have more children when they could help care for children who do not have families of their own. Beverly agrees that there are many children who need help. However, how could the two of them make much of a difference? In the United States alone, 26 percent of all children under six lived in poverty in

1992, a total of approximately 6 million children under six. This is the result of a rapid increase in childhood poverty over the previous twenty years, up from 3.4 million children under six in 1972 (*Child Poverty News & Issues*, Winter 1995, Vol. 5, No. 1; the poverty line in 1992 was an annual income of $14,335 for a four person family, $11,186 for a three person family, and $9,137 for a two person family). The Children's Defense Fund estimates that, according to data available as of June 1995, 2,699 babies are born into poverty in the United States every day, approximately 24.2 percent of all births. Their circumstances are dire. That is about 985,000 children born into poverty every year, approximately one in four. The problem is simply overwhelming.

Beverly does not want them to use birth control or to adopt. She wants to have a large family of her own, like the one she grew up in. Stephen thinks they should not have any more children of their own. He wants to do for at least one other child what his adoptive parents did for him.

The Disposable Hook-Up Dilemma

Reanna had been talking with Julie for a couple of weeks about "hooking up" with Brad. Reanna's suitemates thought Brad was cute, and they had only positive reports from his fraternity brothers about his attraction to Reanna. So when Julie saw Reanna and Brad talking at the fraternity party that weekend, she was pleased. The story Reanna told her the next day, though, bothered her a lot.

Apparently Brad had invited Reanna upstairs from the party to his room. Reanna went with him. She was just as interested in hooking up with Brad as he seemed to be in hooking up with her. Conversation gave way to touching and kissing, and one thing led to another. At some point, three of Brad's fraternity brothers burst into laughter in the closet. They had been there all along. Reanna withdrew in horror and saw that Brad was aware they had been there. They made no advance on Reanna. The brief conversation she heard before she got her shirt on and was out the door suggested that though Brad hadn't "finished," he would be allowed to pass to the final stage of his ordeal, since it was the brothers' fault he hadn't been able to finish.

Julie has seen this sort of thing happen before, and she thinks

Reanna should file formal charges of sexual harassment against Brad and his three friends. Reanna is angry, but mainly she is disillusioned and hurt.

The Elderly Parent Dilemma

Willard and Jerry have worked hard to hold their household together. Willard was laid off ten years ago as the manufacturing company for which he worked for eighteen years was cutting middle management. He had to start his career over, and he has not yet achieved either the salary or the supervisory authority he had as regional director of sales in the Southeastern United States. This has been a cause of considerable stress for the household. Willard feels betrayed and cheated. Jerry wonders sometimes whether Willard wouldn't be better off if he could identify someone to blame, even himself, but he can't. Jerry had started his own real estate business shortly after he and Willard finished school, and he has successfully built the agency to fourteen full and part-time agents and brokers. He had a lot of work during the time Willard was between jobs, but things have slowed since then. Still, he works most weekends and holidays.

There is now an additional strain. Willard's mother, Tarissa, who lives two hours away, is increasingly dependent on Willard. She and Willard's father, Warren, had saved enough money for a secure retirement, but they had not anticipated that the illness that led to Warren's death would drain their savings so much. Insurance covered most of the medical expenses, but not all, and then there were incidental expenses like hotel bills so Tarissa could be near the hospital where the specialists kept Warren for prolonged periods. Tarissa can afford to keep her small house, where Willard and his sister (no longer living) grew up, but if she keeps it she cannot afford to hire either a housekeeper or a nurse, and it looks increasingly like she cannot do without both.

Jerry and Tarissa have never gotten along. Having her move into their house would have been out of the question. But this was before Tarissa fell and broke her hip. If she does not move in with them, nursing care and housekeeping help are going to be necessary. Adequate private care, when added to the cost of maintaining her house, would cost more than would an assisted living arrangement in a facility in a neighboring suburb. But Tarissa simply refuses even to consider entering a "nursing home." She remembers how both her grandmother and her mother withered away in such cramped, smelly places.

In each of these four situations, the people involved are at an impasse. It is not clear what they should do. There is no consensus among the people in any of the situations about what should happen next, and most of the individuals in these situations are themselves conflicted about what they should do.

Heinz can think of reasons for and against stealing the drug, since though he cannot be sure the drug will save his wife's life, even temporarily, he cannot think of anything else to do. Heinz feels the druggist is being stingy and unreasonable, especially in the circumstances, but the druggist is not responsible for the condition in which his wife finds herself.

Beverly and Stephen are deeply committed to conflicting family plans. However, each is also committed to each other and to their marriage too much to insist the other's plans not be honored in some way. Stephen thinks they should help care for needy children already born and suffering. However, Beverly cannot believe she has a duty to make what she regards as the very large sacrifice involved in adopting a child when it will make such a small contribution to solving the overwhelming need in the world.

Reanna wants Brad to acknowledge the wrong in the way he treated her as a mere thing to be used in his own game. She is hurt and embarrassed, though, and does not want to drag it out. Julie knows all too well the hardships that come with accusing someone of sexual harassment, but she also knows that unless men are substantially discouraged from treating women as disposable objects, too much in the culture of the United States encourages them to continue. She also, with and for Reanna, just wants this to be past.

Jerry resents the way Tarissa has always treated him as an incidental and eliminable part of Willard's life, but he thinks Willard might be better off if she moved in with them. Willard doesn't know how well he can deal with the strain this would add to the household, but he can't think of a better option that would be fair to his mother. Tarissa realizes moving in with Willard and Jerry would be difficult for them all, but she doesn't think she can afford any other possibility she can imagine as acceptable, and she does not want to be a financial burden to Willard, only increasing his anxiety about his frustrated career.

Scholars commonly identify Kohlberg with his theory about how our reasoning concerning such situations develops over the course of our lives. In his dissertation at the University of Chicago, Kohlberg (1958) formulated an account of six stages of development through which the moral reasoning of all humans moves, regardless of culture, from childhood to maturity. He identified the stages as six distinct ways of thinking about what morality requires when people are faced with problematic dilemmas, six distinct moral philosophies. Kohlberg devoted much of his thirty-year career to refining and corroborating the revolutionary findings of his initial research.

Kohlberg's stage theory gained prominence in the 1970s and was described in many textbooks in developmental psychology as the best or even the only credible account of moral development. In the 1980s, however, his theory lost much of its support among academic psychologists and social scientists generally. It also came under increasingly harsh criticism among academic philosophers. Many believed it had gone the way of other displaced scientific paradigms. It had had its day. It was no longer scientifically or philosophically viable.

My Revisionist Account

I wrote my dissertation (Reed, 1986) under the impression these critics were right. I focused on Kohlberg's notion of Socratic dialogue as a method of moral education, and I looked specifically at his preference for the teaching method of Socrates in Plato's *Meno* and other earlier dialogues as opposed to the educational recommendations of Socrates in Plato's *Republic*. I argued that Plato meant to show us something Kohlberg hadn't recognized about the inadequacy of Socratic dialectic. But as I looked more into Kohlberg's own educational interventions, I changed my mind. Kohlberg had in fact recognized what Plato meant to show about the importance of the social and political character of education. He simply had not acknowledged— perhaps because there were impediments to full acknowledgment or perhaps because he did not himself appreciate—what this recognition entailed for his understanding of moral development. He had not acknowledged the way his own work mirrored the move Plato himself made from the early dialogues to the *Republic*.

I write this book in order to tell a revisionist story. It is revisionist on two counts. First, I offer a revision of the common understanding of the development of Kohlberg's research program, the understanding I myself held. Second, I suggest revisions of our interpretation of what the overall project was really about and so of how it should be developed more fully.

I can state the four principal themes of my revisionist story as follows: (1) By the time the best known and apparently most damaging criticisms of the Kohlbergian project were formulated and published in the late 1970s and early 1980s, they no longer addressed the central tenets of the project. The project had changed. However, (2) Kohlberg never pointed this out in response to his critics because he never quite realized it himself. (3) He gave a great deal of his time and attention from 1968 to the end of his life to a democratic reform project that was never addressed by his best known critics. This project of reforming the practice of democratic community offered the greatest promise for accomplishing the aim of his larger project—to conceive and do justice in a socially pluralist way that would nonetheless show the Holocaust of World War II to have been ahistorically, cross-culturally immoral. However, (4) Kohlberg continued to understand the aims of his larger project in the idiom of what I will call his structural stage model of moral development. This was the theoretical component of his project most famously challenged by his critics. Yet those aims would have been better formulated in the idiom of the program of democratic reform on which he spent over half his professional career. This I will call, following Kohlberg, the just community model of moral education. It is a model for education conceived as an integral part of the practice of democratic community in a pluralist and intercultural society.

How could Kohlberg have failed to recognize where the promise of his work lay? Let me suggest in a preliminary way two parts to an explanation concerning the second theme. First, Kohlberg was personally intent on moving his larger project forward on multiple fronts—data collection and scoring revisions, prison reform and school reform beginning in the 1970s, philosophical and cosmological reflection about a hypothetical Stage 7, etc. He was also intent on incorporating critics into work on his project, into the discussions and debates of his research team, to which he personally invited them. In fact, he was more intent on incorporating critics and expanding the scope of his larger project than he was on maintaining conceptual coherence among the various theoretical components of the larger project. Vibrant tensions kept him and his research team constantly on the move. Kohlberg was not inattentive to the conceptual coherence of the project as a whole, but that was not his primary commitment. Personally, professionally, and theoretically, tidiness was simply not Kohlberg's number one priority. One colleague reflected that if you sent to central casting for a disheveled, absentminded professor, they would send Larry Kohlberg. Perhaps he thought overall conceptual coherence could wait or that things would eventually fall into place. Kohlberg's first priority, bar none, was to expand the scope of his project of conceiving and doing justice.

The second part of this explanation is related to the first. In January 1972 Kohlberg contracted *Giardia lamblia* on a trip to Central America to collect cross-cultural research data (see Higgins, 1991a, p. 36; Schkolnick, 1992, p. 24). On that trip, Kohlberg did not take adequate precautions to sterilize his drinking water. He also neglected to get timely medical attention, and somehow the protozoa lodged permanently in his intestines. The medications he took to fend off their attacks left him nauseous and feverish and out of sorts, sometimes disoriented and even subject to occasional hallucination. His psychological coherence was sometimes episodic, and there was simply too much to be done during those more or less extended episodes. He never quite pulled everything together conceptually. Other things were just more important to him, until nothing seemed to be important enough.

I refer intentionally to "the Kohlbergian project" rather than to the stage theory typically identified as that project. Kohlberg was in the early 1970s taking his work into prison and school reform programs in ways that would require a more variegated moral psychology than many of his critics would ever appreciate. I want to suggest that Kohlberg himself may never have fully appreciated it either. He continued to defend the structural stage model of moral development on more or less the understanding of it that his critics challenged. He maintained the various components of the project as if they were equally integral. The reason, I suggest, is that Kohlberg himself failed to appreciate the ways in which his work on the practice of democratic community had begun to move beyond the inadequacies of the psychological theory informing the structural stage model of moral development, inadequacies his critics had identified (theme 4). Kohlberg came to an impasse between the structural stage model and the just community model and, I will suggest, never quite resolved it.

In short, then, I tell a story of the development of Kohlberg's project on which Kohlberg's critics have been mostly correct. And yet on my story their success is quite limited. For they have succeeded in limiting the scope of a component of the theoretical apparatus of the project which itself had become more or less inessential to the development of the larger project. The structural stage model continued to attract most of the attention, and it provided Kohlberg the reputation on the basis of which he drew graduate students and postdoctoral assistants and obtained grant money for running his democratic reform projects in the 1970s and 1980s. But except for the fact that many Kohlbergians, including Kohlberg himself apparently, seemed to think the success of the larger project continued to depend on the success of the structural stage model, the stage theory had become more a distraction than anything else.

Plato and Kohlberg

I bring Plato into the story in order to make what will perhaps seem a rather odd suggestion, that following Kohlberg's early development, which is similar to Plato's in two crucial respects, will shed revealing light on the project to which Kohlberg drew such a following, international in scope, and will also help us see how he might himself have envisioned the advancement of his project following the anomaly-ridden troubles of the structural stage model. And *this* would have us following Kohlberg with Plato toward a conception of the social construction of justice. Kohlberg devoted much of his career to advancing a conception of moral development as individual rational [re]construction of principles of justice. Also, however, he developed a conception of the social construction of justice through the practice of democratic community. Plato had come to a nondemocratic version of an account of just community in much the same circumstances as had Kohlberg.

During his career, Kohlberg challenged the moral relativism of the positivist social science of his day and recommended democratic approaches to issues of social justice precisely because, from his own point of view, these two elements—nonrelativism and democracy— were required for an adequate response to Nazism. Kohlberg encountered the effects of Nazism firsthand. As an eighteen-year-old he served in the United States Merchant Marine in Europe in World War II. As a nineteen-year-old he put his new skills to use as a second engineer on the *Paducah,* an old Navy icebreaker used by the Jewish defense force in smuggling Jewish refugees from Europe through the British blockade into Palestine (Kohlberg, 1948).

By the completion of his dissertation at the University of Chicago in 1958, Kohlberg had in all essentials already formulated his theory of an invariant sequence of six cross-culturally universal developmental stages of moral (justice) reasoning. This theory was a deliberate response to the injustices he had encountered before college in the 1940s (Kohlberg, 1991; 1981, p. 407). Thus, the most important influences on Kohlberg, with respect to the formulation of his project, had already occurred by the time he was thirty-one. Much the same is true of Plato.

Plato was born shortly after the beginning of the Peloponnesian War. This war tore apart the tenuous union of independent Greek city-states forged against the attempted invasions of the Persian Empire just years earlier. The war pitted mainly Athens-sympathizing democrats against mainly Sparta-sympathizing oligarchs or aristocrats. When Plato was eleven, the Athenians slaughtered the people of a small Aegean island, Melos, who had refused to give up neutrality in the war. In his late teens and early twenties he witnessed the gradual, impoverishing defeat of democratic Athens. The disgrace was deepened when he was twenty-three, with the overthrow of the democrats and institution of a ruling council of thirty oligarchs, referred to by the democrats as the "thirty tyrants." And, most famously, at twenty-eight Plato was a spectator at the civic drama surrounding the legal execution of Socrates by the reimposed democrats. Socrates was brought to court on charges that he had corrupted the youth and introduced false deities. It had not escaped the notice of many that these were trumped-up charges aimed at silencing this philosophical gadfly who was believed by some to have oligarchic, perhaps even Spartan, sympathies. Plato experienced firsthand the misjudgment and injustice of which democratic regimes are capable.

Son of a well connected, well-to-do Athenian family, Plato may have trained to be a tragic poet. He turned instead to philosophical drama, devoting himself to examining the good and the real. The theme that runs through his work more than any other is the question whether genuine knowledge of the good and the real is possible, rather than only opinion and supposition. His principal concern in this regard, beyond exposing the faults of conventional opinion and conventional virtue, was to examine critically the best arguments available for defense of relativism about the good and the real. If arguments for relativism were sustainable, then so were defenses of the slaughter of the Melians and the execution of Socrates. For the young Kohlberg, the defenses that had to be found lacking were offered by Nazi war criminals at Nuremberg.

Historical Overview of the Project

Kohlberg constructed his project, quite self-consciously, to be politically and personally meaningful (Kohlberg, 1991; see also Kohlberg, 1981, p. 407). In the formulation of his project he aimed at addressing the possibilities of evil made actual in Nazi tyranny—a tyranny the effects of which he had experienced between boarding school and college. Kohlberg's first published article was a narrative of this experience on the *Paducah*, published in 1948 in the *Menorah Journal* (Kohlberg, 1948). He titled it "Beds for Bananas." This was the headline that had appeared in a local port-city French newspaper after the paper's reporters had quizzed the *Paducah* crew about the wooden shelves that lined the cargo area of the ship. The crew had claimed they were hauling bananas. The newspaper story claimed they were smuggling Jews. There was little doubt that this was just what they were doing. Someone at an earlier port had asked about the disproportionate number of Jewish crew members.

Kohlberg's project had to enable him to articulate and go about changing what he found to be ahistorically, cross-culturally immoral in the Holocaust. Kant, whom Kohlberg read as an undergraduate in the Hutchins college at the University of Chicago, seemed to provide the frame for just such a meaningful project. He found Kant stating the underlying principle of what seemed to him so plausible in the competing theories of universal human rights advanced by Locke, Jefferson, and J. S. Mill (Kohlberg, 1991, p. 13). As a graduate student formulating his theory of moral development, he drew on psychologists already committed to Kantian formalism in ethics (especially Baldwin and Piaget), and as he proceeded to work through his project he found invigorating support for that Kantianism in contemporary (1950–70s) analytic moral philosophy (see Kohlberg, 1981, e.g., pp. 94, 159, 191; and Kohlberg, 1984, pp. 274–317, esp. p. 277).

While Kohlberg constructed his project at first within the professional domain of academic psychology, this was simply the avenue he chose for initiating the project. He chose to pursue graduate studies in clinical psychology rather than law—both of which he regarded as professions enabling him to help people—after a summer working as an attendant in a mental hospital. After an unsettling experience during a two-year clinical psychology internship, also in a mental hospital (Kohlberg, 1991, p. 13f), he chose to shift to social psychology and to do his dissertation research on the moral reasoning of children. In the hospital episode, a patient being treated for paranoia appealed to him against the professional staff, which she said was intent on persecuting her. The chief psychiatrist overheard her complaints and prescribed electric shock therapy. When Kohlberg protested to the staff, noting that electric shock therapy could only confirm the patient's paranoia, he was rebuffed and the treatment was administered.

Furthermore, during the first ten years of theory elaboration and empirical substantiation of the research program begun in the dissertation, the practical implications of his theory became more and more clear, e.g., in the research of his students, especially the research of Turiel (1966), Rest (1968), and Blatt (1969). The next frontier was the school itself. Advancing the project, he moved in 1968 from the psychology department at Chicago (where he had been since 1962) to the Graduate School of Education at Harvard. And in 1971, 1974, and 1978, he began pilot programs of moral education in the Niantic Prison in Connecticut, the Cluster School within the Rindge and Latin High School in Cambridge, Massachusetts, and the Scarsdale Alternative School in Scarsdale, New York.

Sheldon White, a colleague of Kohlberg's at both Chicago and Harvard, has suggested that Kohlberg believed his theory was simply misunderstood by his critics (White, 1991). Kohlberg had remarked that he would show them what he meant by doing what Dewey did, by putting his theory into practice in the schools themselves. He made a transition from Socratic dialogue to the social construction of justice, as Plato himself had done. Kohlberg had a project to advance, and if this required him to engage in metaethical debate with moral philosophers or methodological debate with developmental psychologists or pedagogical and political debate with teacher educators and school administrators, so be it. Indeed, he engaged in discussions of all these and other types as well—academic disciplinary boundaries to the contrary notwithstanding.

This is where matters become complex. For there is a fundamental tension in the project as a whole, in spite of the fact that Kohlberg may initially have believed that the work in the schools simply put into practice what he had articulated in the stage theoretical model. I have suggested that the project had changed by the late 1970s (theme 1) and that the structural stage model had become more or less inessential to the development of the larger project. It had become inessential for the following reason. The Piagetian structural stage model of moral development and the neo-Kantian metaethical assumptions orienting it are in basic tension with the other primary element of the project: the just community model of moral education in the schools, a model informed by G. H. Mead's social psychology and by Deweyan educational theory and practice, by the kibbutz ideal of social justice, and by Durkheimian sociomoral assumptions (see, e.g., Kohlberg, 1978, p. 85; Kohlberg, 1980, p. 42; Reimer, 1981, p. 486; Power, 1988a, p. 173; Power, 1988b, p. 198; Kohlberg, 1985; Kohlberg and Higgins, 1987; Power, Higgins, and Kohlberg, 1989, chap. 2; Higgins, 1991b, p. 117). It is in this tension between the two primary models that we can locate *both* the reasons why Kohlberg's project faltered *and* the features of the project which can be carried beyond the anomaly-ridden problems of the structural stage model. Let me state a related thesis before pursuing this matter further.

There is an incongruence in the true tale yet to be told about Kohlberg, related I think to the incoherence I've just suggested. On the one hand, Kohlberg's colleagues, family, and friends express warm regard for him as a caring person, strongly committed to their individual needs and well-being and firmly embedded in close personal and collegial attachments with him (see Fowler, Snarey, and DeNicola, 1988; Rest, 1988; and Kuhmerker, 1991; but see Schkolnick, 1992, for a less memorializing treatment of Kohlberg's character). On the other hand, his account of morality or justice has been criticized for its impartiality and impersonality and for the infamous disconnection and separation it presupposes (Gilligan, 1982). I suggest that the best explanation for this incongruence is that Kohlberg's notion of morality (justice) was never intended to account for the character of his relations with colleagues, family, and friends. It was rather intended to account for the conditions required to protect those relationships and the individuals involved in them from injury or destruction *from the outside*. That is, Kohlberg intended his conception of justice to account for what is ahistorically, cross-culturally wrong in Nazi genocide and every other project of less radical violation of human dignity. Fundamental injustice obliterates people. The maintenance of nonrelative morality provides the conditions for the possibility of relationships of attachment, Kohlberg would suggest (Kohlberg, Levine, and Hewer, 1983). An ethic of care presupposes an ethic of justice, since only the latter assures the possibility of the former. Assuring that possibility against what he experienced as an eighteen- to twenty-year-old, insuring it in both theory and practice—insuring it against both relativism and the authoritarianism for which relativism seems to make room—this task occupied and, to the detriment of his own health, preoccupied the smuggler of refugees to his final days.

Perhaps it is this occupation with the universal, cross-culturally nonrelative nature of cruelty and murderous assault on human dignity that accounts for Kohlberg's captivity to Kantian formalism. Perhaps he failed to recognize that Kantian ethics is no less an expression of a particular historical culture than is, say, Jewish Law. One of the striking features of the Enlightenment culture we inherit from Kant and his predecessors is the conviction that we can give a fully intelligible and yet culturally neutral account of our basic commitments as a people or peoples. That it would be unintelligible to us how any culture or tradition-constituted community could *not* hold these basic commitments (say, to maximizing liberty and opportunities for re-nouncing authority) turns out to be less interestingly a fact about them than it is about us—a fact about what things are intelligible *to us* as inheritors of the Enlightenment. We can locate the primary limi-tation of Kohlberg's project in this formalism, in the particular shape given to it by Kant and the contemporary voices of the Kantian tra-dition in moral theory on which Kohlberg drew. And of course it is to just this formalism that a good deal of recent feminist criticism of Kohlberg is directed (see, e.g., Kittay and Meyers, 1987).

The incoherence that I have suggested lies in the project as a whole can be found in the theoretical resources on which Kohlberg initially drew in formulating his project. Kohlberg spent a year as a graduate student at Chicago (during the second of the internships I mentioned) reading and deliberating over the form his project should take before beginning the interview research that would serve as the empirical basis of his dissertation. In his review of the literature on moral de-velopment in the second chapter of his dissertation (Kohlberg, 1958), he discussed utilitarians such as Hume, Adam Smith, and Sidgwick, as well as the antiutilitarian, antimoralist Nietzsche. He also devoted a section to Durkheim and one to George Herbert Mead. The final three sections of the second chapter were devoted to Baldwin and Piaget. Durkheim, Mead, Baldwin, and Piaget seem to occupy a con-tinuum on Kohlberg's (1958) account, from less to more able to ac-count for the universal and formal character of moral judgments. Kohlberg portrayed Mead as a middle figure who took Kantian in-sight too far in the direction of Durkheim. "It becomes very difficult to isolate any characteristics of morality in Mead which really differ-entiate morality from problem-solving uses of social intelligence. . . . His clearest effort to deal with the motivational side of morality is contained in his article on 'The Psychology of Punitive Justice,' of 1918, an article which seems related to both Freudian and Durkhe-imian views" (Kohlberg, 1958, pp. 46–47). Baldwin and Piaget clearly set the frame for the structural stage model of moral develop-ment. Yet it is to Durkheim and Mead that Kohlberg returned in his endeavors to formulate the just community model of prison and school intervention.

In the Kohlbergian project as a whole, this is the basic tension: the structural stage model on the one hand and the just community model on the other. The tension is, roughly stated, between a liberal notion of justice or right and a communitarian notion of the practice of community (Power, Higgins, and Kohlberg, 1989, esp. pp. 48, 62; see also Sullivan, 1986). I explore this tension in the following chapter by outlining two very different construals of morality.

Two Construals of Morality

A Schematic Dichotomy

I shall explain more clearly what I mean by the tension between the liberal and communitarian features of Kohlberg's project. This will help me illustrate the way in which we can see the just community model as an *alternative* to the structural stage model, such that the latter is inessential to the development of the former. I summarize in table 2.1 (page 18) two ethics, two models of morality. This summary is schematic. I mean it to be ambiguous as between several different dichotomies. For example, one might read this summary as typifying the difference between a masculine ethic of rights and a feminine ethic of relationships, but one might also take it to typify the difference between a liberal individualist political ethic and a communitarian political ethic, both of which might be considered androcentric in light of the feminist critiques of the Kohlbergian project (see Friedman, 1987). But there is more. One might alternatively take the summary to typify the differences between a predominantly urban and a predominantly rural ethic, or between the ethos of commerce and that of the professions, or between the decadent present and the good old days, or between the secular and the ecclesial, or between political relations and domestic relations.

I don't believe the overlap of these different dichotomies schematically described is an accident, and there are clues here about the cultural origins of both of the "voices" Gilligan and her colleagues have so tellingly described (Gilligan, 1982; Gilligan, Ward, and Taylor, 1988). But I will focus here on the version of the summary in table 2.1 that typifies two political ethics, one liberal individualist and the other communitarian. This I think is the way Kohlberg would have approached the matter. He read Plato's *Republic* as communitarian and thus, he thought, as suggesting an indoctrinative, cultural-transmission model of moral education embodying a commitment to a "bag of virtues" conception of morality. His structural stage model was articulated in explicit contrast to this, not in contrast to Gilligan's "dif-

Table 2.1

ETHIC OF RIGHTS (Competition)	ETHIC OF GOODS (Cooperation)
Rule-Based Rights-Centered Hierarchies of Rules Ultimate Principle	Relationship-Based Goods-Centered Hierarchy of Ends Highest Good

Morality keeps us from destroying each other as we each pursue our own self-interest; it's a *necessary frustration* of our natural inclinations, which are selfish.	Morality is a *guide* to follow as we seek to live the best life we can, and coming to enjoy being moral is a crucial part of having the best life we can have; the moral life is the life of happiness.
Humans have to live in community to survive, yet social cooperation is unnatural because it imposes restrictions on the personal pursuit of happiness and satisfaction. *Separation,* not connection, is natural.	Humans are naturally familial and social beings, desiring the company and cooperation of others as essential to their happiness. Socialization is part of natural human development. *Connection,* not separation, is natural.
The principal part of an explanation of what is ethical in general or in a specific case is an account of which rules specify appropriate conduct.	The principal part of an explanation of what is ethical in general or in a specific case is an account of what *goods* are furthered by our conduct, dispositions, and perceptions.
Goods are those desired things and/or activities which we desire independently of whatever rules bind us BUT which may motivate EITHER violation OR compliance with binding rules. (The focus tends to be on individual quandaries about action.)	*Rules* specify means or boundaries on means to the good; they define relationships of community members in the type of social life required for pursuit of the good. (There is no obvious need for rules that are universal in scope.)
The *penalty* for violating rules of conduct or for otherwise rendering social life less efficient and productive is, if you don't get caught, *nothing.*	The *penalty* for violating rules of conduct or for otherwise rendering social life less efficient and productive is *failure and frustration* in one's activities and life as a whole, whether or not one gets caught.
APPARENTLY, there are very different conceptions of the rules that bind human conduct.	APPARENTLY, there are very different conceptions of the highest or ultimate good and so also of appropriate constituent and/or instrumental goods.
YET, surely every person recognizes the immorality of cruelty to the innocent and helpless and of willful and gratuitous betrayal of sincere trust.	YET, surely we all desire pleasure, esteem (honor), certain types of knowledge, a modicum of wealth, and friends and companions.

ferent voice." He regarded her apparent embrace of a version of relativism as a rejection of ethics rather than as an alternative ethic.

I turn now to a description of two rival ways of thinking about and
living out morality. The description is—let me say it again—highly
schematic. I describe thin ideal types, not thick, particular social realities. Still, such a description will help make sense of my claim that
Kohlberg might have come to see the just community model of moral
education as an *alternative* to the structural stage model of moral development. I am not finally satisfied with the dichotomous structure
of the following contrast. On the one hand, there are other options
than these two, though I will not explore any in detail here. On the
other hand, I will myself later describe a kind of synthesis toward
which I believe Kohlberg's work may have been moving. However, if
he ever himself envisioned an overcoming of the liberal individual-
ist-communitarian dichotomy in these terms, he never said so. Since
Kohlberg himself at least initially held that liberal individualism and
communitarianism are incompatible, I will for the moment treat them
as such.

A Rule-based Ethic of Rights

On one way of thinking about and living out morality (see MacIntyre,
1979), living morally is construed primarily as living according to
certain rules or principles. To be moral is to follow certain rules, to
stay within their bounds. A particular notion of human nature, a particular anthropology, underwrites this construal. According to this
ethic, humans are naturally self-interested and so are by nature at
odds with each other over the allocation of desired resources like food,
shelter, prestige in the group, and so on. For we cannot all have as
much of such goods as we would like. Typically, though not necessarily, we do not possess food in unlimited supply. Some edibles are
more scarce than others, and some of the scarce ones are both nutri-
tious and tasty. These are typically the foods over which we have to
compete, say, on the hunt or at the market. Prestige, by contrast, is
necessarily limited. We cannot all have high prestige in the group,
because prestige by its nature is a matter of distinction among persons. With respect to food and prestige, and other goods as well, of

course, there is simply not enough to go around if everyone gets as much as they want.

Therefore, laws of some sort are required as a framework for peaceful coexistence. A community articulates and reflectively reconstructs laws or rules of morality in its educational and cultural activities. In so doing, a community specifies what is and what is not appropriate in its particular circumstances, in the competition for limited resources. Regardless of our circumstances, if we are to coexist peacefully and yet be in competition for the best kinds of food, say, we must not kill each other, must not steal from each other, must not break legally binding agreements or contracts. We must not break good-faith agreements, lie, refuse reasonable requests for help. Also, there are some things that we in our particular circumstances must not do that others might do in their different circumstances, depending on what meanings actions have in different cultures or meaning systems. North Americans typically experience beating a disobedient wife as wrong, whereas Hindu Brahmans do not. Brahmans typically experience outrage at sons who soon after the death of their fathers get haircuts and trim their fingernails (Shweder, Mahapatra, and Miller, 1987), whereas North Americans typically do not. In different meaning systems, very different things may count as harm and as doing harm.

Generally speaking, peaceful competition requires a certain amount of agreement and mutual trust. *Caveat emptor,* but a deal's a deal. Never judge a book by its cover, but if you can't trust your doctor, who can you trust? And so on. In the case of some violations of minimal mutual trust, we are disappointed in the offending parties. They have let us down. With some, we feel the right to seek redress. We want our money back, or we sue for damages in product liability cases. With still others, we are drawn into rebellion, foment revolution. When arbitrary discrimination is systematic and malignant, or when economic oppression quite simply strangles, bringing suit before the powers that be may not in some highly specific circumstances be enough. We have to treat each other with at least minimal kinds of respect if we are to coexist peacefully. Morality, on this way of construing it, is what defines the minimum.

Morality also thereby performs a judicial function. The laws that define what peacefully competitive coexistence requires provide us with standards for appeal when we think we have not been or are not being treated appropriately, fittingly. They enable us to make legitimate claims to things or against others—claiming what we call "rights." To have a right is to have a legitimate (*legitimus:* lawful) claim, a claim that should get a hearing and be honored before the law as an institution of the community. If I say I have a right to life, I am saying either that I have a legitimate or legally defensible claim to be kept alive or that I have a legitimate or legally defensible claim against anyone who wants to have me killed. The concept of a right is therefore secondary to that of a law because rights are explained in terms of laws. Constitutional rights are a clear example. I have a right to free speech, say, because the first amendment to the U.S. Constitution grants it to me. Indeed, one of the principal things to which people typically claim to have a right, on this way of thinking about morality, is liberty—liberty from harmful interference or injury, liberty of thought and of speech, and so on.

Some rights, however, are held to be *natural.* That is, they are held to be legitimate claims independent of any particular legal system. When the United Nations issued its declaration on human rights in 1949, it meant to make claims about how all people everywhere, under any legal system whatever, ought to be treated. My right to life, say, obtains on this view even if I happen to be under the jurisdiction of a legal system in which execution of U.S. citizens is regarded appropriate for no other reason than that citizens of the U.S. are thought to be instruments of Satan. So if my right not to be killed is a natural right, it obtains even though no properly enacted law exists—within the jurisdiction I inhabit at the moment—to which I can appeal in legitimating my claim not to be killed.

(This makes a difference, of course, primarily only if one's would-be executioners are willing to listen to arguments about one's natural rights. Analogously, if a slave appeals to his or her master's own conception of natural rights in defense of a claim to be granted liberty, the slave will get somewhere only if the master regards him or her as a bearer of natural rights, say, as fully human.)

Since the concept of a right is secondary to, derivative from, the concept of a law, those who claim that there are natural rights are committed to holding that there is some sort of natural law (or to explaining how rights originate without being in any sense legislated).

The laws or rules of morality are taken to be natural in the sense that they need not have been enacted by some specific group of consenting legislators to be valid. On the way of thinking about morality that I am now describing, every person is equal before the laws or rules of morality (though every member of the species may not be counted a person). Equality before the law is claimed a natural right, on the notion that treating like cases alike is required by natural law. No one is above the law, and no one has special privileges. The right to liberty is also often held to be a natural right.

This is not only a way of thinking about morality. It is also a way of living it out. Political debate in this type of life often turns on conceptions of what rights are possessed by whom and on how rules of law and of morality are to be interpreted. So, for example, in political debate people oppose the right to liberty from (excessive) taxation to the right to minimally decent living conditions and to equality of access to basic human goods such as food, clothing, and shelter. A, perhaps *the,* crucial device of this way of life is the contract—the binding agreement into which separate individuals, not previously bound to one another, may enter if they freely choose. Thus, the sorts of institution that typify and are characteristic of this type of morality are law courts, legislatures, and legally regulated markets, sometimes including markets designed for the trade not only of products or of labor but also of money and financial instruments themselves (currencies, stocks, precious metals). A principal goal of the moral upbringing of children in this way of life is the development of moral autonomy and of respect for individual freedom and dignity, since these facilitate individual pursuit of self-interest in peaceful, competitive coexistence.

Think about how Heinz's situation is to be understood on this way of construing morality. The problem Heinz finds himself confronting, on this construal, is one of conflicting rights. The druggist has a right to sell the products of his labors at a price he thinks appropriate. He invested in and worked to develop his skills as a medicinal chemist. He invested in the attempt to develop a cure for this special type of cancer, and it paid off. Everything he has (let us assume), including his knowledge and skill, he has legitimately. He has a legitimate expectation that he should be able to benefit from risks and investments on which he made good. On the other hand, Heinz's wife has cancer from no fault of her own (let us assume). Heinz (as stipulated in

Kohlberg's formulation of the dilemma) has done everything legally within his power to secure adequate resources to pay for the drug. Heinz and his wife have (let us assume) every grounds for expecting that if she does not receive this drug, she will die from this disease much sooner and perhaps more painfully than she would have otherwise. She has a right to life. The druggist has a right to his property and to realize a gain on his successful investments. Heinz is bound to honor both rights except when neither can be honored except at the expense of the other. So the question is: Which right trumps?

Think also about how Beverly and Stephen's situation is to be interpreted. On this way of construing morality, their situation is also a situation of conflicting rights. Stephen's contention is (on this construal) that children already born and suffering have more claim on their aid than do children not yet even conceived. Stephen need not contend that "future generations" never have a claim on us, say, on the notion that they are nonexistent. He might think, for example, that the rights of future generations require that we practice environmentally responsible means of production, consumption, and disposal. It would not be fair to future generations to leave them a devastated planet so that we can live as we please. Stephen might argue, however, that children presently suffering have more claim on his and Beverly's assistance than do children whom they can choose never to bring into existence. Those doing damage to the environment are simply not in a position to make this sort of comparison. They cannot say, "if we destroy the earth, there will be no future generations to hold claims against our destructive activities, so let's make hay while the sun shines." We have every reason to assume that there will be future generations if we do not destroy the earth first, whereas if Beverly and Stephen decide not to have any more children, they can see to it that they do not have any.

Beverly's contention, though (on this construal), is that the claims suffering children have on them cannot be thought to trump their own claim to have as many of their own children as they want. For look what this would entail. If the little that Stephen and Beverly have, relatively speaking, can go so long a way in helping the desperately needy in the world—if fifty dollars or fifteen dollars or five dollars a month can provide a starving, diseased child with minimally decent conditions for living—how can they really justify buying their own house or taking a vacation from the grind of their jobs and every-day lives? Indeed, how can they justify going to a restaurant or even preparing more than subsistence-level nutrition at home? In fact, how can they justify providing for themselves any more than minimally decent conditions for living? Beverly's contention is that Stephen's contention would entail taking a virtual vow of poverty and service. So how can the claims of needy children really trump their own claims to plan their family as they choose, provided that they make reasonable sacrifices in giving to agencies that aid the poor and needy? For Stephen's argument applies to everyone, not just to Beverly and Stephen. Surely, on Beverly's view (on this way of construing their situation), we cannot construe the claims of needy others in a way that requires everyone to take a virtual vow of poverty and service. That would be unreasonable. People have a right to plan their families as they see fit and to use the resources they legitimately acquire to that end, as long as they make reasonable sacrifices to help those in need—or perhaps even if they make no such sacrifices at all. As long as people legitimately own what they have, they have a right not to share at all, though, we might say, it would be better if they did.

A Relationship-based Ethic of Goods

On the other way of thinking about and living out morality, people construe the moral life as primarily a matter of the pursuit of certain goods, goods that make human life especially valuable and worth-while. People who construe morality this way commonly list such goods as health, physical comfort and pleasure, adequate material possessions, and the types of knowledge required for worthwhile and fulfilling social and intellectual activities. Notice that material goods are only one of the types of goods we seek, on this construal. We also seek intellectual goods (various types of knowledge and intellectual activity), social or common goods (discussed shortly), and spiritual goods (spiritual peace, interpersonal and intrapersonal spiritual harmony, or ritual, sacramental, and/or personal communion with God or Nature or Being). The nonmaterial goods overlap, of course, many of them being social to some degree, and this categorization should not be taken as exhaustive or necessarily even representative. These material and nonmaterial goods are desired for the sake of *the* good—the worthwhile and meaningful life to which they contribute.

On this way of construing morality, some of the goods that are essential to a fulfilling life are goods that individuals can obtain only in common with others, goods that are correctly described as the possession of a group or community, not of individuals. Such goods include participation in games such as soccer, chess, and a card game I learned as a child called "ten point pitch." The common or social goods also include such things as performance in string quartets, taking part in interesting and stimulating conversations, and participation in politics. On this construal of morality, a life without these, or at least without some subset of common or social goods such as these, would not be meaningful and worthwhile. Thus, it is not surprising that human life, on this construal, is only fully lived as community life. Many have expressed this by claiming that human life is essentially or "by nature" social—in contrast to the anthropology or doctrine of human nature central to the rule-based, rights-centered construal of morality. So, if we are to give a full description of what a good human life involves, we must necessarily include a description of what types of human community best foster human flourishing. Politics and political philosophy are inseparable from individual action and ethical theory. The personal is the political, and vice versa.

Since the fostering and flourishing of human communities is crucial, on this way of construing morality, those types of action that injure or destroy the bonds of community must be prevented. We must at least hold them to a survivable minimum. We need laws that specify which types of conduct are prohibited, and these laws must be enforced if the community is to flourish, even to survive. But notice that the laws that are required are, in this way of thinking, required as minimum conditions for *community*, not as minimum conditions for *peaceful, competitive coexistence*. What is common, and so what provides the possibility of common goods, requires law. Law is required, on this way of thinking, to preserve and foster *community*, not to preserve and foster self-interested *individuals*. On the rule-based, rights-centered way of construing morality, humans are naturally self-interested and at odds with each other, but on this construal humans are naturally together in community in common pursuit of goods they can have only in community. To have a meaningful and worthwhile life is to be connected with others in common pursuits, not to be separated from others in competitive coexistence with them.

On this relationship-based, goods-centered construal, violating the law is but one way a person might fail. First, if one breaks the rules that specify the limits within which common pursuit can proceed, one will necessarily frustrate one's own (as well as the collective) pursuit of common goods—though of course one may not necessarily thereby frustrate one's pursuit of individual goods. For instance, cheaters of various sorts undermine and ruin the game or activity for groups, but of course the cheaters themselves sometimes come out ahead in other ways, say, by taking home bigger prizes of various sorts or a better win-loss record of one kind or another. But, second, one might also fail, on this construal, by falling short of those types of excellence (traditionally called "virtues") that enable one to perform well in the *common* pursuit of *common* goods. This type of failure roughly corresponds to a type of failure on the rule-based construal, failure to achieve the types of skill and prowess that enable one to acquire what will satisfy one's *individual* needs, desires, and wants.

Here is a mundane example. Pitch is a card game for which you need at least four people, two teams of two. It provides an example of an activity or practice in which the goods obtained in the activity itself—enjoyment of a particular type of company and friendly competition—are intrinsically social. It also provides an example of a historically constituted activity or practice in which certain excellences, taught to newcomers by established initiates, facilitate (but do not guarantee) enjoyment of those goods.

I have never been as good as my younger brother at ten point pitch (or at any other card game I can think of). My brother and I learned the game from our maternal grandparents when he was six and I was eight. They had played pitch at Grange meetings while my mother was growing up outside Brighton, Colorado, near Denver. Grange was a farm organization prominent in the western and midwestern United States in the 1930s, 1940s, and 1950s, and some local Granges are still active. The Green Valley Grange Hall was not two miles from my grandparents' house. We played pitch with my grandparents, uncle, aunt, and cousins when we visited them on our grandparents' farm. We also played at home when it was just the four of us. And twice a month we played with couples my grandparents' age at the Prairie View Community Building in the rural northwest Arkansas county where I grew up. This was a one-room schoolhouse that had been a community elementary school in the 1930s and 1940s and was the place where my 4-H club met. Benton County had once been divided into communities the public centers of which were the one-room schoolhouses, and some of the schoolhouses there still held community activities in the 1960s. Well before this, though, the town I "grew up in," Siloam Springs (pop. 7,000, including surrounding communities) had become the public center of growing activity. The couples with whom my parents, brother, and I played pitch gathered every other week, against the tendency of later generations to center everything in town or in small cities in other counties, to play cards and talk about their lives and the strange world in which we lived then in the 1960s. They gathered for the goods internal to and associated by them with ten point pitch. My brother was seven years old and I was nine when we began to join them. The men and women played separately, and they assigned Joe Dan and me to play with the women.

The object in ten point pitch is to take as many of the ten points in suit as one's team can acquire and over the course of a few hands to acquire fifty points before the opposing team does. Suit is determined through bidding. A bid of five points typically prevails. Six is a somewhat daring bid, seven very daring, usually implying that one holds at least the ace and two other face cards of a single suit. Since the object is to reach a score of fifty before the opposing team does, and since the highest bidder names trump in a way that will enable her or him to take the most points *and* is allowed to go through the remains of the deck looking for extra trump cards, each player has an incentive to make the highest bid. However, if one does not make one's bid, not only does he or she fail to add those points to his or her score, the points are actually subtracted from one's overall score. One's team goes "set." Hence, there is incentive not to bid too high. My seven-year-old brother, Joe Dan, playing with three women typically in their sixties (or with two and our mother) at the Prairie View Community Building, relished bidding six or seven. And if his teammate's confidence was not inspired by his tender age, he had a tendency to lead with the two of trump (a point-card which "saves itself," i.e., which cannot be taken even by a higher trump card, but which is the lowest card in suit).

The thing was, he often made such bids. Still, this initially unnerved the women with whom he was playing, and not surprisingly. But Joe Dan had a knack for memorizing the cards that had been played and for learning how people typically played their hands, e.g., laying out trump early on or holding on to them until the end. He learned strategy by picking up on the strategies of others and by trying them out. He would lead with a two of trump, which meant others had to follow with trump he could not take with a two. What if an opponent or, worse still, his teammate had the three of trump (worth three points) and no other trump?! If the three and ten (also a point-card) fell on the first trick and went to the opposing team, Joe Dan and his partner were surely "set." And this did happen occasionally, but usually Joe Dan was holding the three and maybe the king, queen, one of the jacks and one of the jokers. He was flushing out the ace (which his partner might even have been holding) so that he would have the next two or three high cards in trump, and he was flushing out trump cards so that when he ended up leading with the three, it would be the only trump left in anyone's hand.

If I had not seen Joe Dan do this all his life, I would say this was just kid luck. But he has always used complex strategy and his excellent memory in card playing, and he does it in increasingly complex ways. He has perfected the "poker face" and can bluff or conceal his intentions with great subtlety. As a result, when the players involved are of roughly equal skill and when their aim is enjoyment of the particular type of company and friendly competition possible when playing cards, Joe Dan and his fellow players have a great time. These two qualifications are important. First, if the players are not of roughly equal skill, the game does not go nearly as well and is not as enjoyable. If making one's bid is too easy because one's opponents are poor players, or is almost impossible because one's teammate plays unintelligently, the game is simply not as rewarding. The tension produced in the friendly competition is not as engaging, and the company is not as lively. Second, however, if one's aim is not the enjoyment of company and friendly competition but winning, say because there is some kind of tournament prize to be gained and that is the only or primary reason one is playing, then it is actually better if one's opponents are poor players. And if one player's aim is winning whether the game is enjoyable or not, and if that player is preoccupied with the score or the slightest mistakes of his or her teammate, the quality of the company and friendly competition is diminished for the other players.

These two qualifications are true not only of games, such as pitch, soccer, and chess, where the rules are relatively well defined, but also of other rule-governed common activities where the rules are largely unwritten and less well defined, such as in string quartets, conversations, and politics. The deficiencies of one participant diminish the goods gained by all. And an inordinate attention to goods only indirectly connected with the activities or practices in question (like prize money or salary increases or enhancements of prestige) also diminishes the goods gained by all. One can fail not only by violating rules but also, on this goods-centered construal of morality, either by falling short of the excellences that make the practices go well or by missing the point of the practices in the first place.

The excellences that are required not just for good pitch playing but for all common pursuits and activities are an important part of the fulfilling human life. They are traditionally referred to as virtues of character and virtues of intelligence. People fail to achieve such a life not only by failing to follow the laws that specify the minimum conditions of its pursuit but also by failing to achieve the excellences of character and intelligence that go beyond any minimum, boundary conditions.

This too is not only a way of thinking about morality. It is a way of living it out. Institutions and practices typical of this way of life include some or all of those legal institutions I discussed earlier but also those that foster the excellences of shared or community life and that bring about the public recognition of special achievements in it. In previous generations of rural peoples in some parts of the United States, the Grange Hall and the one-room schoolhouse community building were such institutions. Generally speaking, of first importance are educational institutions such as 4-H and the Scouts, elementary schools and their after-school clubs, that promote the development not only of technical skills but also of character and of practical as well as theoretical intelligence. The liberal arts college and the preparatory school are also such institutions (when, that is, they actually do what their "mission statements" claim they do), and so as well are public primary and secondary schools that emphasize the advantages of extracurricular as well as curricular activities in the development of the whole person. Civic clubs that perform public service for the good of the community and which through awards recognize excellence in civic and political leadership are also important.

And whereas we elect legislative representatives whom we believe will be able to "bring home the bacon" for their constituents, we in the United States sometimes elect government administrators such as governors and presidents whom we believe typify our conception of human and civic excellence. George Washington and Abraham Lincoln are mythic heroes of grade school history textbooks in the U.S. because they are portrayed as representing models of public and private virtue. A principal goal of the moral upbringing of children in this way of life is teaching appreciation for what makes life worthwhile and fulfilling as well as appreciation for the models of human excellence and achievement that orient the community's life and activities.

Think now about how Heinz's situation is to be understood on this other way of construing morality. The problem Heinz finds himself facing concerns not his wife's rights or the druggist's rights or his own rights. Rather, it concerns his relationship with his wife in the concrete social, historical, and institutional contexts of their other relationships. On this way of construing morality, the Heinz Dilemma is about troubled relationships, not conflicting rights. The relationship of Heinz and his wife has developed over the course of their acquaintance and over the course of their marriage. Their marriage itself has had particular meanings for them, their families, and others within their broader social and cultural context. Their relationships with each other and with members of their communities have been prefigured by these meanings in that broader context. They have been bound to each other and free with each other, intimate exclusively with each other in some things, intimate with others in other things, in ways framed by their particular context(s). And they have improvised a good deal in their relationship along the way. So in this particular instance, what would constitute being faithful or true to his wife, in the context of this and their other relationships? What goods are to be pursued in this situation in which one or another type of loss and violation of relationship is apparently inevitable?

At this point I find myself at an impasse. Without some additional suppositions about Heinz's situation, I do not know what more to say that is not highly abstract and hypothetical. For Kohlberg constructed the Heinz Dilemma for the purpose of eliciting people's reasoning along the lines of the rule-based, rights-centered, individual-centered construal of morality. For this reason he did not find it necessary to incorporate any detailed information about the relationship between Heinz and his wife or between them and other people. For his specific purposes this information was irrelevant. We know next to nothing directly about their relationship with each other or with others save that the druggist has refused to lower his price or extend Heinz credit and that Heinz has been unable to raise any more than $2,000 to purchase a dose of the drug for his wife's treatment. For the purposes of the present illustration, then, let me make some suppositions.

Taking the information from Kohlberg's formulation of the Heinz dilemma at face value, we know that Heinz has done everything he could do legally to raise $4,000 and has been able to raise only half that amount. Let us suppose, then, that he and his wife have very few assets, indeed, that they have at most $2,000 worth of assets or that the assets they do have were not all marketable. Heinz sold everything they have that he could sell, and he only managed to raise $2,000. Since legally he also had the option of taking a mortgage or a lien on some of their assets, we have to assume that had he attempted to raise money in this way, he would have been unable to raise more than the $2,000 he did raise. We must also suppose that none of Heinz's family or acquaintances were willing or able to loan Heinz much money or to give him any as a gift in his wife's health crisis. In sum, if he tried every legal means to raise the money for the drug, he must have tried to borrow against the family's possessions and, failing this, to sell all that were saleable, and he must have sought to acquire the remaining money needed for the drug as charity from family or acquaintances or social service agencies. Still, he has been able to raise only $2,000. Finally we must suppose that the community and/or state in which Heinz and his wife live has no social service or health care agency designed to help needy individuals in such circumstances. Either such an agency exists but did not find Heinz's wife qualified to receive more than nominal support, say, because the state's resources are extremely tight and Heinz's wife's prognosis is so poor that aid to others took priority over aid to her. Or such an agency does not exist in the area of Europe where Heinz and his wife live. A third possibility is that the state's financial situation is not so bleak, but that its people or officials simply do not place emergency or life-saving medical care to the indigent (as opposed, say, to preventative care) high on the list of their priorities. We need not suppose Kohlberg had any actual country or municipality in mind, for he surely meant this dilemma to be hypothetical.

Suppose further that the druggist would have been able, but felt no special obligation, to help Heinz or his wife. He was not willing either to lower his price or to extend Heinz credit. The druggist must not feel bound to help Heinz's wife through any relationship they have or through any compassion or sense of charity. We need not suppose, though, that the druggist is being especially niggardly in this, for Heinz has not managed to find anyone else willing to provide sufficient assistance either. The druggist's unwillingness to help appears different from the unwillingness of others in the community only in that he actually stands to realize some financial gain from a satisfactory resolution of Heinz's shortfall. Were Heinz to come up with the money to meet the druggist's price, or were the druggist to allow Heinz to take the $4,000 dose for $2,000 cash and a credit of $2,000, the druggist would at least receive five times what it cost him to produce the dose in question. But he is unwilling to do this. Still, can we single out the druggist for being unwilling to do for Heinz what the community as a whole with its combined resources is unwilling to do? Not on this construal of morality.

Famously, some of Kohlberg's subjects (and some of the students with whom I have discussed this dilemma in my classes) have balked at these implications. Surely Heinz did not try *every* legal means. Heinz must have had a house or a car or something to sell or borrow against. Perhaps another druggist could be found who made this drug. Surely Heinz could go to the news media and make an appeal for help. It would make CNN and the evening news and people would send in donations from all over! At the very least the druggist would be shamed into lowering his price. And so on. The critics and uncooperative interview respondents are right in that Kohlberg constructed the Heinz dilemma so that Heinz faces a choice too simple to be realistic in any typical way. Steal or watch your wife die of cancer, period. Things are not usually so simple. However, perhaps these critics and respondents are also to some extent too inclined to denial about how badly off the poor sometimes are, as in the case of Heinz and his wife. Disheartening as it is, we should admit that some people in poverty are this badly off.

Returning to our question, how can Heinz be faithful or true to his wife in the context of what—taking Kohlberg's formulation of the dilemma at face value—we must suppose to be their relationships with others? I would perhaps not oversimplify if I said that Heinz and his wife have been abandoned by their larger community. Heinz and his wife are simply disconnected from those people and processes which manage the flow of resources (e.g., medical care) in their society. From the point of view of a relationship-based, goods-centered, community-centered construal of morality, the first question is not what Heinz is morally required or permitted to do on his own in the circumstances. Instead, the first question concerns the fact of his and his wife's disconnection from the relationships and community which normally should be the context for the pursuit of goods that make life meaningful and worthwhile. The first question is: How could this happen? Something has gone badly wrong.

Let me consider briefly two further possible suppositions. Going beyond the information Kohlberg provided for his interview respondents in the formulation of the Heinz Dilemma, we should ask how Heinz and his wife could find themselves in this predicament. First, perhaps Heinz and his wife live in anonymity in an impersonal, uncaring community, or at least in one in which the poor are overlooked and perhaps despised. A second is that Heinz and/or his wife are scoundrels, criminal nuisances, and notorious gamblers and prodigals (even though their intemperances may in no way be responsible for the cancer). If something like this second explanation of what has gone wrong is adequate, then perhaps it is not surprising that Heinz has not found many willing to give or loan him money. How could they be confident he would actually spend it on medical care for his wife rather than gambling it away or spending it on superfluous entertainments? In the United States, as things stand, Heinz's wife, ironically, might well be better off in prison, for there she would at least be provided this care. Still, it might be prudent in the circumstances for Heinz and his wife to seek reconciliation with their community. The issue on this second hypothetical supposition, then, is not whether Heinz should steal the drug or watch his wife die. The issue is whether he should steal the drug, continuing as a rebel and miscreant, or seek restoration to his and his wife's community. As a question of practical rationality for Heinz, the issue, then, is whether he and his wife would be better off restored to or in defiance against the way of life of their community. So, on this construal of morality, Heinz would have to make a judgment about the value of the life of his and his wife's community before he could decide what is practically rational for him in the circumstances. Perhaps the community does not merit supplication even in these dire circumstances, or perhaps it does. Of course, if Heinz and his wife are scoundrels and prodigals, their judgment about the community's value may be distorted. Be these complexities as they may, our concern and Heinz's has to be with the community and Heinz's and his wife's situation within this community. On this construal of morality, we cannot abstract the situation from the community. If we attempt to do this, we deprive ourselves of the bearings by which we and Heinz might make a practically rational, moral judgment about what he should do.

If, however, something like this first hypothetical supposition is accurate, that is, if Heinz and his wife live in an impersonal, uncaring community, or at least in one in which the poor are overlooked and perhaps despised, then, on the relationship-based, goods-centered, community-centered construal of morality, the question is whether Heinz and his wife would be appreciably worse off, or appreciably better off, if Heinz steals the drug (or the money to buy it). On this construal of morality, the laws and mores of the community specify the minimal conditions of successful pursuit of common or social goods and of the flourishing of the relationships and communities that mediate these goods. In abstraction from those pursuits, relationships, and communities, a person has no good reason to honor the laws and claims based on them (e.g., rights claims). The reason not to steal is that theft undermines the relationships and community through which humans can pursue worthwhile and meaningful lives. On this construal, if one is already deprived of those relationships and community, and hence if one is already excluded from the common pursuits of common or social goods, why *not* steal? The principal reason not to steal *in such circumstances,* which appear to be Heinz's and his wife's circumstances, is that the apparatus of the state may be established so as effectively to discourage and deter theft. Theft may not be a prudent option in the circumstances. But it may be. Ideally of course, on this construal of morality, theft would not be practically rational because theft would undermine the relationships and community through which one's life is worthwhile and meaningful.

Since I have dwelled at length on the Heinz Dilemma in illustrating the relationship-based, goods-centered, community-centered construal of morality, I will offer only a few observations about how we should conceive Beverly's and Stephen's situation on this construal. First, the problem Beverly and Stephen face, with respect to their marriage, can be described as I described the problem Heinz and his wife face. Stephen and Beverly have a relationship that has developed over the course of their acquaintance and over the course of their marriage. Their present disagreement about family planning is the latest passage in that history and cannot be well understood apart from that history. Their marriage itself has had particular meanings for them, their families, and others within their broader social and cultural context(s). Their relationships with each other and with members of their communities have been prefigured by these meanings in that broader context. We know that Stephen and Beverly are Roman Catholic. On this construal of morality, if we are to understand Beverly's notion of what her family is to be and how it is an extension of her parents' and grandparents' families, we should not abstract it from the particular communities in which she and they identify sexual union and procreation as worthwhile and meaningful. The same is true of Stephen's concern for needy children. If we are to understand his sense of relationship to and community with these children, we should not abstract his concern from the particular community(ies) of faith in which he identifies these relationships and this community. On this construal of morality, Stephen would identify a felt obligation to help needy children but not in terms of their rights in abstraction from particular relationships. He would identify an obligation to help them in terms of a notion of universal human community established and sustained by God. The point here is that Stephen's and Beverly's disagreement occurs within a concrete context of community engagements in, and conceptions of, what makes life meaningful and worthwhile. Roman Catholics do not all agree, of course, and so Beverly's and Stephen's disagreement occurs within a context of ongoing dialogue. It is a context of particular broader community disagreements, say, about artificial birth control, abortion, access to adoption, and poverty. These community disagreements provide the terms in which Beverly and Stephen can make sense of their responsibilities to each other and others, including their families, their immediate communities, and thousands of anonymous needy children.

The political culture of the United States is, not surprisingly, a mixture of the two ethics I have outlined as ideal types, one rule-based, individual-centered, and rights-centered, the other relationship-based, community-centered, and goods-centered. The masculine and the feminine, the urban and the rural, the commercial and the professional, the secular and the ecclesial, the political and the domestic all settle in together in life in the United States as in other cultural regions of the world. Liberal individualist and communitarian forms of discourse and practice cohabit more or less comfortably in many political cultures. In the United States, liberals team up politically with socialists, and libertarians with Christian fundamentalists. Rotarians gather for lunch, sing patriotic songs, pledge allegiance to God, country, and helping your neighbor—and return to their offices to resume efforts to get a leg up on the competition so that they can keep up with the Joneses.

One conclusion we might draw from this North American phenomenon, which of course is not peculiarly North American, is that these two ethics are not in fact wholehearted rivals or really incompatible at all. Kohlberg certainly did *not* draw this conclusion, not at first anyway. This is clear from his formulation of the structural stage model which I will discuss in the following chapter. But first, I shall conclude this introduction by relating more explicitly my discussion of the relationship-based, goods-centered, community-centered construal of morality to the Kohlbergian "just community." I will then close with what I take to be the two-part question that from the beginning oriented and can continue to orient the larger Kohlbergian project.

Moral Identity in the Just Community

Though Kohlberg described his just community work in collectivist terms, to my knowledge he never himself fully articulated the extent to which the just community model of moral education embodies "communitarian" assumptions (Kohlberg, 1985, and Kohlberg and Higgins, 1987, do not use this term, but see Power, Higgins, and Kohlberg, 1989, where this term is used). I do not know to what extent Kohlberg would have affirmed the relationship-based, goods-centered, community-centered construal of morality, as I have described it, as a way of making sense of the moral presuppositions of the just community model. However, I suggest that we can best understand the aim of the just community approach to moral education as follows: the aim is to develop thickly constituted selves (not only thinly constituted, abstract justice-reasoning skills) whose primary commitments and projects include participation in a pluralistic democratic community. Certain goods are to be pursued in a particular type of democratic community in which certain types of relationships are nourished and cultivated. Here I anticipate conclusions I will draw later in my argument.

The Stage 6 self has to be especially thin because it is to be genuinely culturally universal, not the thick self of some particular culture at some particular point in its history. It is, however, we were to believe, the developmental *telos* (aim, goal) of a careful crafting of thickly democratic justice-oriented selves. This crafting of selves is supposed not to be indoctrinative of an arbitrarily selected "bag of virtues," for the reason that the aim is such a thin, cross-culturally universal self. It is sufficient, so Kohlberg argued early on (Kohlberg, 1966a; Kohlberg and Turiel, 1971), for persons to be led Socratically to recognize the cognitive-moral inadequacy of their present justice-reasoning stage-perspectives (see Blatt, 1969; Blatt and Kohlberg, 1975). But the very aim of the just community is the inculcation of Deweyan democratic habits. Character is being built. A particular type of excellence or virtue is being instilled. A culture of democratic nonrelativism is being transmitted (see Kohlberg, 1980a). Conceptions of what constitutes the good human life and of the human excellences or virtues which make this life possible are embodied full-blown in the practice of a highly specific and historically and cultur-ally concrete type of community (see Galston, 1991).

Whether Kohlberg could or would have conceded that his own work in the just community projects moved in this direction, *away* from the antiindoctrinative, anticultural-transmission, anti-"bag-of-virtues" stance of the structural stage theory, seems clear. He thought it did (see Kohlberg, 1978, 1980a; Kohlberg, 1985; Kohlberg and Higgins, 1987). However, his account of the structural stage theory did not reflect this change of heart. Rawls, on the other hand, with whom for a time Kohlberg felt in deep philosophical affinity with re-spect to his account of the structural stage model, has moved some-what in this direction. As Galston (1989, p. 723) puts it,

> Rawls's "ideal theory," abstracted from the empirical contingencies that differentiate existing political orders, was designed to judge and (when possible) to improve them. And, he contended, his theory was neither produced by specific historical and social circumstances nor intended to defend any existing order. The theory was rather "im-partial," for it was constructed *sub specie aeternitatis,* regarding the human situation "not only from all social but also from all temporal points of view."
>
> In the Dewey lectures and subsequently, however, Rawls abandons this effort. Political philosophy, he now contends, is always addressed to a specific "public culture." It either appeals to the principles latent in the common sense of that culture or proposes principles "congen-ial to its most essential convictions and historical traditions." In par-ticular, justice as fairness addresses the public culture of a democratic society. It tries "to draw solely upon basic intuitive ideas that are embedded in the political institutions of constitutional democratic regimes and the public traditions of their interpretation." Justice as fairness "starts from within a certain political tradition" and (we may add) it remains there. (Galston quotes from and cites Rawls, 1980 and 1985)

The Rawlsian method of inquiry was to lead any and every fully ra-tional (i.e., cognitive-morally mature) agent to the principles of jus-tice as fairness (Stage 6, more or less). But this method turns out to rely for its conclusions on essentially historical and culture-laden "in-tuitions" and dispositions to judge (and act). Aiming at "reflective

equilibrium" between our principles of justice (the underlying rationales of our reasoning about justice) and our moral intuitions and considered judgments about particular cases, Rawls had originally meant
the method to be ahistorically and cross-culturally applicable. Democratic liberalism was destiny (Shweder, 1982b) precisely because we
were thought not fully able to adapt to the logic of the sociomoral
order, to sociomoral reality as such, *unless* we attained a Stage 6 reasoning perspective informed by the principles of justice as fairness.
But as the metaphysical commitments of this view have been pressed
by critics of both Rawls (see esp. Sandel, 1982) and Kohlberg, Rawls
has abandoned the claim to ahistorical, cross-cultural applicability
for his method. He has adopted the view that the method of inquiry which aims at principles of justice in reflective equilibrium
with our intuitions and considered judgments is a heuristic designed
specifically for negotiating the public, political problems unique to liberal democracies in multicultural societies (see Rawls, 1980, 1985,
1987, 1988, 1993; and see Galston 1982a, 1982b, 1989, 1991).

For the purposes of my argument, this last point can be restated.
The "reasoning operations" that lead justice-reasoners through the six
stages to the *telos* of the stage sequence, the "post-conventional" Stage
6, require that reasoners already *recognize* situations as morally problematic ("dilemmatic"). The projects and commitments that partially
constitute their identities must be such that people already hold fairness and procedural justice to be essential to acting in ways consistent
with their being the types of selves they take themselves to be. These
projects and commitments "define what we would not do, what we
regard as outrageous and horrible; they are fundamental conditions
for being ourselves" (Kekes, 1990). In short, reasoners must somehow
already have come to adopt the projects, commitments, and dispositions to judge and act that would be inspired and instilled in an environment in which justice as fairness is a primary orienting principle
or value. Thickly constituted democratic, justice-oriented selves
would be such reasoners. The Kohlbergian just community would be
such an environment. The goal of a just community is not only the
development of reasoners of a certain stage but also, or perhaps instead, the crafting of selves or persons of a certain sort. We should
not be surprised, then, to find that prior to the institution of such
communities, Stages 5 and 6 and even Stage 4 reasoning have been

found almost without exception only in liberal democracies where justice-centered democratic institutions would already be in place, transmitting a culture of democratic pluralism and nonrelativism.

The Question That Must Be Answered

Rereading "Beds for Bananas" now will remind us of the importance of vital just communities that foster democratic nonrelativism. But if we are to remain true to what is plausible in Kohlberg's larger project, we have to see beyond the relevance of his work for the subcultures of postindustrial, affluent, pluralistic, democratic societies. For I have suggested that what inspired his project, among other things, was the conviction that the project of Nazism is ahistorically, cross-culturally immoral. Kohlberg also held that ethics and moral psychology should be able to articulate this. He had in mind the destruction and human indignities he witnessed at the end of World War II, including of course the Holocaust of European Jews, Gypsies, and others, as he attempted to articulate in moral and psychological theory why we must hold that some things are ahistorically, cross-culturally immoral. Every form of relativism that fails to acknowledge this must be defeated.

Furthermore, ethics and moral psychology should also be able to supply us with the (conceptual) resources with which, through education and community, we can prevent the spread of Nazism and suchlike. But we must be able to prevent the spread of cultural plagues like Nazism without resorting to the arbitrary impositions of oppressive domination that characterize the evil we aim to prevent. We cannot simply impose our favored order, arbitrarily. We *can* seek consensus. And yet, of course, opportunities for reasoned discussion are not always at hand. We must sometimes impose justice if we are to avoid the destruction of those for whom reasoned discussion is to be fostered. I am thinking of atrocities not only under the Third Reich but also recently in Burundi, Rwanda, the former Yugoslavia, Haiti, Argentina, Beijing, Chiapas, Chechnya, and other places. For this reason, our account of justice cannot be merely heuristic and political. That is, it cannot be confined to a particular cultural and political setting at a particular time. We need an account of how justice can be fostered without oppressive domination and also how it can in cases of fundamental threat be imposed nonarbitrarily. We need a nonop-pressive antirelativism.

The conviction that empirical moral psychology is an essential ele-ment in just this sort of account of justice is a Kohlbergian legacy the importance of which it would be hard to overstate.

In my revisionist story I need to address a question that on Kohl-berg's view must be answered by any account of morality and moral development. *How can justice be fostered without oppressive domination and, in cases of fundamental threat, be imposed nonarbitrarily?* The struc-tural stage model was designed for the express purpose of answer-ing this question. On my revisionist story of the development of the Kohlbergian project, we cannot appreciate Kohlberg's mature answer to this question unless we understand his initial Piagetian-Kantian answer to it.

THREE

The Structural Stage Model

Why Principles?

Oversimplifying a bit further, then, it is useful for the moment to imagine that Kohlberg constructed his entire project as a response to a single problem. How do we foster justice, on the one hand, and respond to injustice, on the other, without arbitrarily imposing our own personal or group agenda? His answer, in short, was that whereas we should interpret individual acts of justice as differing across cultural and subcultural regions in particular substantive or material respects, we should understand justice itself as universal when considered formally or structurally. The basic structure of justice is universal. The substantive details vary. This universal formal or structural identity, he thought, could be expressed in an idiom of abstract principles.

Take, for instance, the Disposable Hook-Up Dilemma. What is wrong with what Brad did? He did not force Reanna to accompany him to his room. She came of her own free will. Indeed, she had been hoping to do just that. She also hooked up with Brad, kissing and petting through her own choice. In fact (I am adding new information at this point), Brad was indeed just as interested in hooking up with Reanna as she was in hooking up with him. He was not duplicitous in representing himself as interested in hooking up with Reanna. He finds her attractive and would have sought to hook up with her even if he were not also engaged in an ordeal in his fraternity. And if the evening had gone as planned, Reanna would never have known Brad's three fraternity brothers were hiding in the closet. She would have been saved the hurt and humiliation that were accidental results of Brad's brothers' lack of self-control. She would never have known the difference.

I find it helpful at this point, in discussing this particular case, to understand some of the details of the practice of hooking up among undergraduates. There is a more or less commonly understood culture of hooking up among college students like Reanna, Brad, and Julie—

and though others besides undergraduates hook up, for the purposes of my discussion I want to stipulate that this case does not directly involve them. We can understand the full moral significance of what happened at the party and in Brad's room only if we understand some of the peculiarities of this culture. And so we need to look more closely at the circumstances and their context if we are to describe accurately what Brad did that was wrong. Kohlberg thought of moral principles as interpretive constructs, not fixed rules (see Kohlberg, 1984, pp. 296–304). Expressing what he took to be his agreement with Dewey, Kohlberg understood "a principle as a way of construing a concrete moral situation" (p. 298). In order to complete my discussion of this case, then, illustrating why Kohlberg chose an idiom of principles as a way of construing the formal or structural universality of justice, I need to say more about the undergraduate hook-up culture.

A "hook-up" is a spontaneous sexual encounter involving at least tongue-kissing, possibly but not necessarily involving sexual intercourse. Hook-ups are spontaneous, not prearranged, and in this respect are set in direct contrast to dating. Typically, people meet at parties where alcohol is provided, talk, perhaps dance; then, depending on the party, they may leave the premises, find a vacant room on the premises, or simply occupy a sofa or corner or doorway. Hook-ups can originate in other circumstances as well. There is rough consensus that though a peck on the forehead or cheek is not a hook-up, a passionate kiss is a hook-up even if no further sexual intimacy occurs.

On the one hand, hooking up is "no strings attached" sexual intimacy (not necessarily sexual intercourse). Neither men nor women are assumed responsible for phoning each other in the days following a hook-up. People tend to think someone tacky but not in violation of shared expectations if he or she does not even greet someone with whom he or she hooked up during the previous week. The "one-night stand" is the norm and the default expectation, that is, unless there is explicit agreement to the contrary. This is not to say that no one who hooks up hopes for something more enduring.

On the other hand, undergraduates recognize a type of hook-up that is not a one-night stand. People who regularly hook up with each other, say, when they meet at parties, and who (normally) refrain from hooking up except with the particular other person, are said to be "steady" or "regular hook-ups." Third party flirting with or "scamming on" them is understood to be inappropriate and grounds for censure. Either of the two is liable to censure if he or she "scams on" a third party, provided he or she intends to maintain the steady hook-up relationship. In the hook-up culture, dating is not the norm. Indeed, many tell me that dating is considered abnormal. People who date are considered practically married.

Hooking up is not new. The widely shared vocabulary of "hooking up," "scamming," "playing," "mashing," "shacking," etc., is new, but hooking up is not. (There are, of course, local variations in practice and vocabulary.) What is new in the United States is the relative abnormality of dating, the marginalization of prearranged get-togethers that involve social interaction in relative independence from sexual intimacy. Dating means (at least minimal) commitment, and commitment is out. Commitment makes independence problematic. Spontaneity is in, and with it a highly sexualized social life.

This much detail is sufficient for the illustration at hand. Kohlberg thought he could express the formal or structural universality of justice in an idiom of moral principles. So, we should describe what is wrong in what Brad did by construing particular circumstances of the case as salient and significant in terms of moral principles that are formally identical universally. Cultural anthropologists have catalogued an amazing variety of sexual customs and mores, but that does not show that sexual morality is culturally relative, on Kohlberg's view.

Brad did not force Reanna. She came to the party, drank, and engaged in conversation with Brad by her own choice. She accepted Brad's invitation to his room in full knowledge of the significance and implication of the invitation. She knew—by commonly understood convention—that an invitation to come to Brad's room, away from the crowd and the noise, ostensibly so that they could talk with less distraction, was actually an invitation to retire to a place where they could hook up (in private), should they each consent when it came to that. And it came to that, and each consented. Reanna knew— by commonly understood convention—that hooking up with Brad would not necessarily lead to further hook-ups or to a more broadly intimate relationship, let alone that they would ever date. And she supposed quite reasonably—according to common custom—that hooking up in Brad's room would be hooking up in private, that no one would be concealed in Brad's room for the purpose of observing them. Brad and his fraternity brothers had correctly taken the inquiries of Reanna's suitemates to imply that Reanna was interested in Brad. The interest was mutual, and this was more or less implied in their responses to the inquiries.

However, on Kohlberg's view, this is a clear case of someone (Brad) using someone else (Reanna) for his own purposes. It is a clear case of a violation of the Kantian categorical imperative. One of Kant's own formulations of the categorical imperative was that one should never use another as a mere means to one's own ends (see Kant, 1983 [1785], p. 36). Whether Brad enjoyed himself or not, whether he wanted to hook up with Reanna independently of his fraternity ordeal or not, he hooked up with Reanna as part of his passage through the ordeal. He used Reanna sexually for purposes to which she was not privy and which, unless told otherwise, Brad should assume she would reject were she to know them. It is this fact, that Brad used Reanna for ends that were not her own and about which she did not know, that makes what Brad did wrong, on a Kohlbergian account. To see that this is what Brad did, we have to know some of the details of the context-relative circumstances and shared understandings in which he did what he did. And so, for example, though Reanna could not expect hooking up with Brad would mean anything more than a one-night stand, she could rightly expect that there was no one in Brad's room monitoring their behavior.

However, it is not hard to imagine counterfactual circumstances (circumstances contrary to fact) in which she *would* expect to be monitored or in which she *should* have supposed Brad meant to use the hook-up in some sort of customary, tribal rite of passage. We could describe a perfectly coherent counterfactual social order in which this sort of thing is typical. In such a social order, Reanna thus should have anticipated these features of her interaction with Brad. Even if she didn't like to be in this sort of situation, she would have known what she was getting into and so could be supposed to have chosen autonomously—unless coercion were involved. In order to determine whether coercion was involved, we would need to know more details of the situation and the counterfactual social order. So, in this social order and those circumstances, whether Brad had done anything wrong would depend on yet further substantive details of the situation. And yet I have described what is wrong in what Brad did in the actual circumstances of the dilemma situation in a way that refers to formal features of his action that might be replicated in very different material circumstances, in many different cultures, and in many different historical periods. That is, describing Brad's wrong in this way—his using Reanna as a mere means and for purposes not her own—makes at least implicit reference to details of the material circumstances of the particular case *as they are to be construed and understood by reference to universal principles, not in a way that is relative to the circumstances of this case alone.* On Kohlberg's view, using people as mere means to your own ends is wrong whatever the situation, and there are lots of ways to use people that do not have much or anything to do with hooking up in undergraduate colleges in the United States in the 1990s.

It is this idiom of universal moral principle that Kohlberg believed would solve the problem that defined his project. What made his project unique in the history of moral theory is that he formulated an elaborate account of how our understandings of universal moral principles develop from childhood to maturity. He worked out the empirical details of this otherwise abstract philosophical theory, drawing on various conceptual resources for construing those details. In this chapter I offer an account of that construal, the structural stage model.

First, I offer another angle on what motivated Kohlberg's project. Immediately after that I will begin to explore its outline more fully.

Two Horns of a Dilemma:
Relativism vs. Indoctrination

In some of his early descriptions of his project, Kohlberg began with what he took to be the most important problem facing moral educators (see Kohlberg, 1971c). How can educators avoid indoctrinating students with the values they happen to hold without at the same time teaching them that no values or value systems are better than any others? That is, how can educators avoid indoctrination without teaching moral relativism?

At one extreme, teachers might teach subculture-specific rules of respect, say, requiring particular forms of address when interacting with elders and/or children from different classes or status groups. They might also teach specific gender roles and understandings of masculinity and femininity, or specific understandings of racial difference, and they might indoctrinate beliefs and habits that imply that differences of age, class, sex, or race require certain patterns of deference and respect. Further, teachers might require participation in certain group rituals implying allegiance to a particular state or religion. And they might do all this in the name of what is right and true. At the other extreme, teachers might try to confine such teaching of behavioral norms to those rules alone that will preserve classroom order. They could intend thereby to refrain from imposing their values arbitrarily. We cannot all talk whenever we like because then children will not learn their lessons. For the same reason, we cannot leave the classroom whenever we like. We mustn't hit, because fights disrupt class. And so on. On the one extreme, the rules indoctrinated are arbitrarily selected—even when they are the liberty- and rights-centered rules of an egalitarian culture such as those in North America and Western Europe are thought to be. On the other, they seem to have no bearing beyond the classroom, and teaching only classroom rules may imply moral relativism, which is not a morally neutral stance.

Teachers cannot avoid being moral educators. The question is what morality they teach. Kohlberg's aim was to formulate an account of moral education that satisfies two conditions: the moral theory it presupposes is not relativist and the educational methods it prescribes are not forms of indoctrination.

If Kohlberg's theory is correct, teachers can avoid indoctrinative methods of moral education while at the same time avoiding teaching moral relativism. Justice can be fostered without arbitrary imposition. Kohlbergian Socratic dialectic was intended to be nonindoctrinative, and yet, if Kohlberg was right, it facilitates development toward a nonrelativistic view of justice. The doctrine of moral relativism is false, and teachers can without indoctrination facilitate moral development, the highest, most mature stage of which is an acceptance of something like Rawls's principles of justice (Rawls, 1971). In short, Kohlberg saw his neo-Kantian formalism and structuralism as a way out of the indoctrination vs. relativism dilemma.

On his construal, indoctrinative methods themselves imply relativism, since they involve the arbitrary imposition of one's cultural or personal agenda on others. The only acceptable negotiation of the horns of the teacher's indoctrination vs. relativism dilemma is a neo-Kantian formalist, Piagetian structuralism that reveals how teachers can facilitate students' own self-constructions of nonrelative morality.

Piaget's Cognitive-Developmental Kantianism

Helen Koch, who directed Kohlberg's dissertation at the University of Chicago, introduced Kohlberg to Piaget's work. The Swiss biologist-psychologist was not much read or known in the United States in the mid-1950s. His theories would saturate the intellectual market for child development research, stimulated by the flood of federal dollars from the Johnson administration's Great Society Program, in the mid-1960s. In the mid-1950s, though, Piaget's work and the work of American philosopher-psychologist James Mark Baldwin were touchstones for Kohlberg's project of formulating an empirically elaborate, species-wide account of postwar universal morality. Piaget's important study of moral development is presented in *The Moral Judgment of the Child* (1932; see Flanagan, 1991). Piaget had an ingenious idea. In this work he reports the results of his study of the game-playing of a relatively small group of children at schools in Neuchâtel and Geneva. The particular game in question is the game of marbles as played by boys up to the age of thirteen, who generally lose interest in the game by this age. Older boys had been teaching the game to their juniors for many years. Piaget's idea was to observe the rudiments of moral development in children's development toward full participation in a well defined, rule-governed, social activity—marbles.

On the first page of the first chapter of this book, Piaget states that

> All morality consists in a system of rules, and the essence of all morality is to be sought for in the respect which the individual acquires for these rules. The reflective analysis of Kant, the sociology of Durkheim, [and] the individualistic psychology of Bovet all meet on this point. The doctrines begin to diverge only from the moment that it has to be explained how the mind comes to respect these rules.

For our part, it will be in the domain of child psychology that we
shall undertake the analysis of this "how." (p. 13)

It would be hard to find a more direct statement of a rules-centered
construal of morality. In fact, the influence of Kant arrives at Kohlberg's theory not only through Rawls and the earlier neo-Kantian
analytic moral philosophy of the 1950s and 1960s but also through
the rules-centered metaethical assumptions that guided Piaget's own
research program.

Piaget set out to discover *how* children come to respect rules. This
he took to illuminate in an important way children's moral development, which he equated with the development of children's capacity
to make moral judgments according to moral rules or principles. In
his analysis of the development of boys' respect for the rules of the
game of marbles, Piaget distinguished between children's rule-conforming behavior and their rule-consciousness as exhibited in their
articulation of the rules. He discerned four developmental stages in
respect to the rule-conforming behavior and three in respect to rule-
consciousness. These two sets of stages overlap with each other to
some degree, with children's behavior moving into a new stage before
the child's "consciousness" of rules correspondingly moves. That is,
children can articulate rules only some time after their game-playing
behavior has already come to conform to them. (This is a crucial point
that will come up again in my discussion of Kohlberg's structural
stage model.)

Piaget described four stages in the development of children's rule-
conforming behavior. The four stages correspond to the familiar
Piagetian sequence: sensory-motor, preoperational, operational, and
formal operations. (B1) Children in the motor stage behave as if ignorant of rules, e.g., burying the marbles, throwing them at siblings,
sucking on them, stacking them, etc. (B2) Children in the egocen-
trism stage begin to show behavioral conformity to a few basic rules
but no behavioral acknowledgment that more than one is to play the
game. For instance, children behave in accord with the rules about
the shooting line, the square, the procedure for scoring, but they do
all this while ignoring others who may be playing simultaneously
with the same shooting line, square, and target marbles. (B3) Chil-

dren in the cooperation stage cooperate with others in playing an organized game, obeying the same rules, delighting in cooperative competition. And (B4) children in the codification stage take delight in the codification of rules for the sake of codification. For example, they join their colleagues in trying to anticipate every possible game situation so as to have a rule to cover it.

Piaget described three stages in the development of children's consciousness of rules. (C1) In the first, children take the rules to be nonobligatory motor examples (examples of motion) of the way some children play with marbles, as when children report that some play with a shooting line from which they begin the play. But the respondents do not think this is something they have to do or that always has to be done. (C2) In the second, children take the rules to be sacred and untouchable, never to be violated or altered. For instance, children report that God gave the rules to their daddies and their daddies gave the rules to them when they taught them how to play, or when they report that the local magistrates began playing long ago when they were in school and the game has not changed since then. And (C3) in the third stage, children take the rules to be the product of mutual consent, deriving their authority therefrom. For example, children report that it is permissible to change a rule or to suspend a rule in a particular case, so long as everyone agrees.

Piaget used this analysis as the basis for his conclusion that there are two basic types of respect for rules, and hence two types of morality, corresponding to C2 and C3. He called these two types of respect for rules the morality of constraint or heteronomy (corresponding to C2) and the morality of cooperation or autonomy (corresponding to C3) (Piaget, 1932, p. 197). The last three-fourths of *The Moral Judgment of the Child* is devoted to his formulation of the stages in the development of children's ideas of justice. He conducted his personal interviews with children, the basis of his stage formulations, against the background of his analysis of the development of children's respect for the rules of the game of marbles. He found three stages in the development of children's ideas of justice, stages which variously embody the two types of morality. The first stage in children's ideas of justice he called the stage of Authority (approximately ages 6–8) which he characterized as the stage of (a) heteronomy in the making of rules, (b) unilateral respect of one's elders, (c) obedience to the rules, and (d) expiative punishment. The second stage he called the stage of Equality (approximately ages 8–11) which he characterized as the stage of (a) autonomy in the making of rules, (b) mutual respect for one's peers, (c) cooperation, and (d) reciprocal punishment. The third stage in children's idea of justice he called the stage of Equity (approximately ages 11–13) in which equality is relativized to one's age and status. For example, younger children might be given certain advantages when playing with older children in order to compensate for differences in skill related to age or size. They are given a "handicap," if you will.

In sum, Piaget worked from a basic insight. If morality is primarily a matter of following rules and, when deliberation is required, of making judgments in reference to rules—and so if childhood moral development is primarily a process of learning to respect and follow rules in both judgment and action—then we can learn about childhood moral development from observing children learning how to play rule-governed games. Moral development, then, is at least partly cognitive development, specifically the development of children's capacities to conceive and articulate rules. Yet Piaget found something interesting as he observed children engaged in rule-governed social activity. Children settle into patterns of rule-conforming behavior before they can cite rules as justifications, or requirements, for their behavior. So in describing children's development, Piaget reported finding overlapping stages in the development of their conformity to and respect for rules. He described some cognitive and some behavioral stages. On the basis of these he described two main types of respect for rules (heteronomy/constraint and autonomy/cooperation) and three stages in the development of children's ideas of justice (authority, equality, and equity). We will see, then, that Kohlberg extended Piagetian moral psychology in one of a set of possible directions. He emphasized some things and deemphasized others.

Charges of Sex-Bias

Not only Kohlberg's Kantianism but also his alleged sex bias seems to have roots in Piaget. Piaget found that little boys show more interest in rules, whereas little girls play less legally complicated games, prefering games with greater flexibility and more avenues for creativity.

Since Piaget held that respect for rules constitutes morality, it is a short step to the conclusion that little girls are less morally sophisticated, perhaps even morally deficient. I shall discuss the charge of sex bias briefly now, before proceeding. It is a serious charge and I want to understand it clearly.

We do well to separate two issues. Are girls in fact less legally sophisticated? And does respect for rules constitute morality? Piaget's construal of morality might be sex-biased, or his observations about girls might be. Piaget observed a group of children at schools in Neuchâtel and Geneva in the late 1920s and early 1930s. After presenting his analysis of the game of marbles as played by boys, Piaget examined the game-playing activity of girls at the schools where he did his research.

> Before drawing any general conclusions from the facts set out above, it may be useful to see whether they are peculiar to the game of marbles as played by boys or whether similar examples cannot be found in different fields. For this purpose we studied, with the same method, but questioning only girls, a much simpler game than the game of marbles.
>
> The most superficial observation is sufficient to show that in the main the legal sense is far less developed in little girls than in boys. We did not succeed in finding a single collective game played by girls in which there were as many rules and, above all, as fine and consistent an organization and codification of these rules as in the game of marbles examined above. . . . But each game in itself is very simple and never presents the splendid codification and complicated jurisprudence of the game of marbles. As to the game of marbles itself, the few little girls who take any interest in it seem more concerned with achieving dexterity at the game than with the legal structure of this social institution. (1932, pp. 76–77)

If we observe that girls are by nature less legally sophisticated than boys, we might, on the notion that morality is a matter of respect for rules, conclude that girls are less morally sophisticated. The sex bias here might be in the insistence on a rule-based conception of morality, or it might be in the observation that girls are by nature less legally sophisticated. But the conception of morality is itself sex-biased *only if* boys and girls and/or women and men have different sex-based legal capacities (neurophysiologically speaking). For, if they do not, a rule-based conception of morality may be mistaken, but it is not sex-biased—except perhaps accidentally or contingently. That is, it is possible that there are no sex-based differences in legal sophistication but that as a matter of the historically contingent arrangements of the social and political institutions in a particular culture, rule-based conceptions of morality happen to favor men and boys over women and girls. But if this is the case, we would more properly say not that the conception of morality is sex-biased but that the institutional arrangements are. I will return to this point again in a later chapter.

Since Kohlberg's emphasis on justice reasoning concentrated on the application of principles in dilemma situations, one might expect his results concerning sex-related differences in respect to moral development to coincide with Piaget's—if in fact relevantly similar physiological and social variables obtain across their samples. I say "sex-related differences" and not "sex-based differences" because finding that a subject's sex is a significant variable for the sake of prediction does not give grounds for concluding that a subject's sex is a *cause* of predictable states of affairs. Other variables associated with sex may be the causally relevant variables, e.g., social convention, socialization patterns, and expectations, extending to educational and occupational achievement.

Kohlberg began the empirical work for his dissertation with an all-male sample of Chicago youths, aged ten to sixteen. As a male graduate student in 1955, doing personal interview research about morality with adolescent and preadolescent youths, he chose a same-sex sample. He had studied *The Moral Judgment of the Child* and perhaps expected, influenced by Piaget, that males reason more legalistically than females, and in light of this expectation he no doubt contemplated the advantages of beginning his research program with a more responsive sample. These were possibly the reasons Helen Koch had in mind, in fact, when she counselled her dissertation advisee to select an all-male sample. I believe we have solid grounds for thinking this was a bad idea, that Kohlberg should not have assumed that sex would or would not be a significant variable. However, whatever reasons Kohlberg had in choosing the sample for his dissertation research, his continuing to follow the development of this sample for the sake of collecting needed longitudinal data is understandable on methodological grounds alone. This was not, of course, his only or largest sample.

Carol Gilligan's (1982) charge of sex bias in Kohlberg's theory (discussed in more detail later) is the best known. Because women express moral judgments and engage in moral reasoning on the whole differently from men, Kohlberg's account of moral development, formulated from initial study of boys and men only, is sex-biased. Her challenge to Kohlberg's program is taken to be primarily a charge of sex bias in empirical results in virtue of sex bias embedded in the Kohlbergian research itself. A sex-biased sample led to sex-biased conclusions about how development occurs. Since Kohlberg developed his scale of moral maturity from studying boys and men only, it measures the maturity of all moral judgment and reasoning on a scale derived from the style of judgment and reasoning characteristic of men. Thus, it is no surprise that women typically appear morally inferior to men (assuming men and women reason in different ways).

Kohlberg maintained his position that justice reasoning is the central feature of moral development, and he responded to criticisms that this orientation is sex-biased by pointing out that the crucial variable is not sex but participation in democratic institutions (Kohlberg, Levine, and Hewer, 1983, reprinted in Kohlberg, 1984, pp. 338–370; see Walker, 1991). Since middle-class women in the United States have in the past, on the whole, tended to participate less than middle-class men in the social institutions where justice reasoning is a regular medium of communication and decision-making, they have had less practice employing such reasoning and hence have tended to score lower than men on the Kohlbergian justice reasoning stage scoring test, the Moral Judgment Interview (MJI). However, when studies control for variables of educational achievement and occupational experience, women and men show no differences in moral or justice reasoning (Walker, 1984, 1991).

The Interview Data Base

Although Kohlberg's research program was informed significantly by Piaget's findings, his research differed from Piaget's in that initially it dealt almost exclusively with responses to moral dilemmas posed orally to subjects. There was on the whole little attempt to relate verbal responses on dilemmas to the behavior of subjects in actual dilemma situations (until the just community work began in the early 1970s). Kohlberg's structural stage theory of moral development is a theory about the development of moral reasoning (in a way, of moral theorizing or philosophizing, of reasoning about moral reasoning), and this moral reasoning or theorizing is limited to reasoning about justice in situations of conflicting claims. So there is no parallel in Kohlberg's theory to Piaget's analysis of rule-conforming behavior. However, Kohlberg did have a view about the relationship between a subject's stage of moral reasoning and the subject's moral action, and I will explain this later in the course of my discussion of Kohlberg's theory. There *is* a parallel between Piaget's conclusion that there are two basic types of respect for rules—constraint or heteronomy, and cooperation or autonomy—and Kohlberg's stages of moral reasoning.

Kohlberg incorporated Piaget's conclusion that there are two basic types of respect for rules into his latest formulation of the stages by including a heteronomous and an autonomous substage to each stage, at least at Stages 3 through 6 (Kohlberg, 1984, p. 225). I will explain the conception of these substages later while discussing the current formulation of Kohlberg's theory. Kohlberg also incorporated Piaget's analysis of the three stages of a child's idea of justice: the stages of authority, equality, and equity. Kohlberg elaborates the conception of each of these stages and extends his analysis beyond these stages chronologically.

Owen Flanagan (1984, pp. 155–56, 168–70) has argued that the limitation of Kohlberg's research program almost exclusively to personal interviews about simple, hypothetical moral dilemmas severely limited his claims to having a comprehensive theory of moral development. The dilemmas all present a narrow range of possible choices between rival and incompatible claims to rights or privileges. Kohlberg's moral psychology lacked an account of moral character, and his moral philosophy must be supplemented by an account of the goods toward which a moral life is directed, Flanagan argued.

Kohlberg responded to the criticism that his theory is too narrow by asserting that all aspects or domains of morality presuppose some stage of justice reasoning. An account of why one acts the way one does in a given dilemma situation, indeed, even a description of *how* one acts in the situation, must be articulated in the terms of one of the stages of justice reasoning. Only from the point of view of some conception of morality can moral action, moral character, and moral good be understood and articulated in the first place. Kohlberg, remember, thought of moral principles as ways of construing particular moral situations, not as fixed rules. The principle, for instance, of treating people as worthy of respect in their own right and never as mere means for our own purposes helps us see some features of situations as salient. It helps us construe situations. It is not a fixed rule binding independently of the circumstances. And so what appears from Flanagan's point of view to be the examination of only a small part of moral development appears from Kohlberg's point of view to be a study of the very core.

Kohlberg might well have claimed that criticisms such as Flanagan's about narrowness inadequately differentiate the moral from the nonmoral, and hence that these criticisms amount to faulting Kohlberg's theory for being more advanced along the developmental sequence. The plausibility of this type of response, though, depends on Kohlberg's defense of his thesis that Stage 6 reasoning is the most adequate both cognitively and morally. I address this thesis later.

The Structural Stage Sequence

As early as his dissertation, Kohlberg (1958) offered a theory of an invariant sequence of six cross-culturally universal stages of moral reasoning. He provided a summary account of the six stages in an appendix to each of the two published volumes of his collected papers (Kohlberg, 1981, pp. 409–12, and Kohlberg, 1984, pp. 621–39). The account he presented in the second volume is more detailed, and I rely here on it and on the Moral Judgment Interview manual published shortly after Kohlberg's death (Colby and Kohlberg, 1987a,b; see also Kohlberg, 1984, pp. 170–85.) In formulating this (1958) cross-culturally universal stage sequence, Kohlberg set the research agenda he would follow for the next ten years. He also took empirically elaborated postwar neo-Kantian moral theory far beyond Piaget toward answering the question at the heart of his thirty-year project: how do we foster justice and respond to injustice without arbitrarily imposing our own culture-laden ideals?

Kohlberg claimed that there are six developmental stages or structures of "justice reasoning," which is Kohlberg's expression for reasoning about justice. These stages are to be found in the same order in every cultural context, and at least the first four (or three) have been found in every type of society so far studied. Individuals move through these stages in an invariant sequence, never passing over a stage and never regressing. Each stage is a "structured whole," an internally consistent though not necessarily adequate or complete moral theory. The stages are "underlying thought organizations" that are qualitatively different but that perform the same function, a type of moral reasoning. Each stage integrates the adequacies of the previous stage and makes new differentiations that compensate for the inadequacies of the previous stage. The invariant sequence of stages is cross-culturally universal in the sense that the earlier stages are to be found in all cultures even if some cultural environments are more conducive than others to movement into the higher stages. Cultural environments that are more conducive to advance into the higher stages are sufficiently complex so that in them individuals face conflicts of claims that reveal the inadequacies of lower stages (see Puka, 1982).

One implication of this is that the earlier stages are often adequate to the simple social environments of undeveloped countries and of secluded rural settings, whereas these earlier stages are inadequate in the more complex social and political circumstances of developed countries (see Flanagan, 1984, p. 168). We might imagine this applying analogously to the communities that had gathered at the Prairie View Community Building and the Green Valley Grange Hall, in comparison to the urbanized settings in which my children are growing up. This accounts for why Kohlberg and his colleagues found significantly higher stage scores among older middle-class adolescents in the United States, and to a lesser extent in Taiwan and Mexico, than among older adolescents in isolated villages in Turkey and the Yucatan (see Kohlberg, 1981, pp. 24–25, and Kohlberg, 1984, pp. 56–57).

Kohlberg grouped the six stages into three pairs: the preconventional, the conventional, and the postconventional (Kohlberg, 1984, pp. 44–52). The notion of conventionality Kohlberg employed in this classification is that of a context-specific system of social norms, i.e., the social norms or conventions of some particular society. So reasoning at the preconventional stages is reasoning by individuals prior to their becoming full participants in some particular social system ordered and defined by social norms. Reasoning at the conventional stages is reasoning by individuals who are becoming or have become full participants in such a social system. In conventional "justice reasoning," respondents (seem to) take the social norms that order and define their social system to be the most fundamental principles of morality. Reasoning at the postconventional level is reasoning by individuals who have transcended the social norms of any particular social system and who take as the most fundamental principles of morality those that are universal and valid across particular social contexts.

Notice that this entails that in a "sufficiently developed society" individuals are faced with conflicts of claims the resolution of which cannot be achieved except by transcending the social norms of the society in question, that is, only by appealing to universal moral principles. This is not the case in less developed societies. And since the postconventional stages integrate the adequacies of conventional stages, they prove adequate in all the cases in which conventional stages were adequate, and then some. But notice also that the circumstances to which the postconventional stages are adequate while the conventional stages are inadequate are the circumstances of a "more developed society."

How is it that the social norms of a "more developed society" are less adequate for the conflicts that arise in that society than are the social norms of a "less developed society"? The individuals in the developed society, presumably, are faced with problems that are, if you will, outside the jurisdiction of their society—or rather, with conflicts that are themselves intersocietal. Presumably then, "more developed" societies are multicultural. In them people are forced to adopt a trans-societal perspective in order to be able to adjudicate conflicting claims. The shift in perspective from the conventional to the postconventional stages is the shift from the perspective of a member of a particular society to the perspective of a member of the class of all human beings. Hence, the adjudication of claims shifts from that between individuals qua members of a particular society to that between individuals qua human beings.

Thus, the shift from the conventional reasoning perspectives to the postconventional reasoning perspectives involves a dissatisfaction with (at least an awareness of the inadequacy or limitedness of) the conventions and understandings of one's interpersonal group (at Stage 3) and of one's local society (at Stage 4). One comes to see these conventions and the understandings of society and the world that inform them for what they are. One sees them for the first time as merely local.

The Stages

The preconventional stages are Stages 1 and 2. Kohlberg called Stage 1 "Heteronomous Morality," explicitly recalling Piaget's account of heteronomous as distinct from autonomous morality. He also called the Stage 1 perspective "naive moral realism," in that interview respondents at this stage take norms to be expressions of absolute categories of right and wrong, good and bad. They believe rightness and wrongness, goodness and badness inhere in persons and actions the way weight and color inhere in physical objects. Furthermore, respondents at this stage make no differentiation between perspectives. They assume that everyone perceives the morally relevant circumstances in the same way, in the manner in which people (presumably) perceive color and weight. Also, respondents at this stage take the moral relevance of authority to be absolute, and they take characteristics such as wealth and physical size as signs of authority and so as morally relevant. For children, the authorities in their lives are physically large and powerful. They do not distinguish physical size and power from the basis of adult authority. Further, respondents interpret punishment as a sign of wrongdoing and reward as a sign of righteousness. (Imagine the disorientation induced and the dysfunction created by the reverse assumption, when the authorities in question are those very people on whom one is physically and emotionally dependent, at a time when one is most or most often vulnerable.) This is because they accept the rule of authority as absolute. Typically, if authorities punish them, they must have done wrong. By the same token, if they are not punished, they must have done no wrong.

So from a Stage 1 perspective, the Heinz Dilemma pits the authority of the law and of the state generally against one person's need for something she and her husband cannot afford. A typical Stage 1 rationale is the following: Stealing is wrong because it is against the law, and Heinz would be punished if he stole the drug. If he does not steal it, his wife will die, and this will be sad, but he will have done nothing wrong. In cases of compensation for wrongdoing, respondents at Stage 1 demand strict reciprocity and equality in exchange—an eye for an eye. So certainly no special consideration should be given to Heinz if he does steal the drug. He must pay the druggist for his loss and suffer the penalty imposed by the law.

The notion of equity—of equal treatment adjusted for the circumstances—is absent at Stage 1. Also, respondents at Stage 1 have no conception of rules as the product of cooperative agreement. Rules are passed down by those who know the rules, the authorities. A judge would be wrong to make an exception for Heinz (see Colby and Kohlberg, 1987a, p. 242 and 266f.), and so would a jury or even a general referendum. The law is the law. Respondents at this stage take avoiding punishment and gaining reward to be the best reasons for obeying authority, since they regard these as the direct results of obedience.

I quote an interview transcript that Kohlberg and his colleagues scored at Stage 1. They scored it as a solid Stage 1 with hints of Stage 2 in the responses to questions 7 and 7b. Colby and Kohlberg (1987a) offered this and the following transcripts as unmarked practice cases for those learning to score Moral Judgment Interviews (see Kohlberg, 1985, for other examples selected to illustrate stage descriptions). (The bracketed insertions in these transcripts are not mine but are in the version from which I am quoting.) This transcript is from Case #410.

1. *Should Heinz steal the drug?*
    No, because it's a rule [that you're] not supposed to steal. It's not right. It's a crime.
3. *Suppose the person dying is not his wife but a stranger. Should Heinz steal the drug for the stranger?*
    No, it's not right.
4. *Suppose it's a pet animal he loves. Should Heinz steal to save the pet animal?*
    No, it's not right for him to steal drugs from the store.

6. *It is against the law for Heinz to steal. Does that make it morally wrong?*
   Yes, it's against the law.

7. *Should people try to do everything they can to obey the law?*   ⌐
   Yes. They don't want to get hurt or have accidents and die. It could be safety. Like, you obey the stop signs and street lights and walk beside your bicycle across the street because you could run people's feet over and get them hurt.

7b. *How does this apply to what Heinz should do?*
   The man who owns the store might catch him and put him into jail. (Colby and Kohlberg, 1987a, p. 241f.)

Stage 2 is called "Individualistic, Instrumental Morality." The "naive moral realism" of Stage 1, and the corresponding lack of differentiation of perspectives, gives way to a type of moral relativism. Respondents come to believe that all people have their own interests and pursue them as if they were as valid as anyone else's. The pendulum has swung. The interest of Heinz's wife in recovering from her cancer is no more or less valid than the druggist's interest in turning a profit on his investment in developing the drug, and both of these are just as valid, but no more so, than Heinz's interest in keeping his wife alive, say, because she is his closest companion or because she cooks and cleans for him. They are three individuals, and their interests are equal, whatever they happen to be.

The recognition that there are different perspectives on right and wrong and on good and bad leads to the belief that there are in fact no absolute norms. Hence, respondents' decision-making at Stage 2 is instrumental and pragmatic. It proceeds on the basis of risk/cost-benefit analysis. Would Heinz be better off or worse off if he stole the drug, in light of the risks he would incur? Respondents display the beginning of a notion of equity at Stage 2 when they take the needs and desires (but not the intentions) of each individual to be morally relevant. They hold the needs and desires of each to be equally valid, and "just distribution" is accomplished by equalization according to needs and desires. Relationships are based, whether explicitly or implicitly, on reciprocity as mutual exchange bargaining for the sake of personal need and desire satisfaction. Also, respondents at Stage 2 understand social norms in the idiom of the Hobbesian social contract. Social norms are products of agreements resulting from bargaining, and they assume that the reason for obeying social norms, and for disobeying them, is need and desire satisfaction. Heinz has to strike some sort of bargain. So far, the druggist is not budging and the money is not coming in from any of the legal means Heinz has to employ in raising it. From a Stage 2 perspective, the issue for Heinz becomes whether keeping his wife alive is worth the bargain.

Kohlberg and his colleagues scored Case #168 as exhibiting Stage 2 on the Heinz Dilemma.

1. *Should he have done that?*
    If he liked his wife he should.
2. *Is it wrong to do it?*
    Sure, he could go to court.
3. *Would a good husband have to?*
    He wouldn't have to, no. If he didn't want to. But if he loved his wife, he should.
4. *Should he steal for a friend?*
    If the friend had a lot of money, I wouldn't. He could buy it himself, or maybe they would let the doctor buy it.
5. *Would a good husband do it or not?*
    If he wanted to stay out of trouble, he wouldn't. (Colby & Kohlberg, 1987a, p. 261)

Stage 3 is the first of two conventional stages. Kohlberg called it "Interpersonally Normative Morality." At Stage 3, respondents integrate the separate personal perspectives of Stage 2 into a third-person perspective, the perspective of a generalized member of an interpersonal association. Members of particular interpersonal associations more or less share notions of how "one of us" thinks about things. The interpersonally normative perspective of Stage 3 is characterized by shared moral norms and mutually trusting relationships. Heinz is engaged not in a risk/cost-benefit analysis but in deliberating how to maintain the norms and the shared ideals and expectations of an interpersonal association. The primacy of shared norms is embodied in an emphasis on being, in Kohlberg's phrase, a "good role occupant." Respondents come to conceive the equality of persons in terms of role occupation. What would a good person—as understood by "us"—do in these circumstances? What are Heinz's wife and relevant others (but not *all* others) counting on him to do?

The motives for obeying social norms are the mutual recognition and affirmation of acquaintances that come with being a "good role occupant" and also the related sense of interdependence and mutual encumbrance. The desire and need satisfaction that were primary at Stage 2 are secondary at Stage 3. Heinz will want to do the right thing because he understands himself as a member of an interpersonal association where approval and disapproval reflect directly on one's worthiness and are thus reflected in individuals' self-respect. Shared norms and shared ideals and expectations express the group's sense of how they are to be with and for each other. At Stage 3, respondents ground the notion of reciprocity in a sense of obligation and debt to the interpersonal association, and they hold this reciprocity to be the basis of reasons for norm maintenance and for being a good role occupant.

At Stage 3, respondents recognize intentions to be relevant. Intentional violation of shared norms is far more grave than unintentional violation. Also, consenting, cooperating individuals can make exceptions to social norms for the sake of equity. The exchange bargaining characteristic of Stage 2 is at Stage 3 subject to evaluation according to shared norms, and since shared norms are taken to be valid insofar as they are shared, group members are in a position to make mutually acceptable exceptions and/or revisions.

Kohlberg and colleagues identified Case #247 as a Stage 3 reasoner (with hints of Stages 2 and 4).

1. *Should Heinz steal the drug?*
   He should talk to the man and see if he would let him pay for it on time.
2. *There is no other alternative.*
   Well, depending on what he thinks of his wife, he should steal it, I suppose, if he really wants to save her.
3. *What would he think of his wife?*
   If he really loves his wife, if he didn't want to see her die, he should steal it. It's wrong, but he has no other choice; the man is put in a corner, he has to fight his way out of there.
4. *Why is the amount of love he has for his wife, why is that the important thing?*
   If he didn't care for his wife, if he didn't care what happens

to her; but if he really loves his wife, and doesn't want to live without her, then there is no other choice. He has to steal it or she is going to die.

5. *If he does love his wife should he steal the drug?*
Well, he should because it is not right to let the woman die, but if he doesn't want her around anymore, he would have to break the law to get it, so he could legally let the woman pass on, it would be up to him. Yeah, I suppose he should, if the person is going to die a senseless death, the cure is there, but he just can't get it, legally he can't just go in and buy it or charge it, so he steals it or she dies.

6. *Suppose the person dying is a stranger. Should he steal the drug for a stranger?*
Should he? He shouldn't, because I say it is not right to steal in the first place, he doesn't know the person, really what does he care, if it is a complete stranger, he just shouldn't. Why should he care what happens to a stranger?

7. *But you said he should steal for his wife?*
For a loved one.

8. *Even if he doesn't love his wife?*
If he doesn't love his wife, he should. He knows her, he has to have some feeling for her, it might not be love, but it might be friendship or just knowing of a person, but a stranger, he can't have any emotional attachment, to a stranger.

9. *What is to be said for obeying the law in this situation or in general?*
Well, it's wrong to steal, he can be punished for it. Then again, what kind of law is protecting him from a guy who is jacking the price up to ten times the original amount? He is not breaking a law, he can do just what he wants, but it's wrong, the person would be dying because he was greedy for money and I guess the law is going to be on his side, but again, the guy is wrong, but he is still going to get punished for it if he gets caught. They might, in a situation, justice might be easy on it, but he is still breaking the law.

10. *But what is there about the law that you say in general it is bad to steal, it is against the law? Why is it bad to go against the law?*
Well, they are rules set down by the people over the years, if he has to do it that way, which is the legal way, everybody

else has to do it that way and you know if you don't do it that way you are going to get punished for it, you are breaking the law and going against the majority of the people. They set the laws as standards of the country, so you are breaking something that people are living with. So if you can do it that means somebody else can do it, and if you get a slap on the wrist, that person is going to get a slap on the wrist, or shouldn't get a slap on the wrist, and you are just breaking something that people set up for rules to be followed.

11. *Heinz might think it is important to obey the law and save his wife, but can't do both. Is there a way to resolve the conflict between life and law taking the best arguments for both into account?*
Give me some idea of the way I can get started on this one.

12. *Why don't you just take a crack at it?*
I don't really understand how to get into that. Well, one way, I said it, he is forced if he really wants to save his wife, he is forced to steal, if there is no other way this man is going to get this medicine, but now, like I have been saying, the laws have been set up for everyone to be followed, and if they are not followed, the man is in trouble. Now how can you resolve both of them—the man could steal and the next day the law could be easy on him. Kind of give him his punishment but not to the point where the guy is really going to suffer for it. You don't want to see anybody dying senselessly, which would be if he couldn't get it. I don't know any other way to answer it, he's got to get it, but then he would break the law, and the law could be easy on him, that's about the best I can do for you on that one. (Colby and Kohlberg, 1987a, pp. 246–47)

Stage 4 is also a conventional stage, and Kohlberg and his colleagues called it "Social System Morality." Given Kohlberg's understanding of the conventional stages, it is not surprising that he would have thought the relationship-based and goods-centered construal of morality less advanced developmentally than the postconventional stages, which are rules-based and rights- and individual-centered. At Stage 4, respondents systematize norms for the sake of impartiality and consistency. The Stage 3 perspective of a member of an interpersonal association becomes at Stage 4 the perspective of a generalized member of a particular society, e.g., a law-abiding citizen. Stage 4 respondents think of Heinz's predicament as that of a citizen of a society that has a system of law and extralegal social norms. If Heinz can be morally justified in stealing the drug, there will have to be grounds for supposing that in his situation an exception for theft should be made. Some but not all Stage 4 respondents think an exception should indeed be made in Heinz's case. Also, at Stage 4, respondents recognize that even "good role occupants" can be in conflict, and so they understand the need for a system of rules for resolving legitimate conflicts. They conceive the equality of persons as "equality before the law." The legal system must protect the druggist as well as Heinz's wife, though differences of circumstance can warrant different types of protection. If Heinz steals the drug, he should expect to be treated the same as anyone else in relevantly similar circumstances. What particular circumstances people should regard as exceptional, whether as a matter of law or as a matter of extralegal social norms, varies somewhat from society to society.

Respondents construe the norm of reciprocity as a sense of obligation and debt incurred to society. Because Heinz and his wife have received benefits from membership in their society, they are obliged to reciprocate by respecting the society's laws and extralegal social norms. Also, the legal system, and not some specific other or others as in Stage 3, is responsible for authorizing exceptions to the law for the sake of equity. If an exception is to be made in case Heinz steals the drug, it should not be made, say, by a sympathetic arresting officer. The exception should be legal and aboveboard, the result of discretionary processes built into the system and not of personal fiat. Similarly, if Heinz is morally justified according to the society's extralegal social norms, he should be able to offer an aboveboard justification for his actions. Stealing on the sly in the absence of moral justification is strictly forbidden. So the transition from Stage 3 to Stage 4 is a transition from the norm-maintaining perspective of a member of an interpersonal association to the norm-maintaining perspective of a member of a social and legal system.

Kohlberg and his colleagues scored Case #191 as a Stage 3/4 mix. Here are excerpts from an interview about the Heinz Dilemma (Dilemma III) and a related dilemma (Dilemma III') which they scored as Stage 4 responses. The respondent has said that she or he thinks Heinz should definitely steal the drug. "There is no dilemma—life is more precious than anything else."

Dilemma III

7. *Why should people generally do everything they can to avoid breaking the law, anyhow?*

   I don't think it should be "avoid" if you agree to it. It's unhealthy to be a servant of society, not its master. If it's possible to change things you should do it out front—actively try to change. You have a responsibility to accept the results of what you do. Just to know that if you challenge the law, why are you doing it and what you are going to do.

7a. *How does this apply to what Heinz should do?*

   The law is the line, it provides. Reason may be example why and how [*sic*]. A person should be responsible. The laws are made [by] people—people like you. Everyone has more or less an equal chance. [I have substituted "by" for "like" which is printed.—DR]

Dilemma III′

2. *Officer Brown finds and arrests Heinz. Heinz is brought to court, and a jury is selected. The jury's job is to find whether a person is innocent or guilty of committing a crime. The jury finds Heinz guilty. It is up to the judge to determine the sentence. Should the judge give Heinz some sentence, or should he suspend the sentence and let Heinz go free?*

   Punish him. Explain to the court why. He should show everyone what he did that was wrong, what he did that was right. Any court ruling sets a precedent.
   Why?
   This isn't the only case like this—in morals you just can't measure. He is a servant of the law. He is not omnipotent. If I were Heinz, I'd explain why I did it. I don't think they would be so heartless so as not to understand.

3. *Thinking in terms of society, should people who break the law be punished?*

   I wouldn't necessarily call it punished. It depends on the crime—how it was done and why it was done. A person who

> commits the crime should be put in a situation where he benefits and society benefits because he is part of society. Society is made up of individuals just like him. (Colby and Kohlberg, 1987a, pp. 259–60)

Stage 5, which Kohlberg called "Human Rights and Social Welfare Morality," is the first of two postconventional stages. Whereas Kohlberg thought of the conventional stages as "society-maintaining" perspectives, he thought of the postconventional stages as "society-creating" perspectives. At Stage 5, respondents understand the social system as a whole to be an embodiment of universal moral principles. As such, society as a whole is subject to evaluation in terms of those principles. The laws against theft, for instance, are justified by reference to universal moral principles, and reference to these principles in particular cases may also justify morally appropriate exceptions. We can understand the crucial shift from a "society-maintaining" perspective to a "society-creating" perspective as follows: it is the shift from an understanding of the moral validity of law as certified by social consensus to an understanding of the moral validity of law as constituted by reference to universal moral principles. So from a Stage 5 perspective, if moral principles suggest Heinz should steal the drug, he should steal it, even if he breaks the law doing so and even if social consensus is against it.

Respondents may conceive these universal moral principles as based either on a (deontological) theory of human rights or on a (utilitarian) theory of the maximization of human welfare. Deontological theories concern what must be done, irrespective of consequences. For example, it is wrong to kill an innocent person regardless of the benefits to be gained. Utilitarian theories define what must be done by reference to likely and foreseeable consequences for maximizing human welfare. Would raising the minimum wage increase the well-being of those working for the minimum wage enough to offset the harm done to those who might lose their jobs or fail to secure work because of the increase, when we take into account other effects of the change as well? In either case, respondents conceive the equality of rights and the equal worth of persons in terms of the universal value of human life and liberty. In addition, they believe that

the claims and opinions of all individuals are to be considered in resolving conflicts, regardless of an individual's political power or social
role. So, for example, Heinz should consider how his stealing the drug
would be understood and experienced by all the relevant parties
in the situation, the druggist, his wife, local law enforcement, his and
his wife's relatives and friends, the druggist's creditors, etc., as well
as himself. Heinz should steal the drug only if he can weigh the
claims of all relevant parties and reconcile them in an imaginative
dialogue in which each understands the other's claims as they understand them themselves, and only if the imaginative consensus is that
he should steal the drug. In this case, he should steal it—even if no
one of the actual parties agrees in real life, where their perspective
may be partial and selfish.

Finally, taking a deontological perspective, respondents conceive
equity in terms of equal respect of all human beings as ends in themselves (never merely as means to another's ends), and they conceive
the reciprocity of relationships in terms of free rational agreement
in social contract. Kohlberg and his colleagues scored Case #7 at
Stage 5.

1.   *Should Heinz steal the drug?*
     Yes.
1a. *Why or why not?*
     This has to be one of the cleanest-cut dilemmas possible. It
     comes down to simply a question of two values: what's more
     important, respect for life or respect for property. As we
     know, Heinz will break the law but this isn't really all that
     important. Laws are designed to protect life and property,
     and are tools to this end, not sacred ends in themselves. So
     Heinz has a very simple problem and very simple solution:
     steal the drug, as life is more important than property.
2.   *If Heinz doesn't love his wife, should he steal the drug for her?*
     Yes.
2a. *Why or why not?*
     It is not Heinz's love for his wife that is paramount, but the
     life itself. Heinz is possibly under a greater obligation than
     most as this is his wife, but it seems to me that anyone else

who hears of the problem would be under an obligation to act similarly. To repeat, it is not the relation of someone to the life that's important, but rather the life.

3. *Suppose the person dying is not his wife but a stranger? Should Heinz steal the drug for the stranger?*
Yes.

3a. *Why or why not?*
As stated above, the feelings someone has for the person in question are irrelevant. The importance of life over property transcends the relationships or feelings involved.

4. *What's to be said for obeying the law in this situation or in general?*
The laws are tools for the protection of life and property. They have no meaning unless they serve this purpose. If in a situation, the ends are not served by the laws, then one is no longer under any obligation to obey the laws. To do so would be counterproductive. If though, one is not in a situation where the laws and the laws' ends are not at cross-purposes [*sic*], then it could be argued that one should obey the laws. Whether or not it is a moral duty to obey the laws is highly questionable though, and personally, I doubt it.

5. *Heinz might think it's important to obey the law and to save his wife, but he can't do both. Is there a way to resolve the conflict between law and life, taking the best arguments for both into account? Why or why not?*
As stated above, you obey the laws if you feel the laws will help you to reach the proper goals. If they don't, you don't. I am not at all sure what you mean by resolving the conflict. He cannot serve both masters at once in some situations. In conflict situations, he should perform his moral obligations, not his legal ones.

It could be argued that he solves the situations by serving the law's ends rather than their specific means[*sic*]. This argument has some validity, but it does not take into account that generally speaking laws value property as much, if not more, than life. This is possibly necessary so to promote a more harmonious society which benefits the individual and therefore is valid on a global level. On an individual level, one should choose life over property.

So, while one can resolve the conflict in terms of what one actually does on an individual level, because of global considerations, it seems impossible to resolve the conflict so that one serves both laws and life. (Colby & Kohlberg, 1987a, p. 262f.)

Stage 6 is the final stage in Kohlberg's stage sequence and is called the "Morality of Universalizable, Reversible, and Prescriptive General Ethical Principles." Kohlberg called this "the perspective of 'the moral point of view'," the perspective of impartial, reversible role-taking. A reversible judgment is one that takes into account the interests, opinions, and claims of every individual affected by a justice decision. As I described earlier, each individual affected by a decision is to reverse perspectives with all other individuals involved, imagining that she or he is each one in turn. A judgment that would satisfy all perspectives involved is reversible. The principal difference between Stage 5 and Stage 6 is that respondents at Stage 6 make self-conscious use of criteria of universalizability and reversibility as principles of normative validity. Respondents at Stage 5 aim to protect the universal value of human life and liberty and the universal right to fair treatment, but at Stage 5 they do not systematize these into principles. At Stage 6, respondents make universalizability and reversibility explicit criteria for moral judgments. This difference between Stage 5 and Stage 6 can be thought of as representing the time lag between the beginning of unselfconscious reversible reasoning (Stage 5) and the ability to articulate the principle of reversibility (Stage 6). The Stage 6 "moral point of view" (perspective) approaches justice judgments by explicitly and self-consciously invoking universalizable and reversible moral considerations.

Kohlberg and his colleagues did not find many Stage 6 respondents, so few in fact that they dropped Stage 6 from the sequence for which they claimed empirical verification. It is not hard, though, to imagine an example of Stage 6 reasoning on the Heinz Dilemma. Let me invent such an example.

1. *Should Heinz steal the drug?*
    Yes.
1a. *Why or why not?*
    The issue here is the right to life versus the right to property. Heinz should steal the drug because the right to property in

this situation is outweighed by the right to life. If the druggist were to consider the situation from Heinz's and his wife's point of view, he would think Heinz should steal the drug rather than let his wife die. If Heinz and his wife were to consider the situation from the druggist's point of view, they would still think Heinz should steal the drug. They would understand that the druggist has to ignore their predicament to refuse to sell the drug at a lower price or at least to arrange for a purchase on credit. This is what the druggist himself recognizes if he considers their point of view, that he has to be far too partial to his own interests to insist in these circumstances that he has a right to whatever price he asks regardless of the consequences for those who need the drug to live.

2.   *If Heinz doesn't love his wife, should he steal the drug for her?*
Yes.

2a. *Why or why not?*
It doesn't make any difference morally whether Heinz loves his wife or not. The point is that his wife's right to life outweighs the druggist's right to his property.

3.   *Suppose the person dying is not his wife but a stranger? Should Heinz steal the drug for the stranger?*
Yes.

3a. *Why or why not?*
A stranger has a right to life just the same as Heinz's wife. Heinz might have more personal motive for stealing to save his wife's life, but there is no moral difference between his wife and a stranger. If Heinz were to consider the situation from the point of view of the stranger, he would see that there is no moral difference.

I began this chapter by suggesting we might imagine that Kohlberg constructed his entire project as a response to a single problem: how to foster justice and respond to injustice without arbitrarily imposing our personal or group agendas on others. With the structural stage model Kohlberg explained how we can construe justice as universal in spite of substantive differences in details in different cultural regions of the world. Human understandings of justice develop in the same way human understandings of space, time, mass, and so on develop. As Kohlberg knew from Baldwin and Piaget, such cognitive development can be seen as a feature of human biology broadly understood. With the structural stage model, Kohlberg charted and constructed empirical measures of this development of understandings of justice more fully than had any of his predecessors. And though he always retained the basic features of his description of this sequence as set out in his 1958 dissertation, he was led by critics and by his own data to make revisions on some important points. To these I now turn.

FOUR

Revisions of the Model

Are They "Piagetian" Stages?

I explained earlier that in order to meet what Kohlberg took to be Piaget's criteria of developmental stages, Kohlberg's six stages of cognitive-moral development have to be culturally universal structured wholes, progression through which proceeds in an invariant sequence, without passing over a stage and without regression. Each stage, each structured whole or underlying thought organization, must integrate the adequacies of the previous stage with new differentiations that compensate for the inadequacies of the previous stage. Kohlberg and his collaborators had empirical data that they believed supported the conclusion that his six, or at least his first three or four, developmental stages are culturally universal and that they occur in invariant sequence. Kohlberg argued that his stages *are* structured wholes and that they *do* satisfy the criterion of progressive integration and differentiation.

Kohlberg gave an account of these "four general criteria [that] have been used to identify Piagetian (1960) cognitive stages" (Kohlberg, 1984, p. 238). Flanagan (1984, pp. 157–62) has expressed doubts that Kohlberg's stage sequence satisfies these stage criteria. First, he argued that Kohlberg's sequence fails on two counts to be universal in the Piagetian fashion. On the one hand, not all stages are found in all cultures; on the other, not all (biologically normal) individuals go through all the stages to reach the most advanced stage. Kohlberg, however, need not deny this to maintain his claim to universality for the stage sequence.

Given the differences between the physical world (which are the same universally, we might suppose) and the sociomoral world (variable locally) to which subjects adapt, we should not expect Kohlberg's stage sequence to be universal in the same way as the Piagetian cognitive stage sequence. Kohlberg claimed that all (biologically normal) individuals *who receive the appropriate stimulation from their environment* do in fact develop into the postconventional stages of reasoning. If his data and his interpretation of them on this count are sound, then Kohlberg had a plausible and empirically testable explanation for an otherwise embarrassing finding—that not all individuals in any given culture and no individuals in some cultures reach the most advanced two or three stages. Simply put, they are understimulated in a way in which Piagetian subjects adapting to the physical world are not. Everyone falls off things as a child, has experience with objects that disappear behind foreground objects only to reappear from behind them later, and so on. But not everyone has adequate role-playing opportunities in which they are expected, say, to make decisions for the good of a group and hence from the perspective of the group as a whole, and so on.

Hypothetically, if we could systematically ensure that significant populations were understimulated in adaptation to the physical world, it seems quite likely that we could find stage-sequence results similar to Kohlberg's. Similarly, if we could systematically ensure that all people received adequate sociomoral stimulation, on the Kohlbergian account of what this would involve, we would find a distribution across the Kohlbergian justice-reasoning stages much more like that found across the Piagetian cognitive stages.

Second, Flanagan asserted that, as described, Kohlberg's stages do meet the structured wholes criterion. "Each Kohlbergian stage is a neatly packaged, internally consistent, moral philosophy" (Flanagan, 1984, p. 157). However, on the basis of what seem to be data to the contrary, Flanagan had reservations about Kohlberg's claim that "on the average two-thirds of an individual's thinking was assignable to a single modal stage." Flanagan correctly noted that if Kohlberg's stage theory is to apply to real people, individuals must be found to reason characteristically, although not necessarily exclusively, from the perspective of one specifiable stage. Many respondents give answers to interview questions that contain elements scorable at three or even four different stages. The transcripts I quoted in illustrating the stage definitions were practice cases for those learning to score MJIs and were selected for their relative clarity (twice over: by Colby and Kohlberg, 1987a, and then by me from their selection). Still, they were not unmixed. Often less than two-thirds of each subject's responses over several dilemmas are scorable at a single stage.

Third, verifying the invariant-sequence criterion depends on having data that indicate characteristic response from a single stage. To the extent that these data are unclear, we have to withhold judgment on invariant sequence.

Fourth, verifying the no-regression criterion also depends on data concerning response consistency, because it too depends on being able to discern a definable progression of reasoning. However, on inspiration from data that seemed to indicate stage regression (especially during the college years for those who attended college, see Kohlberg and Kramer, 1969), Kohlberg and colleagues revised their stage-scoring criteria, eliminating significant evidence of the existence of Stage 6 (see Kohlberg, Levine, and Hewer, 1983). Flanagan interpreted this revision as a case of grasping the nettle to save the paradigm. He queried,

> why not just accept the intuitively plausible regression evidence and give up the no-regression claim? Kohlberg, as far as I can tell, obstinately refuses to consider this possibility. But he does so without any convincing argument. . . . the theory is a mess with regard to the no-regression requirement. (Flanagan, 1984, p. 159f.)

Flanagan seemed to ask, "Why sacrifice Stage 6—the terminus of development in relation to which the other stages are defined and interpreted as inadequate approximations—for the sake of the no-regression criterion?"

In his "summary scorecard" Flanagan said that Kohlberg's sequence fails the no-regression criterion, but he reached this conclusion without convincing argument. A close examination of the data and revised stage-scoring criteria is required to support Flanagan's conclusion, and he has offered no account of such an examination. Furthermore, until some argument is given that shows that abandoning the claims to empirical evidence for the existence of Stage 6 is fatal to Kohlberg's theory, the jury is still out on the no-regression criterion. Flanagan does concede that "The scorecard, of course, could improve depending on how data gathered by independent researchers [turn] out" (Flanagan, 1984, p. 162; cf. n. 66, chap. 5, p. 307).

Gilligan and Murphy (1979) argued that Kohlberg's stage-regression data and his failure entirely to compensate for these anomalous data by revising his stage-scoring criteria can be explained by reinterpreting the data as follows. Kohlberg's longitudinal data on the original sample seem to show stage regression in the reasoning of a significant number of subjects—20 percent (Gilligan and Murphy, 1979, p. 90)—in late adolescence and adulthood. Many subjects seemed to regress from principled moral reasoning to what appeared in the Kohlbergian scheme to be Stage 2 relativistic reasoning. College-student relativism is a clear and common case of the type of apparent regression that presented anomalous data. Kohlberg's failure, according to Gilligan and Murphy, was in not noticing that this apparent regression was in fact a *progression* toward a more complex understanding of the application of formal, universal moral principles in real-life situations. This progression is elicited by a recognition of the "actual consequences of choice."

Murphy and Gilligan (1980) noted that while some psychologists have argued for the rejection of Kohlberg's theory as a whole, others have directed their criticisms toward Stages 4–6 or 5–6.

> This line of criticism has been supported both longitudinally and cross-culturally by empirical work which has confirmed the sequentiality of the first three of Kohlberg's six stages, while at the same time presenting evidence against invariant sequence for stages 4, 5, and 6. Based on these and other studies, one of Kohlberg's closest associates claims that stages 5 and 6 are best considered not as naturally occurring stages in the strict Piagetian sense, but rather as metaethical or philosophical reflections upon the normative judgments of earlier stages. (Murphy and Gilligan, 1980, p. 78; the reference is presumably to John Gibbs, 1977, 1979)

Murphy and Gilligan rejected this line of criticism on the grounds that it fails to account for moral development beyond adolescence. They argued that the data collected by Kohlberg and others can be interpreted as conforming to the invariant sequence and no-regression criteria and as supporting the existence of both Kohlberg's postconventional stages *and* a post-postconventional stage(s) which they called "contextual relativism." Kohlberg's version of the stage sequence stops short of what is required to account for the data, but it is correct as far as it goes, Murphy and Gilligan (1980) suggested. Keep Stage 6 and add a post-postconventional form of contextual relativism.

According to Gilligan and Murphy (1979), individuals in late adolescence and adulthood come to recognize the insufficiency of formal (context-independent) principles alone for determining the objectively correct moral judgment and action. In struggling to come to terms with the vagueness of real-life moral problems and the uncertainty of judgments in these particular contexts, individuals develop a commitment to responsibility for their judgments, acknowledging them to be contextually relative. Hence, their moral reasoning *appears* to embody a regression to a Stage 2 type of relativism while *in fact* it embodies a progression to post-postconventional "contextual relativism." Murphy and Gilligan (1980) called this "postconventional contextual," in distinction from the developmentally antecedent "postconventional formal" (Murphy and Gilligan, 1980, pp. 80–83). "[T]he regressors are progressors," Murphy and Gilligan contended, "when evaluated against a standard of commitment in relativism instead of absolute principles of justice" (Murphy and Gilligan 1980, p. 77).

Finally, in respect to Kohlberg's increasing differentiation and integration claim, that the stages in his sequence integrate the conceptual adequacies of the previous stages while making new and more adaptive conceptual differentiations, Flanagan noted that "it depends on exactly how the stages are described, but a plausible case can be made that they do." Yet he cited what he took to be "one possible snag, having to do with the relativistic substage 4½" (which was what Kohlberg had provisionally called the anomalous [college student] relativism). Flanagan stated his worry as follows: "it is hard to see how stage 4½ integrates the concern with doing one's duty, the acknowledgment of social responsibilities, and the nonegoistic features of stages 3 and 4, all of which return at stages 5 and 6." But this is a "snag" only if either 4½ is a genuine stage rather than a transitional phase or, even if a phase, 4½ must satisfy the integration criterion. Indeed, Kohlberg eventually held that 4½ *does* integrate a conception of the Stage 4 perspective and *does* preface Stage 5.

> For all these reasons, we have given up calling relativism and subjectivism "Stage 4½," a transitional stage. We do, however, retain our conviction that some form of subjectivism or relativism is a necessary but not sufficient condition for movement to Stage 5. This is because a conception of liberal tolerance and universal individual rights represents a Stage 5 principle that presupposes a questioning of the legitimacy or

absoluteness of the culture's rule system (Stage 4). (Kohlberg, 1984, p. 440f.)

On this account, Flanagan saw Stage 4½ as a problem or "snag" because he failed to see that it integrates the conceptual perspective of Stage 4, even if not retaining the sense of obligation to social convention characteristic of Stage 4.

In short, Kohlberg reinterpreted his data as evidence for a subjectivist or relativist transition from the conventional to the now apparently far more rare postconventional stages (which he was still committed to holding as adequate and final). Gilligan and Murphy interpreted the same data as evidence for a post-postconventional contextual relativism, more advanced developmentally than Kantian formalism. And Flanagan interpreted the data and the rash of interpretations as evidence of serious problems with the theory.

Early Reformulations of the Model

As I have noted, there were many criticisms of early versions of the structural stage model. Some critics contended that the problems were symptoms of fundamental flaws in the design. Kohlberg and his colleagues, meanwhile, were constantly discussing needed revisions. By 1973, Kohlberg (1973; see 1984, pp. 250–52) had come to believe that his original (1958) construction of the moral stages confounded the formal properties of a justice judgment with the content and explanation of the dilemma choice (see Colby, 1978). The dilemmas he posed to his subjects presented them with choices between two alternative courses of action. In the case of the Heinz Dilemma, the choice is between Heinz's obeying the law and his stealing the only known remedy for the special kind of cancer from which his wife suffers. Kohlberg initially identified the choice to obey the law whatever the cost with a heteronomous obedience to authority, whereas he identified the choice to steal the drug in order to save Heinz's wife with an autonomous ranking of the value of life over the value of property. Kohlberg then inferred the stage content from the content and explanation of the dilemma choice, and from this assessment of stage content he inferred the formal structure of the stage as an "ideal type" reasoning perspective.

Using this earlier method for constructing the structural stage model, Kohlberg (1958) found some youths of fourteen to sixteen years of age reasoning at Stages 5 and 6. However, using this early stage-scoring system, he also found anomalous longitudinal data of the sort examined by Flanagan and Gilligan, which I have mentioned. As I have indicated, he found that some of his subjects regressed in their stage development and that many subjects tested as occupying three and even four stages at the same time (across several dilemmas), with no stage predominating in the dilemma choices and explanations. Reexamining the formulation of the stages and the stage-scoring mechanism and refining both, Kohlberg believed that he eliminated the anomalies (see Colby, 1978, for an account of the three stages in the "evolution" of the theory).

Kohlberg and his colleagues made a crucial theory refinement as a result of this reexamination. They referred to this refinement as the clarification of the distinction between the formal properties and the content of the reasoning at each stage. In Kohlberg's penultimate formulation of the theory, the formal properties or deep structure of the reasoning about justice at each stage, the "justice structure" of each stage, consists of two levels: the social-perspective level and the moral or prescriptive level. The social-perspective level is the individual's understanding of her or his relationship to the particular society of which she or he is a member, although not necessarily a full participant. The moral or prescriptive level is the understanding of the definition and role of rights and duties as structured by three "justice operations": equality, equity, and reciprocity. The content of justice reasoning at a given stage is composed of the issue or dilemma choice, as described earlier, and the norms and considerations of consequences that Kohlberg called the "elements" (Kohlberg, 1984, p. 309).

Kohlberg further refined the theory by discerning two substages that occur at each of at least Stages 3 through 5 (Kohlberg, 1984, pp. 252–57 and Appendix C). He describes the substages as midway between the form and content of each stage. They are the heteronomous A substage and the autonomous B substage. B substage reasoning is distinguished from A substage reasoning by its preference for the autonomous choice in a dilemma plus certain formal features of reasoning. The autonomous choice is the choice agreed upon by Stage 5 and 6 reasoners because of its characteristic ranking of the value of life over lesser things such as status or property. Norms and considerations of consequences are brought to bear on a dilemma choice in B substage reasoning, whatever the justice stage, such that the autonomous choice is preferred. The formal features of B substage reasoning include the Kantian criteria of prescriptivity, universalizability, and "intrinsicality" (respect for the intrinsic value of human life, the intrinsic moral worth of persons), and the Piagetian criteria of cooperation, mutual respect, contract, and reversibility.

Where there is intrastage change, it is characteristically from A to B rather than vice versa, and interstage change or development of justice reasoning sometimes occurs, in Kohlberg's terms, "implicitly," e.g., 3A to 4A to 5A, or "explicitly," e.g., 3B to 4B to 5B. Also, Kohlberg contended that B substage reasoners act more consistently in accord with their judgments than do A substage reasoners (Kohlberg, 1984, p. 255). Perhaps this last could be accounted for by noting that heteronomous reasoning is an articulation of what we conceive as expected of us by others, whereas autonomous reasoning is an articulation of what we expect of ourselves, and we are perhaps more likely to do what we expect of ourselves than what we perceive as expected of us by others.

It is easy to see at this point—and hard to overemphasize—that as the stage definitions became more fine-grained, the scoring tasks became more technically complex and demanding. Kohlberg and his colleagues had to redesign the interview and scoring manual to be far more sensitive to subtle variations. Several major revisions occurred during the three decades of Kohlberg's career (see Colby, 1978, and Colby and Kohlberg, 1987a and 1987b). Initially, Kohlberg had noted the content of the dilemma choice (e.g., steal or do not steal) and the explanation given for the choice (e.g., Heinz should steal because he loves his wife and needs her). He had inferred from the dilemma choice and explanation the content of the various stages: roughly, the naive moral realism of Stage 1, the relativism of interests and claims of Stage 2, the interpersonal norms and perspective of Stage 3, the social norms and perspective of Stage 4, the universal principles of Stage 5, and the explicit formulation of a criterion of reversibility of Stage 6. And he had inferred from the stage contents the basic structure of the justice reasoning of each stage, say, the conception of reciprocity or of equity at each stage level. Now, though,

Kohlberg and his colleagues had concluded that they had to refine the definitions of the stage structures in order to be able to make "Piagetian" sense of the dilemma choices and explanations, that is, in order to preserve what Kohlberg understood to be the requirements of the Piagetian stage criteria. For instance, they articulated two levels of stage structure (the social-perspective level and the moral/prescriptive level) and two substages for each stage (at least for Stages 3, 4, and 5). Each new theoretical distinction they articulated in order to make sense of the data required elaborate operationalization in the scoring mechanism. The interview and scoring manual (finally published as Colby and Kohlberg, 1987a and 1987b) became more and more complex, and people who wanted to learn to give and score Kohlbergian Moral Judgment Interviews (MJIs) were advised to attend training seminars offered in the summers at the Center for Moral Development, operated out of Larsen Hall at Harvard.

In short, as the stage theory became more complex, the revolutionary work of empirical explication and corroboration began to seem to some almost baroque; to others it was reminiscent of Ptolemaic epicycles (Phillips and Nicolayev, 1978; Shweder, Mahapatra, and Miller, 1987). On the other hand, why assume human moral development is uncomplicated? Why suppose a theory adequate to the facts would be elegant and simple? There is a difference between requiring theories to be no more complicated than necessary and requiring them to be simple. The ontological implications of requiring theories to be elegant and simple, in the name of requiring them to be no more complicated than necessary, are not insignificant. Nonetheless, it is not surprising in this one respect at least that Kohlberg and his colleagues would have hesitated and even balked at the suggestion—often from the same critics who supposed the theory had become too complex— that the dilemmas themselves were too abstract and coarse-grained. Imagine the coding nightmares of introducing even further complexity by making the dilemmas, the moral reasoning prompts, even more likely to call forth ambiguities and subtleties of multistage reasoning.

The Disappearance of Stage 6

In addition to more clearly distinguishing between the form and content of justice reasoning, Kohlberg modified the presentation of his stage theory by diminishing his claims to the empirical verification of Stage 6. "Stage 6 has disappeared as a commonly identifiable form of moral reasoning as our stage-scoring concepts and criteria have developed from continuing analysis of our longitudinal data" (Kohlberg, Levine, and Hewer, 1983, in Kohlberg, 1984, p. 270). As the anomalous longitudinal data were for the most part eliminated by refining the theory and the stage-scoring mechanism, Kohlberg and his colleagues came to interpret the empirical evidence for Stage 6 as inconclusive. For example, data that seemed to indicate stage regression were reinterpreted to adjust chronologically prior stage-scoring down, as from a scoring of Stage 5 or 6 to a scoring of B substage at Stage 3 or 4. Dilemma responses they had interpreted as postconventional came to be interpreted as autonomously conventional, and so apparent regression either diminished or disappeared altogether. What had, for example, appeared to be a transition from Stage 4 to Stage 5 and then back to Stage 2, 3, or 4 could now be interpreted as a transition from, say, Stage 3A to 3B to 4A. Kohlberg explained the newly recognized difference between these as follows: Substage B orientations at the conventional stages lack the organization of moral judgment around a clearly formulated moral principle of justice and respect for persons that provides a rationale for the primacy of this principle. Substage B represents an intuition of parts of both the form and content of solutions reached with Stage 5 or 6 reasoning but cannot yet articulate the central principle of justice which rationally justifies this content and form (Kohlberg, 1984, p. 271). The upshot was that taking care of anomalies required conceding that the case for Stage 6 was empirically very weak.

Kohlberg continued, however, to postulate Stage 6 as the final or terminal Piagetian stage of moral development because, as he had argued all along, the developmental sequence as a whole must be conceived in terms of its terminal or final stage. In what Kohlberg understood as a developmental sequence, all preterminal stages are by definition, and to different degrees, inadequate versions of the terminal stage. Also, the moral theory of which a cognitive-moral developmental sequence is an embodiment must be defended in part by defending the normative claims of the terminal stage. On Kohlberg's Piagetian view, the terminal stage is the most cognitively and the most morally adequate, so that rendering a philosophic defense of the moral theory embodied in Stage 6 reasoning is an important part of defending the conception of the developmental sequence as a whole. The terminal stage must embody the most adequate moral theory, and the claim that it does requires moral philosophic defense. Kohlberg referred to Rawls's theory of justice as "a rational description of parts of the sixth stage," e.g., the notions of equilibration and reversibility (Kohlberg, 1984, p. 272). I will return to Kohlberg's adequacy thesis later. Aside from this moral philosophic defense, however, the empirical evidence for the claim that Stage 6 embodies the most adequate moral theory fell short of conclusive support for Kohlberg's normative views.

> At this point, our stage findings do not allow us to claim evidence for certain normative ethical conclusions which nevertheless remain my own philosophic preference for defining an ontogenetic end point of a rationally reconstructed theory of justice reasoning.
>
> In particular, we cannot claim either that there is a single principle which we have found used at the current empirically highest stage, nor that that principle is the principle of justice or respect for persons. There may be other principles. (Kohlberg, Levine, and Hewer, 1983, in Kohlberg, 1984, p. 273)

Stage 7

However, even though Kohlberg reduced the strength of his claims to empirical verification of the Piagetian Stage 6, he postulated a hypothetical, non-Piagetian Stage 7 that embodies a "religio-cosmic perspective." Though Kohlberg and Power (1981) first published the idea of Stage 7 two years before Kohlberg would withdraw the claim to verification for Stage 6, Kohlberg continued to affirm Stage 7 as a hypothetical, quasi-stage, not meeting the criteria for Piagetian stages. (Kohlberg, Levine, and Hewer, 1983, in which the claim for empirical support of Stage 6 is withdrawn, also discusses Stage 7 as part of the current formulation of the theory.) Stage 7 dilemma choices and explanations are "based on constructing a sense of identity or unity with being, with life, or with God" (Kohlberg, 1984, p. 249). The impetus for constructing this sense of unity, Kohlberg thought, is the perception that the "universe [is] filled with injustice, suffering, and death." Why be moral, why be just in such a universe? The endeavor to find meaningful solutions to moral and religious problems and the more encompassing endeavor to find personal meaning for one's life, Kohlberg and Power (1981) argued, takes one beyond the postconventional stages of justice reasoning (Kohlberg, 1981, pp. 311–72; and see p. 172).

> Unlike the analytic and dualistic development of justice reasoning (i.e., reasoning based on the differentiation of self and other, subject and object), ethical and religious non-Piagetian "soft" stage development culminates in a synthetic, nondualistic sense of participation in, and identity with, a cosmic order. The self is understood as a component of this order, and its meaning is understood as being contingent upon participation in this order.
>
> From a cosmic perspective, such as the one just described, postconventional principles of justice and care are perceived within what might be broadly termed a natural law framework. From such a framework, moral principles are not seen as arbitrary human inventions; rather, they are seen as principles of justice that are in harmony with broader laws regulating the evolution of human nature and the cosmic order.
>
> Thus, in our opinion, a soft Stage 7 of ethical and religious thinking presupposes but goes beyond postconventional justice reasoning. More generally, we believe that the development of soft stages toward the cosmic perspective just described informs us of trends in human development which can not [sic] be captured within a conceptual framework restricted to the study of justice reasoning per se. (Kohlberg, 1984, p. 250)

Kohlberg regarded Stage 7 as non-Piagetian in the sense that it does not meet the structural stage criteria explained earlier, and it is hypothetical because Kohlberg had insufficient data to verify its existence (beyond his own pantheistic, Spinozan cosmology). Kohlberg postulated Stage 7 in order to explain what he took to be an aspect of moral development in maturity, development that supplements but presupposes the terminal, adequate stage of justice reasoning. (I note with interest that Kohlberg and Power formulated this super-postconventional reasoning perspective at about the same time [see Kohlberg, 1981, p. xvi, which dates the Kohlberg and Power essay at 1979] that

Gilligan and Murphy [1979] proposed a post-postconventional reasoning perspective, one they dubbed "contextual relativism.")

I mention Kohlberg's hypothetical, non-Piagetian Stage 7 because of its relevance to discussion of the terminal stage in a developmental sequence. Some philosophers, most notably Elizabeth Anscombe (1958), have claimed that the modern liberal ethics of universal moral law, upon which are based universal rights, presupposes a divine law conceptual framework. For how are we to conceive laws without a legislator? And do not universal moral laws require a universal legislator?

If, as Kohlberg held, Stage 7 is arrived at through attempts to understand the meaning of a just life in a universe that appears to be filled with injustice, through attempts to answer the question "Why be moral?" which the stages of justice reasoning, unsupplemented by a religious or cosmic perspective, cannot answer, then should we not say that the postconventional stages of justice reasoning are inadequate? If the answer is that they are by themselves inadequate, then some version of a religio-cosmic perspective is the genuine terminus of Kohlberg's cognitive-moral developmental sequence—not the Rawlsian Stage 6 for which at any rate there seems inadequate empirical support. Kohlberg contended that Stage 6 is adequate for the adjudication of conflicting claims among persons, but he did not suppose that it can provide a full justification for abiding by Stage 6 conflict resolutions. He did not suppose a Stage 6 perspective would account for why one should be moral. Is this type of justification required from any moral theory deemed adequate? That is, is the requirement for this type of justification one of the criteria of adequacy of a moral theory?

The notion that a postconventional justice-reasoning perspective such as Stage 6 could be adequate without a divine law conceptual underpinning is required by the modern moral philosophy from Hobbes to Sidgwick, as Anscombe argued, and perhaps also from Sidgwick to, e.g., Dworkin, Gert, Gewirth, and Gauthier, not to mention Rawls. The reason Kohlberg stood with liberalism on this point was he saw that religio-cosmic perspectives are obviously not culturally neutral. Accordingly, as I suggested in the beginning, Kohlberg believed he could not save antirelativism if he embraced a culturally nonneutral, religio-cosmic perspective. (An important question is whether in fact Stage 6 is culturally neutral at all.)

Justice, Attachments, and Special Responsibilities

In addition to the modifications of the original six-stage sequence incorporated into the penultimate formulation of the theory, Kohlberg extended his structural stage model in two important ways. First, in response to criticisms from Gilligan (esp. Gilligan, 1982) and others, Kohlberg began to incorporate considerations of particularistic social relationships. He attempted to bring personal loyalties and attitudes of caring, love, and special responsibilities to family and friends into his conception of morality as deontological, i.e., morality as the universal prescriptive language of rights and duties (Kohlberg, 1984, pp. 224–36, and see pp. 338–70, and Kohlberg, 1982, pp. 513–15). Second, Kohlberg began the elaboration of the stages as a basis of a theory of moral action (Kohlberg, 1984, pp. 257–70), relating the justice stage structure to the content of deontic choice (choice with respect to rights and duties), recognizing the relevance of judgments of interpersonal responsibility to moral action, and extending the stage theory into an analysis of "moral atmosphere," i.e., the collective norms of a group or community.

I discuss what came to be called the "judgment-action problem" in the next section and describe the moral-atmosphere research briefly there but more fully later. I now take up the somewhat knotty and occasionally confusing matter of the relationship between the ethics of justice and care.

In their formulation of the theory, Kohlberg, Levine, and Hewer (1983) explained the justice-centered, deontological basis of the early formulations of Kohlberg's moral theory. Kohlberg derived the construal of morality with which and in terms of which he began his psychological research and theorizing

> from R. M. Hare's (1963) neo-Kantian definition of morality, phrased in formal terms [i.e., prescriptivity and universalizability].
> . . . In other words, I assumed that the core of morality and moral

development was deontological; that is, it was a matter of rights and duties or prescriptions. My assumption about the deontological form of mature moral judgment was associated with the assumption that the core of deontological morality was justice or principles of justice. My assumption concerning the centrality of justice derived directly from Piaget's (1932) own study of the development of moral judgment and reasoning. (Kohlberg, 1984, pp. 224–25)

Kohlberg's initial work presupposed what he took to be a neo-Kantian, deontological conception of morality and a Piagetian assumption of the primacy of "justice reasoning" in the domain of morality (Kohlberg, 1984, p. 228). However, while Kohlberg's research focused on what he called "justice reasoning," or reasoning about conflicts of claims between persons, he recognized that reasoning about justice does not exhaust the domain of morality. Since the mid-1970s, Gilligan and then some of her colleagues have been conducting research about moral reasoning in "real-life," as opposed to hypothetical moral dilemmas. Gilligan began her work as a research associate conducting Kohlbergian interviews with respondents about dilemmas they had actually experienced, for instance, whether or not to have an abortion. They have found an approach to moral dilemmas not captured by Kohlberg's theory of justice-reasoning stages and which, following Gilligan (1977, 1982), has come to be called a "different voice."

They discerned and formulated "an orientation of care and responsibility" which they sometimes seemed to regard as distinct from and independent of Kohlberg's justice orientation. Gilligan and Murphy (1979) had suggested a developmental successor to the six-stage sequence, but the different voice hypothesis has seemed for the most part to suggest an independent, "non-Piagetian" stage sequence. Another result of their research was the finding that significantly more women than men reason from the perspective of the care orientation, while significantly more men than women reason from the perspective of the deontological, justice orientation. Both orientations are nonetheless employed by most subjects some of the time. Lyons (1983), one of Gilligan's colleagues and a former student, gave a statement of this sex-difference thesis cast in high relief, and Walker (1984) offered the best known challenge to the sex-difference thesis.

Kohlberg, Levine, and Hewer (1983) characterized the distinction between these two orientations as follows:

> This and other material does *not* indicate to us that there are two
> separate general moralities, one morality of justice and generalized
> fairness and another completely separate or opposed morality of
> care. In our view, special obligations of care presuppose, but go be-
> yond, the general duties of justice, which are necessary but not suf-
> ficient for them. Thus, special relationship dilemmas may elicit care
> responses which supplement and deepen the sense of generalized ob-
> ligations of justice. In our standard dilemmas considerations of spe-
> cial relationship are in some sense supplementary, since they go be-
> yond the duties owed to another on the basis of a person's rights.
> These considerations, however, need not be seen as being in conflict
> with a justice ethic; in our example, Heinz's care for his wife deep-
> ened his sense of obligation to respect her right to life. Thus, those
> responses to our justice dilemmas which articulate these special con-
> siderations use them as *supplements to, rather than alternatives for,* jus-
> tice solutions to the problems posed. We believe that what Gilligan
> calls an ethic of care is, in and of itself, not well adapted to resolve
> justice problems, problems which require principles to resolve con-
> flicting claims among persons, all of whom in some sense should be
> cared about. (Kohlberg, 1984, p. 229; my emphasis)

The care orientation by itself, on Kohlberg's view, cannot resolve a
wide range of moral problems that require for their adjudication the
application of principles of justice. In conjunction with the justice
orientation, however, as Kohlberg saw it in 1983 (Kohlberg, Levine,
and Hewer, 1983), the care orientation enhances the generalized obligations of impartial principles of justice and is more comprehensive
than the justice orientation's limitation to impersonal rights and duties. The formalistic justice orientation is characterized by impartiality and universality and aims at consensual agreement with all human beings qua human beings concerning the "right" adjudication
of conflicting claims. The care orientation, by contrast, is particularistic in the sense that it regards partiality to family and friends as morally appropriate and, in general, regards considerations of care and
special responsibility to be contextual rather than universalizable.

As I mentioned earlier, on the revisionist story I am telling,

Kohlberg never intended his account of morality to make interpersonal responsiveness central. It is not clear he even thought it morally relevant in earlier formulations. In 1983 he conceded its relevance as a supplement to justice, but he continued to maintain that justice is the core of morality. Kohlberg meant primarily to show why fundamental violations of human dignity such as the Holocaust of World War II are cross-culturally, ahistorically wrong. He meant to formulate a philosophical account of morality—and to elaborate and corroborate it empirically—that would articulate justice as the universal condition for the possibility of interpersonal responsiveness. He meant to show how we can foster justice and respond to injustice without arbitrarily imposing our own cultural or personal agenda on others. Justice protects and fosters individuals. Interpersonal associations presuppose just conditions. Care presupposes and supplements justice. Many students and colleagues worked closely with Kohlberg during his thirty-year career. They speak of him as a person who was responsive almost to a fault, well beyond what many university professors deem required in their dealings with the personal and professional concerns of their associates. Through a single-minded devotion to his work and his associates, Kohlberg gathered an intensely loyal following, many of whom continue his work. But on Kohlberg's account of morality, personal loyalty and responsiveness presuppose conditions of fundamental justice.

Kohlberg explained the difference of Gilligan's findings from his own as resulting from the difference in the type of dilemma she discussed with her respondents. She discussed "real life" dilemmas (such as whether the women with whom she was talking should go ahead with their plans for an abortion) that evoked considerations of care and special responsibility, dilemmas that in their lived context are adequately described and adequately addressed only by taking into account interpersonal relationships of care and loyalty. The idea was that some dilemmas draw more on concrete, interpersonal considerations, while some draw more on abstract, impersonal considerations. For instance, the Elderly Parent Dilemma evokes considerations based on interpersonal relationships in a way the Needy Children Dilemma does not, since Beverly and Stephen have no particular children in mind whom they might adopt. The dilemmas Gilligan discussed were dilemmas that did not explicitly evoke impartial justice considerations but which, Kohlberg argued, nevertheless presupposed a framework of impersonal rights and duties. Further,

> At the postconventional level of justice reasoning the distinction between these two kinds of dilemmas is understood. Reasoning at this postconventional level leads to a *tolerance* about the resolution of personal dilemmas of special obligation while at the same time upholding a general framework of nonrelative justice that provides the context within which individually varying personal moral decision making takes place. (Kohlberg, 1984, p. 232; my emphasis)

Different types of dilemmas evoke different types of moral considerations, but considerations of care and special responsibility presuppose a framework of impersonal rights and duties, and the mature moral reasoner is the most capable at bringing the various considerations to bear on moral problems, allowing (showing "tolerance") where appropriate for the importance of special relationships and obligations. The mature moral reasoner best understands the distinction between the justice orientation and the care orientation and best knows how to bring these orientations to bear on moral problem situations. The implication of this response, intended or not, would not have escaped Gilligan.

Moral Atmosphere and the Judgment-Action Problem

Finally, Kohlberg also undertook the elaboration of the structural stage model as a basis of a theory of moral action. This elaboration has three aspects, as mentioned above: relating the justice stage structure to the content of deontic choice, recognizing the relevance of judgments of responsibility to moral action, and the sociological extension of the stage theory into an analysis of "moral atmosphere," i.e., the collective norms of a group or community (Kohlberg, 1984, pp. 257–70 and 498–581).

Kohlberg analyzed moral action into three steps as follows: the deontic choice of rightness or justice in the particular situation, the judgment that the self is responsible or accountable for carrying out the deontic judgment in moral action, and carrying out the deontic judgment in moral action (Kohlberg, 1984, p. 258). So on Kohlberg's account moral action involves two types of judgment and a sub-

sequent carrying out of the action in question. How are these judgments correlated empirically with moral action?

First, Kohlberg believed he had empirical support (Blasi, 1980;
Rest, 1983, 1984) for the notion that the higher a subject's stage of
justice reasoning, the more likely the subject's action would be consistent with her or his deontic choice. Hence, Stage 5 and 6 reasoners
act more consistently in accord with their moral judgments than do
individuals at the earlier stages, and Stage 4 reasoners more consistently than individuals at earlier stages, and so on. Kohlberg accounted for this correlation with a hypothesis for which he also
believed he had empirical support (Helkama, 1979): "there is a mono-
tonic increase in consistency by stage between the deontic judgment
made and a judgment of the self's responsibility to carry out this judgment in action" (Kohlberg, 1984, p. 258). So the positive correlation
between the justice-reasoning stage and moral action is mediated by
a positive correlation between the justice-reasoning stage and the
judgment of responsibility for carrying out the action in question.
Kohlberg accounted for this correlation by claiming that each pro-
gressively advanced stage of justice reasoning is more prescriptive
than the preceding stage. Each subsequent stage more adequately distinguishes the moral (prescriptive and universal) from the nonmoral
considerations that apply to particular judgments. Hence, the higher
the justice-reasoning stage, the more likely the reasoner is to judge
that he or she is personally responsible for carrying out the action,
and consequently the more likely the reasoner will actually carry out
the action. So the moral stage influences moral action in two ways:
through the deontic choice or judgment and through a judgment of
responsibility (see Kohlberg, 1981, pp. 183–89).

In addition to the correlation between the justice-reasoning stage
development and moral action, Kohlberg claimed that there is a correlation between the justice-reasoning substage and moral action.
Those using B substage (autonomous) reasoning are more likely than
those using A substage (heteronomous) reasoning to perform the
"right" action (the one most often judged right at Stages 5 and 6).
Kohlberg accounted for this correlation by claiming that B substage
reasoning is more prescriptive, reversible, and universalistic than is
the A substage reasoning, and so B substage judgments of rights and

responsibilities are more like those of Stage 5 and 6 than A substage judgments are (Kohlberg, 1984, p. 260). So individuals who reason at either Stage 5 and 6 or the B substage at a conventional level are *both* more likely to make judgments of responsibility and perform actions consistent with their deontic judgments *and* more likely to perform the "right" action, i.e., the action prescribed by philosophic principles and postconventional reasoning (1984, p. 261).

For a thoroughgoing developmentalist, the following question inevitably arises: is moral action always preceded by judgments of justice and responsibility that develop prior to and independently of action patterns, or do judgments of justice and responsibility develop only after consistent patterns of moral action are established, and then as an articulation of the rationale for ongoing action patterns? I mentioned earlier that Piaget believed that patterns of behavior in conformity to rules precede consciousness (or articulation) of rules as the rationale for action patterns. My description of Kohlberg's view perhaps gives the impression that Kohlberg believed determination runs the other direction, from rationale and judgments to action. However, he cited a study by Gilligan and Belenky (1980) that supports the view that determination runs both ways. Kohlberg held that the coordination of structures of reflective moral reasoning with structures of practical moral decision-making seems to be a process of coordination between action and reflection rather than a one-way determination of action by reflection or vice versa (Kohlberg, 1984, p. 262). This understanding of the relationship is similar to the Rawlsian conception of reflective equilibrium between principles and judgments.

Finally, what is the relevance of sociomoral atmosphere to judgments of justice and responsibility as they influence moral action? Kohlberg, Levine, and Hewer (1983) remarked,

> So far we have discussed moral action as if it were something determined solely by internal psychological factors in the subject. This is not the case, for moral action usually takes place in a social or group context, and that context usually has a profound influence on the moral decision making of individuals. Individual moral decisions in real life are almost always made in the context of group norms or

group decision-making processes. Moreover, individual moral action
is often a function of these norms or processes. (Kohlberg, 1984,
p. 263)

Since action is *not* determined "solely by internal psychological factors
in the subject," Kohlberg undertook the sociological extension of the
structural-stage model into an analysis of "moral atmosphere"—constructing democratic just communities in prison and school settings
in the 1970s. One of my theses in this book, as I have already stated
it, is that this sociological extension led to a deep incoherence in
the Kohlbergian project. I return to this in more detail later, but note
for now that at least initially Kohlberg undertook this "extension" to
solve a certain problem. Power and Reimer (1978) had remarked that

> such studies have led us to see that sufficient attention has not yet
> been given to the role that membership in a group plays in the rela-
> tionship between moral judgment and action. . . . Moral acts are un-
> dertaken within a certain ideological context and community atmos-
> phere. Yet most psychological studies have treated their subjects as if
> they were lonely men of morality, acting alone and relying only on
> their inner moral principles to determine which moral action to take.
> (p. 107)

Power, Higgins, and Kohlberg (1989, p. 50) wrote more recently that
"Durkheim's social psychology offers Kohlberg a vehicle for redressing an imbalance that arises from his focusing on individual development." The judgment-action problem, the problem of explaining
how moral judgment relates to moral action, was in part—in large
part perhaps—the result of failing to attend sufficiently to "moral atmosphere." Durkheim would help here.

How do group norms and decision-making processes influence individual moral judgment? First, they influence the content of individual moral judgment or deontic choice. Kohlberg began to argue that
collective community values and norms can be analyzed in a manner
similar to his analysis of the individual justice stage structure.

> Norms shared by the group can be discriminated from individual
> moral judgment in both group discussions and in moral atmosphere
> interviews. The distinctions these studies make rely heavily on
> Durkheim's (1961) notion of norms as prescriptions arising from

shared expectations in a group. In addition to collective norms, both Durkheim and ourselves have studied the sense of community or the sense of group solidarity and cohesion attained in a group. It is this sense of community, solidarity, and cohesion that we call moral atmosphere.

With regard to collective norms, we have taken the position that there is a collective stage interpretation and justification of norms somewhat distinct from the individual's moral stage. (Kohlberg, Levine, and Hewer, 1983, in Kohlberg, 1984, p. 264f.)

As the justice stages lead to deontic content choices, collective norms prescribe shared values and expectations. These shared values and expectations influence content choices especially at the conventional stages of justice reasoning, but they also set the context of preconventional reasoning. Kohlberg, Levine, and Hewer (1983) described research done at the Cheshire reformatory in Connecticut (in 1970) where inmates who tested as Stage 3 reasoners on nonprison, hypothetical dilemmas conceived dilemmas based on their own accounts of prison life in Stage 2 instrumental terms. The "moral atmosphere" of the prison seemed to pull them down. They also described the situation at the Cambridge Cluster School (1974–79) where at the beginning of Kohlberg's research stealing was endemic. Subsequently, collective norms of trust and collective responsibility developed to the point that individuals reimbursed a student theft victim collectively and agreed, quite contrary to their tendencies before and outside Cluster, to report thieves. The community virtually eliminated stealing within Cluster. The deliberately cultivated "moral atmosphere" of the school within a school seemed to pull them up. Kohlberg, Levine, and Hewer (1983) explained that "moral atmosphere differences in normative perception appear to be related to actual differences in behavior" (Kohlberg, 1984, p. 265). Changes in the normative perception of the moral atmosphere lead to changes in deontic content decisions and actual behavior.

They noted, however, that "it appears that the influence of moral atmosphere may be limited to the situational and institutional context of the group" (Kohlberg, 1984, p. 269). Shared attitudes against stealing, for example, may influence action only in the context of the group—whereas Kohlberg had thought of the justice-reasoning stages as global, all-purpose reasoning perspectives. Individuals who share a group's expectations concerning the prevention of theft may nonetheless pilfer and loot to their heart's content outside the context of the group. (There can be honor among democrats that is more or less strictly local.) However, Kohlberg, Levine, and Hewer (1983) contended that "moral atmosphere influences not only the content but also the form of moral reasoning and action" (Kohlberg, 1984, p. 269). Participation in, e.g.,

> democratic alternative schools as well as a developmentally oriented program for juvenile delinquents (Jennings and Kohlberg, 1983) [has] produced conditions conducive to moral [stage] growth more successfully than have their traditional counterparts. The conditions to which we refer are (a) a sense of the degree to which moral discussion and taking into account others' viewpoints occurred within the school; (b) the extent to which subjects felt a sense of power and participation in making rules; and (c) the extent to which existing rules were perceived as fair. (p. 269)

So Kohlberg, Levine, and Hewer (1983) contended that the study of sociomoral atmosphere contributes to the study of moral action in two ways: understanding the collective norms and expectations of a group or society helps us understand the content of moral choices in dilemma situations set in the context of the group or society, and studying participation in democratic institutions can contribute to the study of moral stage development.

We can begin, though, to see how this sociological (Durkheimian) extension of the psychological (Piagetian) structural stage model might have caused difficulties, as we turn now to the neo-Kantian metaethical assumptions of the model as Kohlberg described them. For these assumptions seem to betray a preoccupation with "lonely men of morality, acting alone and relying only on their inner moral principles." The coincidence of the metaethical assumptions of the structural stage model, the individualist anthropology of the rules-based, rights-centered construal of morality, and the study of lonely men of morality is not, I want to suggest, an accident.

FIVE

The Rationale
for the Stage Model

Metaethical Assumptions

I have described some of the more or less specifically psychological aspects of Kohlberg's stage theory. On the revisionist story I am telling, Kohlberg formulated the structural stage model as, among other things, a response to a problem posed for him during his late teens in his experience in World War II and immediately after while a second engineer on the *Paducah* (Kohlberg, 1948, 1991). How can we foster justice and respond to injustice without arbitrarily imposing our own cultural or personal agenda on others?

I suggested that Kohlberg employed the idiom of universal moral principles for responding to this problem. He conceived moral principles not as fixed rules but as interpretive constructs (cognitive schemata), making salient some among the innumerable features of any concrete moral situation. He thought of principles as formally or structurally universal, whereas the substantive features of concrete situations are always more or less context-specific. With the structural stage model, Kohlberg articulated not only an antirelativist, neo-Kantian moral philosophy of justice, he also extended Piaget's work on childhood moral development into an empirically elaborate psychological account of the development of our conceptions of justice from childhood to maturity. That extension is the structural stage model I have described. I continue my revisionist story later as I tell in more detail how in the early and mid-1970s Kohlberg took his psychological theory into prison and school moral education projects. He was led, I will suggest, further and further away from some of the basic philosophical and anthropological assumptions of the psychological theory. But first I need to relate Kohlberg's own account (Kohlberg, Levine, and Hewer, 1983) of those assumptions.

I turn now to the moral-philosophic underpinning of Kohlberg's psychological theory. There are two parts to the rationale Kohlberg offered for his construal of morality, the construal embodied in the definition of the terminal stage and hence in the sequence leading up to the terminal stage. Both are required for the distinctively "Kohlbergian" interpretation of the data collected over his thirty-year career by him and his colleagues. First, Kohlberg made certain assumptions about what morality is, and he argued that, without these or some other initial assumptions, the empirical data could not take on significance (Kohlberg, 1971d). A rationale for the structural stage model as a whole must include a rationale for these initial assumptions. Second, Kohlberg offered a justification for believing Stage 6 is adequate as a sociomoral reasoning perspective about justice. He not only made initial assumptions about morality that he called "metaethical" assumptions. He also formulated a moral theory of justice based on those assumptions. I address Kohlberg's claims to adequacy for his theory of justice in the following chapter, but since the defense of those claims in part presupposes and in part corroborates the initial, metaethical assumptions of the model, as Kohlberg saw it, I describe Kohlberg's account of the metaethical assumptions first.

Construals of Morality

On the way to Kohlberg's account, however, let me illustrate again the contrast between a rules-based, rights-centered construal of morality and a relationship-based, goods-centered construal of morality. This will set Kohlberg's metaethical assumptions in high relief. I return for this illustration to the Elderly Parent Dilemma. Recall that Tarissa (Willard's mother) has become more and more dependent on Willard since Warren (Willard's father) died. Having recently broken her hip, Tarissa is newly disabled and is experiencing some complications related to her injury. She will need nursing care and housekeeping help if she stays in the house where she raised Willard and his sister, but she cannot long afford these herself if she keeps the house. Tarissa and Jerry have never gotten along, and there is enough tension in Willard's and Jerry's household already, given Willard's frustrated career and Jerry's weekend and holiday hours—and many other details related to these. All things considered, and without eliminating options out of hand, three possibilities seem worthy of consideration for the purposes of this illustration. Since my point here is to illustrate different ways of reflecting on the relative merits of available options, rather than to reach a final judgment about what should be done, I will explore here only these three obvious possibilities which suffice for my present purposes. First, Tarissa could move in with Willard and Jerry, selling her house as a way of helping pay the costs of her care. Second, Willard and Jerry could help pay for nursing care and housekeeping help in Tarissa's home. And third, Tarissa could move into an assisted-living facility nearer Willard and Jerry, selling her house as a way of helping to finance her new living arrangement.

From the perspective of a rules- or principles-based, rights-centered construal of morality, such as the Kohlbergian Stage 5 or 6, we can conceive the basic issues in the dilemma in terms of rights, special responsibilities, and reversibility. Tarissa has a right to life. However, she is not in immediate danger of dying as a result of her new physical disability and related complications, though she will be unable to care adequately for herself in the long run. Tarissa does not have a right to control Willard's life, say, by determining with whom he may live or how he will spend his income or use his assets. So, though Tarissa may have some claim on Willard's assistance, she does not have a right to call all the shots. In particular, she does not have a right to insist that Willard rescue her from having to sell her house in an effort to provide for herself. Her right to her own property does not justify requiring others to sacrifice their property in protecting her life and property. Only if one has done everything reasonable within one's means to help oneself, on this construal of morality, are others morally required to lend assistance. Because Tarissa has equity in her house which she can use in providing for her own care, she is not, at least not yet, in a life-or-death predicament—as is Heinz's wife in the Heinz Dilemma. Hence, whereas Kohlberg thought that not only Heinz but also total strangers are duty-bound to help Heinz's wife acquire the drug, Kohlberg would not think the same holds for Tarissa in her present circumstances. The Elderly Parent Dilemma, to put it crudely, pits property against property, not life against property—at least in the short run.

What sort of claim does Tarissa have on Willard's assistance? Does Willard have a special responsibility to help Tarissa? That is, in the absence of impartial grounds for thinking Willard has an obligation to come to his mother's assistance at this point, is Willard obliged to be partial because of his personal relationship with Tarissa? Let us note two important points. First, impartial justice does not demand that Willard help Tarissa. It is not a question of (impartial) justice. The conflict of life vs. property that we see in the Heinz Dilemma does not obtain here in the same way, because Tarissa has discretion over property sufficient to maintain herself, for the time being at least. Recall that Kohlberg thought the care orientation supplements and deepens but presupposes the justice orientation. Willard might be bound to respond to his mother's need, but the duty in question would be a supplement to the demands of (impartial) justice, not an instance of them.

Second, we can see why justice does not demand Willard assist his mother at this point by invoking explicitly (in Stage 6 fashion) the criterion of reversibility. Would a claim—were Tarissa to make such a claim, even hypothetically—that Willard must allow her to move in with him or else must pay for nursing care and housekeeping help in her present home be reversible? If everyone involved in this situation (and everyone else for that matter) were to consider this claim from the point of view of each of the other parties in turn, on their own terms from their perspectives, would an ideal consensus in favor of this claim against Willard for assistance result? No, it would not. For though this claim might seem acceptable from Tarissa's point of view, even Tarissa would have to admit that it is not binding as a matter of impersonal duty from, say, Jerry's point of view. While Jerry might imagine that, were he in Tarissa's situation, he would like to have this claim honored, Tarissa cannot imagine that she would expect it to be honored were she in Jerry's situation. The claim against Willard for assistance is not reversible. (The implications, were it to be reversible, are on the order of those Beverly seeks to press against Stephen's position in the Needy Children Dilemma. A virtual vow of poverty and service would be required of almost everyone were this claim to be reversible as a matter of impartial justice.)

Does Willard have a special responsibility to help Tarissa keep her house and still receive the in-home care she needs, or perhaps to invite her to move in with him and Jerry and to provide the care she needs himself? Since this would be a question of *special* responsibility, we would be free to consider relationship-specific and context-relative factors in determining whether such a responsibility obtains. It is not hard to imagine scenarios on which Willard surely would be obliged and others on which this would be less clear. Imagine, for example, that Tarissa had been Willard's confidant and confessor during much of his confusing and troubled adolescence, that Warren and Tarissa had made significant sacrifices to put Willard through college and further sacrifices to help him with the down payment on his and Jerry's first home, and that though she disapproved of and refused to come to terms with Willard's relationship with Jerry, she had never failed to support him emotionally and with her confidence. Or imagine that Tarissa and Warren disowned and disinherited Willard thirty-five years ago, that they did not help him pay for college and even forced him to move out of their house when he turned sixteen, and that Tarissa had hardly communicated with Willard until Warren's illness and death, after which she has expected support from Willard in ways that ignored the bad history between them. Also, it is easy to imagine cultural conditions in which people would think the fact that Tarissa is Willard's mother settles the matter, whatever the facts of their particular relationship. And it would also be easy to imagine other cultural conditions in which people would think that the fact of Tarissa's being Willard's mother is almost irrelevant. And this is perfectly consistent with Kohlberg's rules- or principles-based, rights-centered construal of morality. For if this is not a question of justice, all sorts of contextually relative facts may be relevant.

On a relationship-based, goods-centered construal of morality, the question is not one of rights, special responsibilities, and reversibility. It is rather a question of preserving and fostering those relationships in which the goods can be enjoyed that make life meaningful and worthwhile. So the question is, what resolution of Tarissa's, Willard's, and Jerry's present predicament will best facilitate their joint and separate pursuits of the goods that make life meaningful and worthwhile? Stated this way, we can see how this question calls us to reflect on the larger context of their present predicament. For the range of goods (not only commodities) available materially, culturally, and environmentally, etc., as well as the available methods of their pursuit, depends on the larger context, economic, cultural, and environmental, etc. The enjoyments and accomplishments available to musicians in string quartets and to participants in local, face-to-face democratic politics, for instance, are not universally available. Neither are the rewards of vegetable gardening and of out-of-doors athletic competition nor the benefits and enhancements of life available in financially secure, harmonious households.

Putting the matter this way also calls us not only to consider the history of the particular relationships in question, as on the rights-centered construal when the question is one of special responsibility. We are called to consider as well the history of the contexts of the particular relationships—the activities and institutions that have given them their shape. For as I described earlier and as we saw in particular in the case of ten point pitch, we have some of the goods without which (or without all of which) life would not be meaningful and worthwhile only in particular activities, activities accessible to us solely because of their peculiar histories and institutional settings. The Green Valley Grange and the Prairie View Community made ten point pitch available to my parents and then to my younger brother and me. Many trace the origins of local, face-to-face democratic politics to fifth century B.C.E. Athens, and of course the history of democracy from then to the Kohlbergian just communities, here in the United States and elsewhere, is checkered and not unbroken. Recall the Peloponnesian War and Plato's early experiences with Athenian democrats. Recall that in the United States many of the so-called "founding fathers" owned slaves and that through the Civil War some state statutes defined persons of African descent as less than fully human—much as the ancient Athenians had regarded "barbarians." Different organizations of family and different forms of household-ing also have their own peculiar histories and culture-laden varieties. And so on. So resolving Tarissa's, Willard's, and Jerry's present predicament will require reflecting in more detail on their circumstances than the description in the dilemma makes explicit for us. Once again, then, we find that whereas I described a dilemma adequately for the purposes of the rules-based, rights-centered construal of morality, I have described the Elderly Parent Dilemma inadequately for the purposes of a relationship-based, goods-centered construal.

Let us suppose that Tarissa was Willard's confidant and confessor through his adolescence and that she and Warren made many sacrifices to enable Willard to achieve what he has today. Because of this, and because Tarissa has never failed to support Willard emotionally and with her confidence, and because of the way Tarissa cared for Willard's sister before her death, Willard wants very much to work this out to both Jerry's and his mother's satisfaction. He understands his own household as an extension of the household in which he grew up, and he identifies with his mother and is responsive to her situation. Willard knows how clearly Tarissa remembers her mother and grandmother "withering away in cramped, smelly places," and Tarissa has told him recently more of the details than he had gathered himself about her failed attempt to have her mother live with them when Willard and his sister were off at college. Tarissa felt very guilty about putting her mother in the "nursing home." But the pressure from Warren's job and her mother's constant arguing about the smallest things made this seem the best thing at the time. Still, most of Tarissa's neighbors are new in the last few years, and her old friends from the neighborhood have either died or moved away to be near their children and grandchildren. So while Tarissa has many fond memories of times in the house—her quilting circle that lasted for twenty-four years, Warren's work on the Eisenhower campaign in 1952, etc.—which are not insignificant as incentives to stay, there is little else besides memories and her identification with the place to keep her there. These are not negligible, as Willard knows. What is more, the neighborhood is gentrifying and is close to the commuter train, and Jerry thinks the modest house would bring as much as $250,000. However, Willard's and Jerry's tastes in music, furniture, art, food, and so on are very different from Tarissa's tastes. If she could ever get up out of those chairs in the living room, she is not sure she could eat what they cook or abide their music. Jerry is allergic to cats, and Tarissa simply will not hear of parting with her two calicoes. The three of them have been through too much for that now.

In short, all the options are unsavory and what they need is some ad hoc improvisation. Jerry's parents moved to the assisted-living apartments near Willard and Jerry fifteen months ago, and though Tarissa has always been cool to meeting them, now may be the time to suggest and arrange it. Jerry has mentioned to Willard that even if Tarissa did not get along with his parents, meeting them might be a way for her to begin to adjust to the idea of moving into a living environment in which she will be closer and receive the care she needs.

Notice that even in this summary description, omitting much that complicates real life, there are many factors that I cannot neatly organize in support of one or another available option. There are many goods to be pursued without a tidy overall organization to them. Tarissa's being able to live in the place with which she identifies her life and herself, for example, is incompatible in the circumstances with her receiving the care and assistance she now requires, unless Willard and Jerry take on a larger financial commitment than is compatible with their present life. Willard's desire to continue to balance his relationships with Tarissa and Jerry requires tradeoffs, as it always has. Jerry cares for Willard too much to force him to compromise his relationship with Tarissa any further, but at fifty-one he is settled into their habits and furthermore is not up to adding two cats to his complicated juggling of allergies. In the circumstances, their joint task is to save as much as possible while honoring established commitments and encumbrances—hence the need for ad hoc improvisation and impromptu deliberation.

This "in the circumstances" is important. For turning to improvisation here does not require us to deny that there are some goods that are not to be compromised. For instance, Willard simply will not leave his mother to fend for herself. He will do what he can, and he will not force her to face withering away in a cramped, smelly place, period. He identifies with Tarissa's well-being, and her good is part of his good. Her well-being is a good they share that he will not sacrifice. But the fact that some goods are not to be compromised does not entail that we can access a complete, hierarchical ordering of all goods worth pursuing. Life is too complicated. Many priorities are set only when we are forced to do so. But from the point of view of a relationship-based, goods-centered construal of morality, the fact that we often have to improvise does not entail that anything goes or that all our encumbrances are or could be up for grabs.

Recall that I suggested earlier that there are some requirements we must honor, on this construal of morality, because they are conditions for the possibility of the common pursuit of common goods. Some actions and some action patterns cannot but frustrate or destroy our common pursuits. Killing for personal gain, lying to cover up our failings, taking what belongs to others in order to avoid the effort of acquiring things honestly—such actions deplete the trust and good will required for cooperative and shared endeavors. We must forbid and prevent such actions if we are to pursue a full complement of the goods that make life meaningful and worthwhile. I think two things are notable here.

First, there is an important similarity between, on the one hand, Kohlberg's notion that if it is not a question of justice, a great many contextually relative facts may be relevant, and, on the other hand, what I have just observed about the flexibility we have in improvising when there are no overriding considerations in favor of a single option. However, on this construal of morality, Tarissa, Willard, and Jerry are still trying to resolve a moral predicament. And the same types of considerations apply in their case as would apply if one overriding consideration weighed in favor of a single available option. For in each case people deliberate about the pursuit of goods that make life meaningful and worthwhile. It is just that in some cases the range of viable options is narrower than in others. On a Kohlbergian rules- or principles-based, rights-centered construal of morality, considerations of special responsibility or of worthwhile goods have weight only if considerations of justice are either equal or moot, but on a relationship-based, goods-centered construal, (impartial) justice is an extremely important good that must be weighed in the balance with other, occasionally equally important goods. Sometimes being partial is more appropriate than being impartial, as when a family has only enough resources to support its own children.

Second, this partly explains why my initial dilemma descriptions are adequate for the one construal and inadequate for the other. For all sorts of details are simply irrelevant on the rules- or principles-based, rights-centered construal. And since I modeled my initial dilemma descriptions on the Heinz Dilemma, which as I have noted Kohlberg wrote to elicit rules- or principles-based, rights-centered reasoning, I initially left out details that are relevant on the other construal.

I turn now to the details of Kohlberg's construal of morality, as Kohlberg, Levine, and Hewer (1983) elaborated them. Kohlberg thought that the results of his empirical research had implications for normative ethics. He believed his data corroborated his claim that the structural stage model captured how moral development occurs and how moral maturity is exhibited cross-culturally. He was careful, though, to distinguish the conclusions that could be drawn from his work from the assumptions that oriented his research. Kohlberg accepted Frankena's (1973) distinction between descriptive empirical inquiry, normative-ethical theorizing, and metaethical theorizing (Kohlberg, 1984, p. 276). So, on Kohlberg's view, before one can understand how moral development in fact occurs (descriptive ethics), he or she must define morality (metaethics). Only with a construal of morality in mind can one conduct empirical research on moral development, because only then can one delineate and define one's subject matter. Further, the plausibility of the results of empirical research, on Kohlberg's view, reflects the validity of one's assumptions about morality. If one's hypotheses and explanations seem to fit the facts, if they provide an adequate interpretation of the phenomena, then and only then are one's assumptions tentatively vindicated.

Kohlberg argued persuasively that much that had gone wrong with the study of moral development by social scientists resulted from their failure to begin with an adequate conception of morality—which he thought should be articulated in the idiom of universal moral principles. He explained his conception of morality in detail, explicitly contrasting several aspects of it with what he held to be mistaken rival conceptions of morality (Kohlberg, 1984, p. 277). I will retain the names Kohlberg gave to his assumptions.

Value Relevance vs. Positivist Relativism

The first of Kohlberg's metaethical assumptions encompasses all the others, he thought. That assumption is that "conceptions of morality cannot themselves be morally neutral" (Kohlberg, Levine, and Hewer, 1983, in Kohlberg, 1984, p. 279). He noted that social scientists studying morality had for the most part tried to define their subject matter in a value-free manner, thinking that this would relieve their research of any moral bias. On the positivist assumption that science is value-neutral, social scientists had given what they took to be value-neutral definitions of morality, for example, "moral values are evaluations of action believed by members of a given society to be right." But as Kohlberg, Levine, and Hewer (1983) pointed out, such a definition "*assumes* moral relativism, it does not find it. . . . Such a definition takes a stand on morality without justifying it, without even admitting it" (Kohlberg, 1984, p. 279). Of course, a definition of morality that implies moral relativism could be correct *if* some version of moral relativism were true, but such a definition is *not* value-neutral.

On Kohlberg's cognitive-developmental view, morality must be defined in a "value-relevant" manner. His concept of development itself implies an internal standard of adequacy, a standard toward which developmental change moves. Development is not mere change. It is

> change toward greater differentiation, integration, and adaptation. In other words, the theorist has to take up a position as to what "more integrated" and "more adapted" means. One cannot study the *development* of moral reasoning without some assumptions as to what it means to be moral, without the definite assumption that morality is a desirable thing, not a value-neutral thing. (1984, p. 279)

Phenomenalism and Cognitivism vs. Emotivism

Kohlberg, Levine, and Hewer (1983) described the metaethical assumption called "phenomenalism" as "the assumption that moral reasoning is the conscious process of using ordinary moral language. This assumption distinguishes Kohlberg from behaviorist and psychoanalytic theorists" (1984, p. 280). Kohlberg, Levine, and Hewer explained that, according to psychoanalytic theory, moral activity and the use of moral language are a function of *unconscious* guilt avoidance, and according to behavioristic theory morality can be studied only by observing *nonconscious* overt action, that is, behavior and the responses of individuals to the consequences of their behavior. According to these theories, the conscious processes that Kohlberg took to be essential to morality are either self-deceptive (on the psychoanalytic construal) or meaningful only as pieces of verbal behavior (on the behaviorist construal). Kohlberg thought both these types of theory assume emotivism, "that [moral utterances] are simply emotive expressions" (1984, p. 280).

By contrast, on Kohlberg's view, morality, as moral reasoning and action issuing from this reasoning, is essentially conscious and reflective. This is why we can assess the morality of action only in reference to conscious processes, e.g., beliefs and intentions.

> Moral conduct is conduct governed by moral judgments; while moral judgment is not always translated into moral action, the assessment of an action as moral depends on the imputation of judgment to the action. . . . [T]he study of moral conduct and moral development per se must consider the motives and the constructions of moral meaning that are expressed in behaviors. (1984, p. 282)

As against behaviorism, we can judge an action moral or immoral, or nonmoral for that matter, only by imputing to the person performing it certain intentions and motives. Otherwise it is impossible to isolate and identify the subject matter under empirical investigation. For we cannot individuate actions (delineate and identify individual actions) without reference to intentions. What is the person standing on the corner doing? Is she hailing a cab, greeting a friend, shooing a wasp, loosening her elbow, or hawking tickets? Imagine that a cab pulls up beside her but that she turns and walks away.

As against psychoanalytic theory, the intentions and judgments that constitute morality are by definition conscious rather than unconscious or self-deceptive. We do not hold anyone morally responsible, and it would be wrong to hold someone morally responsible, for an action she or he did not consciously intend. (The idea seems to be that unless one has direct and autonomous control over one's actions and intentions, one should not be held morally accountable for them. Actions done from unconscious motives, then, would not be blameworthy, perhaps because they would be construed as resulting from some sort of coercion. But even if on a psychoanalytic model we had some sort of indirect control over our unconscious motives, say, through self-discipline and habituation, still, this control would not be direct enough for a Kohlbergian understanding of autonomous moral choice. Autonomous moral choices are made in the reckoning of a single moment. They are free reflective acts, ultimately immune from the weight of custom and habit.)

Kohlberg's metaethical assumption of cognitivism is closely related. This is the notion that "moral judgment is cognitive in that it involves reasoning to and from principles" (1984, p. 290). Kohlberg, Levine, and Hewer also called this assumption "rationalism," and they contrasted it with emotivism, as they did the assumption of phenomenalism. On the emotivist construal of morality, moral judgments and declarations are all simply expressions of emotion. One who says "capital punishment is wrong" is really saying something like "I abhor capital punishment and wish you would too." But moral judgment on the Kohlbergian view is essentially rational in the sense of being reasoned, even if particular moral judgments are not always ideally rational or adequately reasoned. Moral judgment is not essentially emotive, on Kohlberg's view, even though it is often accompanied by emotional fervor and conviction. This does not mean, then, that morality does not involve emotions and passions in an important way.

> While emotivism excludes the rational component of moral judgment, our assumption of cognitivism, unlike Kantian rationalism, does not deny affect as an integral component of moral judgment or justice reasoning. For example, our theory recognizes affect in appeals to respect for the dignity of persons, as well as in appeals to caring and responsibility between persons. Our theory recognizes affect but always as mediated by, or as structured by, cognitive processes such as role-taking, or putting oneself in the place of the other. This structured affect could be manifested as sympathy for the moral victim, indignation at the moral exploiter, and/or concern for care and taking responsibility. (1984, p. 291)

Morally appropriate sympathies and passions are structured by rational judgment and cognitive role-taking. But while admitting the important role of emotions, Kohlberg insisted that "the quantitative role of affect [in moral judgment is] relatively irrelevant for understanding the structure and development of justice reasoning" (1984, p. 292). "Thus, while morally relevant emotions and sentiments are part of moral development, it is important to distinguish between the description or expression of a feeling about a moral situation and the making of a moral judgment about it" (1984, p. 293). The cognitive-structural development of moral reasoning is the heart of moral development, on the "Kohlbergian" view of the structural stage model. The development of morally appropriate sympathies and passions presupposes and supplements cognitive-moral development since sympathies and passions presuppose beliefs and judgments that themselves presuppose stages of justice reasoning. For instance, moral abhorrence of capital punishment presupposes the judgment that capital punishment is immoral, and this presupposes a justice-reasoning perspective on the terms of which the judgment is formulated and rationally defended.

So Kohlberg's construal of morality is not emotivist, and on Kohlberg's account it contrasts with psychoanalytic and behaviorist construals of morality in precisely this respect. It is worth remembering that Kohlberg was finishing his dissertation and beginning to gather a following for his project in the very years in which R. M. Hare, to whom Kohlberg later acknowledged debt, was locked in dispute with emotivists on the one hand and descriptivists or naturalists on the other (see Anscombe, 1958; Foot, 1958, 1958–59, 1961; Geach, 1956, 1969; Hare, 1952, 1957, 1963; MacIntyre, 1959; Murdoch, 1964; Rawls, 1955, 1958; Stevenson, 1944, 1963; von Wright, 1960; Winch, 1959–60).

Prescriptivism and Principledness vs. Naturalism

The metaethical assumption of prescriptivism is the assumption that moral judgments and moral theory are about what ought to be as well as about what is. They *pre*scribe rather than simply *de*scribe. Kohlberg, Levine, and Hewer (1983) contrasted prescriptivism with naturalism, the view that, according to Gilbert Harman whose introductory ethics text (Harman, 1977, p. 14) they quote, "moral judgments and experiences are reducible to underlying natural states" (Kohlberg, 1984, p. 288). Kohlberg, Levine, and Hewer held that ethical naturalism results from the view that rational moral discourse about what ought to be the case that ventures away from what actually is the case is impossible. This is because naturalism, on Kohlberg's understanding of it, presumes that discourse about values in contrast to facts cannot be rational.

> [T]he ignoring of the possibility of rational moral discourse distinct from scientific discourse about facts leads to the assumption that whatever is not scientific is relative and arbitrary. . . . We hold with Hare (1952, 1963) that, as opposed to naturalism, moral language and judgments are fundamentally *pre*scriptive, not *de*scriptive. (Kohlberg, 1984, p. 288)

Of course moral language and judgments have a descriptive component, but they also have an essential prescriptive meaning, according to Hare (1963). Moral judgments are inferences from prescriptive principles conjoined with the facts of a case; hence they are essentially prescriptive. And since the moral principles and rules from which inferences are drawn are by definition universal in application, moral judgments are universalizable prescriptions.

It is important for my argument in this book that Kohlberg, Levine, and Hewer were wrong here. They conflated naturalism with positivism (value-neutralism) and hence counted it as a form of relativism. They thought naturalism was committed to relativism perhaps in part because they took Skinner's relativism to be a consequence of what they took to be Skinner's naturalism (Kohlberg, 1984, p. 287f). But Skinnerian behaviorism is not the naturalism of Hare's critics. The naturalist or descriptivist, as opposed to the prescriptivist, uses the moral term "good" as roughly equivalent to the functional term "good." The functional term "good" applies to objects such as a wristwatch, a vegetable steamer, a garden tiller, and a raincoat. In this way, even as a moral term, "good" is descriptive as much as it is prescriptive. "Good" applies to things, persons, events, and actions that perform the task or activity characteristic of items of their type, that fit their "function," as a matter of fact. A good wristwatch is one that keeps good time, wears well on the wrist, and so on. To judge that a wristwatch is good is, on this understanding, automatically to attribute to it a certain sort of description, and vice versa.

Naturalists or descriptivists of the late 1950s and 1960s, such as Foot, Anscombe, and Geach, are distinct from prescriptivists such as Hare or Harman of the same period *not* in holding that moral judgments *de*scribe without *pre*scribing but rather in holding, with Aristotle, that it makes sense to talk about humans as having an activity characteristic of them as humans. This human activity is performed to a certain end, often called happiness but perhaps better understood as the type of fulfilling and complete life (meaningful and worthwhile *on the whole*) of which humans are uniquely capable. So a moral judgment prescribes inasmuch as it implies what is to be done to that end. Being a dishonest person is bad precisely because and to the extent that it frustrates efforts to lead a fulfilling and complete life. The rejection of just this sort of teleology (goal- or *telos*-directedness) in ethics led those who identified themselves as prescriptivists to insist that moral judgments prescribe but without there being some further point to the matter, some ultimate purpose. Prescriptivists construed principles as independent of, rather than as directives toward, an aim or *telos*.

The description Kohlberg, Levine, and Hewer gave of the assumption they call "principledness" is largely a response to Brenda Munsey's statement of "contextual relativism." Munsey, the editor of a volume of essays on Kohlberg's theory (Munsey, 1980), "takes the position, primarily a metaethical position, of what she calls John Dewey's 'act theory' and contrasts this position with Kant's or Rawls's 'rule theory'" (Kohlberg, 1984, p. 296). Kohlberg, Levine, and Hewer contrasted contextual relativism with Kohlberg's conception of transcontextual, universal moral principles. However, they were careful here as well as elsewhere, as I have described, to show the extent to which Kohlberg's conception of morality can incorporate the orienting intuitions of contextual relativists and still prevent a lapse into relativism. Kohlberg's disagreement with Gilligan was not far in the background on this point. In particular, Kohlberg, Levine, and Hewer pointed out the extent to which Kohlberg's theory is consistent with Dewey's.

> Dewey's questioning of fixed principles, and his equation of them with conventional as opposed to postconventional moral reasoning, is very appropriate in thinking about moral problems as issues of social or public policy. Judgments about, for instance, divorce and abortion as social issues, inextricably mingle issues of fact about the consequence of public acceptance or rejection with issues of "principle." This inextricable integration of factual and "principled" reasoning is obviously historically and contextually relative, since the very meanings of abortion or divorce change historically. (1984, p. 297f.)

But while Kohlberg, Levine, and Hewer admit what they take to be Dewey's critique of conventional morality as fixed absolutes, they consider Dewey's ethics to be a version of ethical naturalism (and hence relativism) and so do not accept it in its entirety. They do, however, accept what they take to be Dewey's understanding of the application of moral principles in concrete situations.

> We agree that in principled morality choice is not dictated by "absolutes" or by rigid or exceptionless rules. Our conception of a princi-

ple, like Dewey's, is not one of principle as a fixed rule; rather, we too understand a principle as a way of construing a concrete moral situation. It is true that principled reasoning leads to an understanding of the value of respecting human personality, phrased by Kant as "Treat each person as an end in himself and not merely as a means." However, it is principled reasoning that does *not* employ this value as a fixed rule, because it understands this value as needing interpretation in concrete situations.

Thus, it is principled reasoning that understands the value of human personality as a way of constructing a resolution of a moral dilemma, but it does not understand this value as a substantive rule dictating *a priori* what the resolution should be. (1984, p. 298)

As I have suggested, Kohlberg conceived "principled morality as a way of seeing human perspectives in concrete situations" (1984, p. 299), not as a system of fixed rules that are to be applied to an independently intelligible set of moral facts. Principled morality structures the interpretation of or gives significance to the morally relevant facts, and the development of this type of interpretive capacity *is* the cognitive-moral developmental sequence described in the structural stage model. To put the matter slightly differently, we might observe that in the way that no psychological or sociological study of morality can begin without a nonneutral understanding of what constitutes morality, no apprehension of what facts are salient in any morally problematic situation can occur without a *structure* for interpreting the situation. This structure, on Kohlberg's view, is some version of a principle-informed moral or justice-reasoning perspective.

One of the *cognitive* aspects of moral development, on Kohlberg's view, is the development of the capacity to understand a situation of conflicting claims from the perspective of others. Kohlberg called this capacity to take the perspective of others "ideal role-taking." "This conception of ideal role-taking attempts to synthesize Dewey's views, G. H. Mead's (1934) reconstruction of Kant's categorical imperative as universalizable role-taking, Rawls's social contract theory, and Habermas's (1979) conception of discursive will formation" (1984, p. 299). The development of the capacity for ideal role-taking is the development of the ability to understand from the point of view of others as well as one's own the morally relevant facts in a situation of conflicting claims, since reversibility is a criterion of moral adequacy. This ability to understand involves the development of one's conception of the principles of morality. "Reversibility is that quality of a justice structure which enables the structure to construct solutions to dilemmas in such a way that these solutions can be considered acceptable or just from the points of view of all relevant parties" (1984, p. 310). And since an interpretation of the morally relevant facts is of necessity tied to a particular social and historical context, Kohlberg's conception of principled morality takes contextually relative considerations into account.

> From our point of view, one could say that some general commitment to principles of justice enjoins the moral reasoner to engage in ideal role-taking in order to resolve moral dilemmas. In this sense, our view of moral principles acknowledges the situational context of each moral problem. . . .
>
> Having stated our claim that adequate moral principles consider context, as Dewey himself holds, we should also note and agree with Dewey's emphasis that the most problematic, changing, historically relative aspect of moral choice is attending to the factual aspects of a moral dilemma. For example, the factual meaning of issues of life quality, seen in real-life abortion and euthanasia dilemmas, changes with each new biological or technological advance in knowledge. We agree that such changes cannot be overlooked by principled reasoning. (1984, pp. 299, 300)

Each new advance in the technology of neonatal care, each new drug enabling nonsurgical abortion, each new anesthesiological innovation in palliative treatment for suffering patients at the end of life changes the moral issues at stake in "real-life abortion and euthanasia dilemmas." So Kohlberg, Levine, and Hewer held that Kohlberg's theory can accommodate the orienting intuitions of contextual relativists without itself lapsing into relativism.

In summary, Kohlberg believed that his assumption and conception of principled morality is sensitive to the specifics of real-life situations that are the concern of contextual relativists. In contrast to contextual relativism, however, he assumed that universal principles that are contextually applied are not thereby rendered arbitrary in the face of changing historical circumstance. This notion of principled stability, Kohlberg, Levine, and Hewer claim, is unavailable within a relativist position (1984, p. 300). They were right on this point, but we should note that their account of prescriptive principles requires two theses that must both be true. First, moral principles can in fact be both universal and sensitive to the most context-embedded features of particular situations insofar as they are interpretive constructs that render the utterly particular morally intelligible. They are not fixed absolutes too general to apply unambiguously in all but a few types of cases. Second, however, universal moral principles have a prescriptive meaning distinct from whatever descriptive meaning they may have, and to hold otherwise would render them contextually relative since, e.g., the very meanings of abortion or divorce change historically. On the "Kohlbergian" view, universal principles must serve both as interpretive constructs and as prescriptions. Unless moral principles are both universal heuristically and prescriptive universally they cannot be *moral* principles. They cannot be postconventional.

Kohlberg thought his commitment to rejecting relativism committed him to denying that moral principles could be articulations of the enactments that accomplish distinctively human ends or purposes. That is, he thought moral principles could not be characterized as directives to some end or ends since conceptions of the good are all relative. And he thought avoiding relativism required rejecting the naturalism or descriptivism of Dewey and the critics of Hare's prescriptivism, namely Foot, Anscombe, and Geach. So he rejected what he considered Deweyan "act theory" in favor of what he considered Kantian "rule theory" because only that could save the most important weapon against relativism, namely, universalizability.

Universalism and Formalism vs. Relativism

The assumption of universalism is that moral judgment is in every case at least putatively universalizable. That is, when someone makes a *moral* judgment, she or he intends it to be applicable to every individual who finds her- or himself in relevantly similar circumstances, irrespective of cultural or historical setting. So if one judges some action morally right in a given set of circumstances, she or he judges it right universally, whenever relevantly similar circumstances obtain. The same holds for what is morally wrong. Referring to Hare (1952) and Habermas (1982) as philosophers who offer accounts of universalizability, Kohlberg, Levine, and Hewer invoke the example of Nazi genocide.

> One can judge Nazi genocide to be wrong not only in terms of some non-Nazi cultural norms but also in terms of standards having more universal application or meaning. The ordinary moral language user could say, "I judge Nazi genocide to be morally wrong not simply because it's not good in my culture but because it's not good in any culture, even Nazi culture." (Kohlberg, 1984, p. 283; see also p. 287)

Nazi genocide is cross-culturally, ahistorically wrong, and the criterion of universalizability shows why. Nazis cannot consistently hold that genocide is right in all relevantly similar circumstances, because were roles reversed, Nazis could themselves be put to the flames. The moral judgment supporting genocide is not reversible.

So stated, universalizability is simply a matter of consistency. How, for example, could Gilligan's contextual relativism involve the denial of such a simple matter of consistency? Treat like cases alike. In similar circumstances, similar actions are appropriate—even when roles are reversed. Everything turns, though, on what counts as relevant similarity and on how one determines it. Kohlberg's genius here is to have constructed a stage-sequential model of the development of interpretive structures for recognizing or, shall we say, cognitively construing, relevant similarity.

This assumption of universalism is in contrast with both "cultural relativism" and "ethical relativism." Kohlberg, Levine, and Hewer referred to Brandt (1961), who identified these two types of relativism as follows. Consider three beliefs: (1) Moral principles are culturally variable in a fundamental way. (2) This fundamental variability is logically unavoidable; there are no rational principles or methods that could reconcile the observed divergences. And (3) people ought to live according to the moral principles that they themselves in fact hold. The cultural relativist holds belief (1). The ethical relativist holds all three beliefs. One can be a cultural relativist without being an ethical relativist but not vice versa. As Kohlberg, Levine, and Hewer pointed out, (1) is a question of empirical fact, and they believed it false; (2) is a question of methodology, a philosophic doctrine that they rejected in favor of a methodological nonrelativism (Kohl-berg, 1984, pp. 284–85).

In regard to belief (1), Kohlberg, Levine, and Hewer held that while particular social customs and practices may vary in detail, the moral norms that structure social institutions and the moral elements or consequential considerations taken into account in making moral judgments are common to all cultures. In regard to belief (2), they held that the structures of justice reasoning are culturally universal.

> We claim that there is a universalistically valid form of rational moral thought process which all persons could articulate, assuming social and cultural conditions suitable to cognitive moral stage de-velopment. We claim that the ontogenesis toward this form of ra-tional moral thinking occurs in all cultures, in the same stepwise, invariant stage sequence. (1984, p. 286)

Kohlberg, Levine, and Hewer argued that much of the failure to un-derstand the claim of universalism results from the failure to recog-nize two distinctions: first, the distinction between moral impartiality or fairness and value-neutrality, and second, the distinction between tolerance as respect for the liberty of conscience (which is a univer-salizable principle) and relativism. Kohlberg incorporated impartial-ity and tolerance and rejected value-neutrality and relativism (see Kohlberg, 1981, pp. 105–14).

Kohlberg, Levine, and Hewer advanced the metaethical assumption of universalism in two respects. They accepted the Kantian criterion of universalizability, and they believed Kohlberg's data show that this criterion is in fact a developmental assumption in moral reasoning in all cultures.

> [O]ur claim about universalism is first a claim that the development of structures of justice reasoning is a universal development. Second, we claim that the moral norms and elements listed . . . are norms and elements that have been used by moral reasoners in all cultures we have studied. We do not claim that this list of moral norms and elements is necessarily a complete list. (Kohlberg, 1984, p. 287)

Kohlberg, Levine, and Hewer observed that Western liberal Kantian-ism is *as a theory* culturally relative, but they claimed that the basic principles derived from Kantian or neo-Kantian moral theory are universal in use (see Kohlberg, 1981, p. 222). The theory of gravity, after all, is culture-specific *as a theory*. The laws of gravity obtain universally, nonetheless—so an analogy might run.

The assumption of formalism is closely related as central to the Kantian insight. It is the metaethical assumption that moral reasoning moves to and from formal moral principles, e.g., always treat others as you would have them treat you, rather than from content-specific normative rules, e.g., never take another's property without his or her consent. Content-specific normative rules assume such culturally relative notions as personal property, whereas formal moral principles do not.

> Our psychological focus on form comes from the form-content distinction central to structural stage psychology. Our psychological formalism requires, however, a philosophic or metaethical conception of moral form if it is to constitute an appropriate perspective for defining moral judgment as opposed to any other type of judgment. (1984, p. 293)

What defines morality and hence what distinguishes moral reasoning from nonmoral reasoning is its formal properties (e.g., reversibility), not its content. And this is required as a metaethical assumption by the psychological formalism of the structural stage model.

Kohlberg, Levine, and Hewer identify the formalist conception of morality with that of several modern moral philosophers, Baier (1965), Hare (1963), Peters (1971), Frankena (1973), and Rawls (1971). "For them, a moral point of view is something that can be agreed upon in defining morality without achieving necessary agreement on the content or substantive principles of morality" (1984, p. 293), principles which can be worked out in debate, given agreement on the formal characteristics of the "moral point of view." Kohlberg, Levine, and Hewer agree with Frankena's (1973) description of the moral point of view and quote at length from his discussion of it in his introductory ethics text. The following is an excerpt from that quotation:

> If this line of thought is acceptable, then we may say that a basic moral judgment, principle or code is justified or "true" if it is or will

be agreed to by everyone who takes the moral point of view and is
clearheaded and logical and knows all that is relevant about himself,
mankind, and the universe. . . . He is not claiming an actual consensus . . . he is claiming an ideal consensus that transcends majorities
and actual societies. . . . What is the moral point of view? . . . My
own position, then, is that one is taking the moral point of view if
and only if (a) one is making normative judgments about actions,
desires, dispositions, intentions, motives, persons, or traits of character; (b) one is willing to universalize one's judgments; (c) one's
reasons for one's judgments consist of facts about what the things
judged do to the lives of sentient beings in terms of promoting or
distributing nonmoral good and evil; and (d) when the judgment is
about oneself or one's own, one's reasons include such facts about
what one's own actions and dispositions do to the lives of other sentient beings as such, if others are affected. One has a morality or
moral action-guide only if and insofar as one makes normative judgments from this point of view and is guided by them. (Frankena,
1973, pp. 112–14, as quoted in Kohlberg, 1984, pp. 294–95)

This conception of the "moral point of view" is formal, Kohlberg,
Levine, and Hewer contended—following the moral philosophers
they cited—in the sense that agreement about it can be reached independently of agreement or disagreement about the content of particular norms.

Notice that this conception of the "moral point of view" includes
the assumption of prescriptivism and universalism as well as consideration for the consequences of actions. Notice also that there is a
parallel between the form-content distinction in the characterization
of the "moral point of view" and the form-content distinction in
Kohlberg's conception of stage development. "Thus, the development
of moral reasoning is, we claim, a movement toward constructing
the formal characteristics of a moral point of view" (Kohlberg, 1984,
p. 295). The terminal, Stage 6 justice-reasoning perspective is the developmental instantiation of the "moral point of view." Moral principles, on this view, are formal (content-free), prescriptive (imperative,
not indicative), and heuristic or interpretive (meaning-constructing).
Such moral principles perform a complex set of tasks, to say the least.

The idea of form-content independence here is not altogether unproblematic. Flanagan and Adler (1983, pp. 581-84) described the tension between Kohlberg's assumption of formalism in respect to moral principles and his denial of the moral relevance of a sophisticated knowledge of a "bag of virtues" embodied in any particular social context. One can interpret the formal principle, for example, never to treat an other as a means to one's own ends but always as an end in her- or himself, as relevant in some particular instance of moral choice only if one understands the concrete social relations among the parties involved. For example, one needs to understand the details of what it means to relate as a woman and man qua wife and husband, or qua employer and employee, or qua physician and patient, or qua counsel for the prosecution and witness for the defense.

However, as Flanagan and Adler pointed out, if the application of formal principles in moral reasoning depends on such a knowledge of specific roles, values, and virtues, then moral reasoning would seem to suffer from the same lack of unity and relativism for which Kohlberg criticized the "bag of virtues" understanding of moral maturity. Kohlberg *did* claim, in response to criticisms from Flanagan (Kohlberg, 1982, pp. 520–21) and Gilligan (Kohlberg, 1984, pp. 363–70), that a sensitivity to contextually specific circumstances is essential to mature, i.e., Stage 6, moral reasoning. I think Flanagan and Adler are right here but that Kohlbergians do not have to concede too much.

Recall that on Kohlberg's view, moral principles can in fact be both universal and sensitive to the most context-embedded features of particular situations because they are interpretive constructs rendering the utterly particular morally intelligible. They are not fixed absolutes too general to apply unambiguously in all but a few, paradigmatic types of case. To save context sensitivity here, Kohlbergians have to accept that a knowledge of moral particulars, including historically and culturally concrete roles, values, and role-defined virtues, is required for adequate moral reasoning. I think they can concede this point. Moral reasoners have to be *in* the world of conventional morality though they don't have to be *of* it, we might say. They may have to know the relevant "bag of virtues," but they don't have to conceive morality on the "bag of virtues" model.

A problem remains. If universal moral principles are interpretive constructs, if they are the deep structure of mature interpretations of moral phenomena, not fixed rules, how can they be stated or understood independently of historically and culturally concrete roles, values, and virtues? How *can* content-independent, formal moral principles be intelligible except through specific contexts? Kohlberg, Levine, and Hewer explain this in part in their discussion of constructivism.

Constructivism and the Primacy of Justice

"Constructivism" is the view that moral principles are reached through active interaction with the sociomoral environment by a process of moving toward reflective equilibrium between moral principles and considered moral judgments.

> In the context of the issues raised by Munsey (1980), my view of moral principles is that they are developmental constructions and not *a priori* axioms or inductions from past experience. This view derives from Piaget's central constructivist assumption, that is, the assumption that mental structures are neither *a priori* biological innates nor inductive habits passively learned from sense experience but are, rather, active constructions assimilating experiences while accommodating them. (Kohlberg, 1984, p. 301)

Moral principles are not "constitutive rules," because they are not a priori. That is, moral principles are not conceptually prior to social interaction. They are not "summary rules" either, because they are not empirical generalizations from social interaction. Moral principles are constructions reached through the cognitive-moral process of assimilating while accommodating social experiences, a process aiming at reflective equilibrium.

In discussing the relationship of reflective equilibrium between "moral intuitions" and moral theories, Kohlberg, Levine, and Hewer quoted Dworkin's (1976) article on Rawls's conception of "The Original Position." Dworkin drew a contrast between the "natural model" and the "constructive model" of the relationship between moral intuitions and moral theories. According to the natural model, moral intuitions can be understood as the apprehension by the conscience of objective moral reality. However,

> The second model treats intuitions of justice not as clues to the existence of independent principles but rather as stimulated features of a theory to be constructed, as if a sculptor set himself to carve an animal that best fit a pile of bones he happened to find together. The "constructive model" does not assume, as the natural model does, that principles of justice have some fixed objective existence, so that descriptions of these principles must be true or false in some standard way—It makes the different assumption that men and women have a responsibility to fit the particular judgment on which they act into a coherent program of action. (Dworkin, 1976, pp. 27–28; quoted by Kohlberg, 1984, p. 302)

Moral principles do not reside in some Platonic realm, there to be apprehended if we are up to it, and even if we are not. Rather, the effort to fit one's judgments into a coherent program of action leads one through a process of reconciling one's reasons for different judgments into a coherent pattern of reasoning. New action situations give rise to new reasoning that is sometimes contrary to one's established reasoning structures. This sometimes leads one to accommodate the new reasoning, but it may lead one to adhere to one's present reasoning structure at the price of changing an action judgment. The endeavor to maintain a coherent structure of reasoning is the endeavor to reach reflective equilibrium between one's moral principles and one's intuitions and considered judgments about appropriate actions and evaluations, i.e., between the reasons one takes to hold for acting in a particular way in all cases relevantly similar to the one at hand and what one thinks should be done in a particular case.

For instance, Julie (Disposable Hook Up Dilemma) is convinced that if the sexual exploitation of women is to cease, women who have been harassed must file formal complaints. Nothing short of this seems to have worked, and even women's success at formal complaint is mixed at best. Anita Hill's is a dramatic case. Hill endured intense and extended public scrutiny in order, Julie believes, rightly to expose Clarence Thomas, then a nominee for the United States Supreme Court, for sexual harassment in the workplace. She underwent extensive, televised cross-examination by senators and was the object of countless news reports and endless bad jokes, from CNN and *The New York Times* to late-night television and bars and locker-rooms all over the country. But she focused the nation's attention on the problems of workplace sexual harassment as no one else in recent memory had done. Lorena Bobbitt, too, became a national symbol of resistance in quite a different set of circumstances, resistance to abuse in the home within marriage. The trials of William Kennedy Smith and Mike Tyson, of Mel Reynolds and Bob Packwood (to mention only the first cases that come to Julie's mind) show the hardships women have to endure to show that sexual harassment and sexual assault cannot be tolerated. For only if people bring abuse to light, however painful this may be for the victims, will people stop simply turning their heads and looking the other way. Julie herself reported the beer-company posters in the campus pub that she found offensive, depicting women in sexually objectifying and suggestive ways. The posters have been removed, though not without Julie taking some grief from some of her friends, both male and female.

But now Julie talks with Reanna. Reanna is hurt, humiliated, angry, disillusioned, and resigned, off and on and all at once. Julie has talked to Reanna about filing a formal complaint of sexual harassment against Brad and his three fraternity brothers, but Reanna refuses to take part in any public examination of her situation. She just wants to learn her lesson and move on—no need to make a spectacle of her victimhood, she says, in more circumspect moments of cynicism. They both know how influential the fraternity seems to be with the college administration, having been given little more than slaps on the wrist for what everyone knows were major alcohol and hazing violations. The fraternity's alumni are supposed to be among the most forthcoming with contributions to the college's operating budget and endowment. If Reanna were to go outside the college to the courts, what kind of evidence does she have that anything harmful really occurred? Reanna seems to have been a willing participant, and everyone knows fraternity houses are not exactly havens of virtue, or of privacy for that matter. And so, understanding how this situation must appear and feel from Reanna's point of view, Julie is not inclined to push, in the circumstances.

But this puts her in a quandary. For she finds herself believing that women must be strong in the face of resistance to reporting harassment and abuse—this is the way she has put it to herself—and also believing that Reanna may be right not to file a complaint, given Reanna's ambivalence and the strength of the resistance she'd likely experience in this case. Julie's intuition and considered judgment in this case is not consistent with her principles. She might decide Reanna should file a complaint anyway. Look at what Anita Hill faced and went through. She might modify her understanding of the responsibility women have to each other and to men as well to report abuse. Maybe reporting is admirable but not obligatory. Or maybe more depends on the circumstances than Julie has thought until now. However Julie resolves her quandary, she must make reflective adjustments to bring her principles and considered judgment into reflective equilibrium. In this and many other circumstances Julie has constructed and reconstructed for herself a set of principles that mediate coherent patterns of reasoning and coherent patterns of action.

Kohlberg, Levine, and Hewer (1983) noted that their description of the principled perspective of Stage 6 may be misunderstood as describing something other than the terminal stage of reflective construction of principles of reasoning. Stage 6 might be interpreted as an a priori system of principles reached through the illumination of conscience. This would be incorrect.

> My discussions of Stage 6 in terms of moral musical chairs or ideal role-taking, however, makes [sic] it fairly clear that Stage 6 principles are necessarily social constructions preparing the person for a process of moral dialogue. Such principles structure an imaginative process in the individual's mind which attempts to produce an ideal moral dialogue for resolving conflicts. The adequacy of the conflict resolution proposed is determined by the achievement of social consensus under dialogic conditions. (1984, p. 303)

Stage 6 is the result of constructive cognitive-moral development through complex environmental and "dialogic" stimulation. The most adequate moral theory is not apprehended a priori, nor is it inferred through empirical generalization from experience. The most adequate moral theory is constructed through reflective interaction with the social environment, assimilating while accommodating social experiences.

In summary, through interaction in a sociomoral environment, people construct universal moral principles as interpretive structures for making sense of the sociomoral phenomena in their environments.

The remarkable thing, on Kohlberg's account, is that if we hold relevant environmental and dialogic conditions constant, all individuals in all cultures will develop their own interpretive constructs in more or less identical fashion through an invariant sequence of construct types. All relevant differences among (biologically normal) individuals are to be accounted for by reference to differences in sociomoral environment, including experiences in moral dialogue and role-playing. Stage 6 is adequate, finally, to all sociomoral conditions, to all the curves and fastballs the sociomoral world throws our way, because— we might suppose—it is adequate to the social world *simpliciter*. Universal moral principles need have no standing *outside* particular contexts because mature, principled interpretative constructs are the same, as a matter of empirical fact, in every particular context. They are not like Platonic forms (*eidē*), separated off in their own pure realm, but they *are* like Aristotelian *eidē*, in the particular things themselves.

The deep structure of the mature interpretation of sociomoral phenomena is the same in every single historically situated, culturally concrete dilemmatic situation. Different situations evoke different aspects of this deep structure, and of course the *content* of the situations varies enormously, but their sociomoral *form* is invariant. For just this reason impartial justice is primary with respect to other sorts of moral consideration that admit more variation.

Kohlberg believed that his metaethical assumptions suggest the normative-ethical thesis that justice is primary in defining the moral domain. That is, justice is the primary feature of morality, rather than, say, emotion and empathy, caring and responsiveness, character and intelligence, identity and self-understanding, or community and solidarity. In relation to justice other features of morality are secondary, either supplementary or derivative. He also believed that his empirical research bore out this suggestion.

Following Piaget's lead, I thought that justice reasoning would be the cognitive factor most amenable to structural developmental stage analysis insofar as it would clearly provide reasoning material where structuring and equilibrating operations (e.g., reversibility) could be seen. With the moral domain defined in terms of justice, we have been successful in (a) elaborating stages which are structural systems in the Piagetian tradition and (b) honoring the metaethical assumptions we have made prior to research. To imply that justice is the *first* virtue of a person or a society, as did Kant and Plato, is a more controversial normative claim that is not required for establishing the validity of our measure and theory of justice development. It seems to us, however, that morally valid forms of caring and community presuppose prior conditions and judgments of justice.

Thus, our assumptions prior to research, as well as the results of our research, have led us to hold that the prescriptivity of moral judgments is a fundamental component of justice reasoning which bases prescriptions and duties on a recognition of others' rights.

The universalizability or impartiality criteria of moral judgment also implies [*sic*] that moral reasoning, as we have studied it, constructs judgments of justice. A universalizable judgment that appeals to norms implies a fair or impartial application of norms. (1984, pp. 304–5f.)

Justice reasoning is, on Kohlberg's view, the use of the moral language of prescriptivity and universalizability. He began his research with this assumption and found that, indeed, moral development consists in the structural stage progression toward the ideally prescriptive and universalizable perspective of the "moral point of view."

"To summarize, the focus of Piaget and ourselves on morality as deontological justice springs from a number of metaethical considerations" (Kohlberg, 1984, p. 305). First, the "prescriptivist conception of moral judgment" lends itself to a conception of morality as conflict resolution in terms of rights and correlative duties. Second, the assumption of "cultural and ethical universality in moral judgment" accounts for the aim of agreement on formal principles of justice as the minimal commonality that allows for diversity in conceptions of the good and of human excellence. Third, the "cognitive or 'rational' approach to morality" makes reasoning from principles central to morality. And finally, as just noted, "justice . . . is the most structural feature of moral judgment." The assumption of the primacy of justice in the domain of morality "springs from" and gives normative-ethical definition to the metaethical assumptions with which Kohlberg oriented his research program (1984, pp. 305–6).

However, as Kohlberg, Levine, and Hewer pointed out, Kohlberg's assumptions did not guarantee the success of his research program. His results might have been different than they were. Also, his assumption of the primacy of justice does not rule out the expansion of the study of the moral domain. Rather, the assumption of the primacy of justice merely, but importantly, designates the best starting point (1984, p. 307). Further, "While the assumption of the primacy of justice has not been 'proved' by our research, the fact that data collected under this assumption meet the requirements of sequentiality, structured wholeness, and relationship to action indicates the empirical fruitfulness of the assumption" (1984, p. 308). No theorist could hope for a stronger type of corroboration of a theory. The nature of theory-laden empirical inquiry is such that the results can never prove theoretical assumptions. For all theorists employ their theories in construing the sort of data to be sought in the first place. Data are not wholly independent testimony. But if Kohlberg's results were as he asserted them to be, they gave him a strong claim to having the best, the heuristically most adequate theory (see Kohlberg, 1981, pp. 175–76).

Lonely Men of Morality

At the close of the last chapter I suggested that in at least one respect Kohlberg's metaethical assumptions made the structural stage model a model of "lonely men of morality, acting alone and relying only on their inner moral principles." We can now add to our reckoning on this point the normative-ethical (as opposed to metaethical) assumption of the primacy of (impartial) justice, as suggested by Kohlberg's metaethical assumptions. And we can note two crucial similarities between Kohlberg's characterization of his and Piaget's construal of morality (as focusing on deontological justice) and the rules-based, rights-centered construal of morality I discussed earlier.

First, both Kohlberg's justice-centered conception of morality and the rules-based ethic of rights approach conflict resolution by reference to rights and derivative duties. The occasions on which it is relevant to claim a right to something or against someone are characteristically occasions on which there is a conflict of claims. When there is no conflict to resolve, there is no point to claiming rights or asserting duties of others. Indeed, we might even say that it makes no sense to assert one has a right to something over which we cannot imagine a conflict of claims, say, the equilateral triangle or the number 39 or the atmosphere of Mars. If it does not make sense to claim a right to such things because it is unintelligible how we might make conflicting claims for them, then the very idea of rights presupposes not only rules but also conflict, conflict that cannot be resolved without appeal to some standard or rule external to the relationship between the conflicting parties. But this shows that a rules-based, rights-centered construal of morality presupposes either insufficient coalescence of, or a breakdown in, relationships between persons such that external standards and/or authorities must be called on. Rights-centered moralities presuppose certain types of community.

Second, both Kohlberg's justice-centered morality and the rules-based ethic of rights prescribe a minimal commonality allowing for diversity in conceptions of the good and of human satisfaction and excellence. Each aims to be neutral with respect to alternative conceptions of the good, to provide a minimal, neutral framework for managing potentially conflicting pursuits of rival human aims and projects. The framework has to be neutral so that those holding rival conceptions of the good—of what makes life meaningful and worthwhile—can accept it independently of their disagreement on the good. The assumption here, too, of course is that we need a standard that will enable contending parties to adjudicate disputes, and so again the models assume the absence of common understanding sufficient to enable settlement of potential differences without appeal to an external standard or authority.

There is no reason internal to either the Kohlbergian deontological justice ethic or the rules-based ethic of rights not to extend these points to their extreme. Both ethics are designed *not* to rely on or require bonds of friendship or personal attachment. Both make room for community among persons but deliberately (obstinately) avoid assuming it. They assume competitive independence rather than cooperative interdependence, separation rather than connection. Both, that is, are designed for "lonely men of morality, acting alone [or at least separately] and relying only on their inner moral principles," not on any shared purposes or common aims. Community might supplement loneliness, but it presupposes it.

I should note that Boyd (1980) objects to this characterization of the Kohlbergian model in his discussion of "the Rawls connection."

> Persons are not thought of as independent, isolated "rule-followers," with greater or less direct access to the moral truth, but rather as rule-followers-in-relation who must construct and continually re-construct through public dialogue the perspective from which rules governing their action have validity. (p. 204, quoted in Kohlberg, 1984, p. 302)

It is instructive that Kohlberg's gloss on Boyd's objection was that "the constructivist model conceives persons as having attitudes of mutual respect" (1984, p. 302). Independent, isolated rule-followers can have attitudes of mutual respect, but presumably rule-followers-in-relation have more. "Rule-followers-in-relation" are committed to a common (democratic) project of public moral and political discourse. They share purposes and cooperatively pursue them, and they socially construct their shared morality. Boyd's remark in an important way already presupposes the "sociological turn" toward the just community model and the social construction of justice in the practice of democratic community. To this I will return again. Before that, I examine Kohlberg's argument for the sociomoral adequacy of Stage 6 justice and justice reasoning. This will throw into even sharper relief the tension between the structural stage model and the just community model.

SIX

The Cognitive and Moral
Adequacy of Stage 6

Adequate to What, and by What Criteria?

Kohlberg claimed adequacy for what he described as the Stage 6 justice-reasoning perspective. Whereas other stage perspectives would
in certain circumstances prove inadequate to the cognitive and moral
challenges presented in those circumstances, a Stage 6 perspective
would meet the challenges of any circumstances. It would be adequate both morally and adaptively. Kohlberg was explicit in what he
thought was entailed in claiming cognitive-moral adequacy for Stage
6, but before I describe his contention, let me suggest why I think he
came to give the adequacy thesis the form he gave it.

On December 9, 1941, two days after the Japanese attacked Pearl
Harbor and one day after the United States declared war on Japan,
Assistant Secretary of the Navy Artemus L. Gates received a letter
containing the following offer:

> I am 47 years old, have 846 hours of certified solo time all on single
> engine jobs of 450 horsepower or less, mostly cross-country, includ-
> ing some blind flying. I feel competent, after a little checking, to fly
> anything and am willing to dive into any objective my commander
> would consider worth-while. Can you use me? (quoted in Keeley,
> 1969, p. 35)

Assistant Secretary Gates knew Alfred Kohlberg and knew he was
serious. He also knew Kohlberg was no crackpot. Alfred had been a
private pilot for eleven years and had been traveling to East Asia on
business for twenty-five. He knew Japan and China well. He was
deeply troubled by Japan's aggressions against China, where he had
made many friends and had established lucrative business contacts.
Now Japan had struck his own soil.

Gates responded thoughtfully to the letter but declined the offer.
Two years later Gates received another letter from Alfred Kohlberg.

This time Kohlberg had read a newspaper story reporting on what were supposedly bombproof submarine hangers at L'Orient. He had a more specific proposal this time. Kohlberg speculated that it would be worth testing just how bombproof these hangers actually were. How would they stand up to a direct hit from a plane with a full load of explosives? (Keeley, 1969, p. 35). Assistant Secretary Gates once again declined the offer.

Lawrence Kohlberg's father had lied. In 1941, the year of the attack on Pearl Harbor, Alfred was *not* forty-seven years old. This was the year a judge ruled to dissolve the nine-year-long joint custody arrangement between Alfred and Charlotte Kohlberg. Alfred and Charlotte had separated ten years earlier when the youngest of their four children, Laurence, was not yet four (Laurence changed the spelling of his name to "Lawrence" when he was a young man). Alfred was forty-four years old in 1931 when he and Charlotte separated, divorcing a year later, and so he was fifty-four years old in 1941, the year he told Assistant Navy Secretary Gates he was forty-seven. This lie was understandable, though. The year before, on Memorial Day in 1940, Alfred had flown his own single-engine plane to Toronto to enlist in the Royal Canadian Air Force. Even though he fudged a few years on his true age of fifty-three, they wouldn't take him. He was too old.

When Alfred graduated from high school in San Francisco in 1904, he had already become a writer (Keeley, 1969, pp. 16f.). He published a small newspaper called *The Westerner* for family and friends. Then, while at the University of California, he moonlighted as a reporter for the *Oakland Enquirer* and the *Oakland Tribune* and then wrote for the *Daily Californian,* the campus newspaper. After the great earthquake of 1906, Alfred left school. He ran his own printing and publishing business for two years. But in 1908, after a frustrating experience with the printers' union, he sold the business and went to work with his father in his accessory dry-goods business. Lawrence's grandfather discouraged his eager son, Alfred, from enlisting before being drafted for military service in World War I. Alfred's draft notice finally came only days before the Armistice on November 11, 1918, and Alfred never got the chance to serve.

These two early, pre–World War I ventures, in publishing and dry goods, would define Alfred's career. His work with dry goods continued in 1916 when he made his first trip to Japan and China and began his work as an entrepreneur in Chinese silk, especially handkerchiefs. The newspaper and publishing experience prepared Kohlberg to become an outspoken and prolific letter writer. During Lawrence's childhood, Alfred Kohlberg wrote hundreds upon hundreds of letters to newspapers, members of Congress, members of various administrations, college presidents, and others, expressing his views on U.S. relations with China. He was distraught by what he believed was U.S. complicity in the Communist takeover of the people with whom he had established friendships and business relationships. He did not keep his thoughts to himself. Everybody who was anybody in Sino-U.S. relations received letters from Alfred Kohlberg.

Alfred made a lot of money as an importer of Chinese silk, and Lawrence's early life and education were richer for it. Lawrence was affected in another way as well. Alfred devoted an enormous amount of energy to redressing what he saw as the errors of the leftist press and the educational establishment and of those he regarded as pro-Communist members of Congress. One could even say he was obsessed with what he saw as Communist injustices and U.S. complicity in them. Young Lawrence and one of his older sisters chose their father in 1941 when the judge dissolved the joint custody arrangement mandating sole custody by one parent or the other. His other older sister and older brother chose their mother. Lawrence identified with his intense and undaunted father (Keeley, 1969, p. 25). He grew up in the cyclone of this international entrepreneur who devoted enormous energy to politics and morality on an international scale.

In 1939, when Lawrence was twelve, his father was active on another front as well (Keeley, 1969, p. 34). That year Alfred was made chair of the United Jewish Appeal, an organization devoted to providing financial assistance to Jews in a Europe that was being more and more ravaged by war. Some thought Alfred's efforts were heavy-handed, but he did what he thought was necessary to raise funds to help fellow Jews on the other side of the Atlantic. As we know now and as Alfred and Lawrence would learn all too clearly, this provided little more than an umbrella in a hurricane.

In 1945, when Lawrence finished boarding school at Phillips Academy, he joined the U.S. Merchant Marine and spent two years in

Europe. In 1947, following his time in the Merchant Marine, he began a year of work with Haganah, the Jewish defense organization.
He served as second engineer on an old Haganah ship attempting to
smuggle Jewish refugees from Eastern Europe through the British blockade into Palestine. Their ship, dubbed the *Paducah,* was captured by the British and the crew and refugees were interred in a
concentration camp in Cyprus before escaping to a kibbutz in Israel
(Kohlberg, 1948). Lawrence returned to the States in 1948 to attend
the "Hutchins college" at the University of Chicago, where he was a
student with both Allan Bloom and Richard Rorty, and where he took
his A.B. by examination in one year. In 1950 he was twenty-three,
and his father's efforts to redress flawed U.S. relations with China
continued unabated. That year Lawrence began graduate work in
clinical psychology at Chicago; he wanted to help people (Kohlberg,
1991, p. 13). That same year his father began a relationship with
Joseph McCarthy, soon becoming one of McCarthy's most resourceful
colleagues in the senator's campaign against so-called anti-American
activities (Keeley, 1969). (It was at about this time that Lawrence legally changed the spelling of his first name to "Lawrence," possibly
to change his nickname from "Laurie" to "Larry.")

   If Larry Kohlberg did not share his father's political views—he
clearly rejected them—he certainly did learn one thing from him.
Obsession with injustice in the international arena is no vice. Alfred's
concern was directed east across the Atlantic toward injustices suffered in Europe by fellow Jews and west across the Pacific toward
injustices suffered by friends and workers in Nationalist China gone
Communist. His moral and political arena was the entire northern
hemisphere. Kohlberg rejected the content of his father's commitment, but he embraced its form. His moral and political arena would
include the southern hemisphere as well.

   In formulating his account of morality in neo-Kantian, Piagetian
terms, I believe that Kohlberg was working through the experiences
of his late adolescence and his young adulthood. These experiences
included, on the one hand, his growing awareness as a young boy of
what his father did, not only for a living but also for what he thought
was right, in China and also in Europe, and, on the other hand, his
growing sense of the enormity of the evil being done to the Jews his

father was raising money to help. Reflecting on his experiences in World War II, in a speech he gave in Tokyo in October 1985 (see Kuhmerker, 1991, p. 3), Kohlberg recalled,

> I reached Europe in the fall of 1945 as a member of the United States merchant marine. Having a Jewish father, what struck me was not only the wreckage of buildings and lives due to the war but getting to know the plight of the survivors of the Nazi holocaust or genocide of Jews, Gypsies, and other non-Aryans. This was not only destruction and horror but injustice such as the world had never known. (1991, p. 12)

Kohlberg formulated his account of morality in response in part to problems he experienced in an international arena and on a model provided by his father's international moral and political activism.

An international arena requires a universal morality. Offering a rational justification for intervening, e.g., to prevent the spread of genocide in another nation, or to redress injustice against racial minorities generally or even against racial majorities as in South Africa, or to correct the widespread effects of sex-based oppression and discrimination, requires a conception of morality that extends beyond personal relationships and attachments and beyond the limits of self-interest or regional and national identity. It requires something like a secularized account of divine moral law, of a law given for all, ideally of a law developmentally emergent in all biologically normal members of the species who engage in adequate sociomoral interaction.

I am suggesting that we can understand Kohlberg's account of morality as designed to address a problem that required (or at least seemed to Kohlberg at the time to require) a principled universalism as a solution. He needed an account that was nonrelativist but that would not require a chauvinistic ethnocentrism about justice. Looking back on the year he spent in the great books curriculum at the "Hutchins college," the year after his experience on the *Paducah,* Kohlberg stated the following:

> Through studying John Locke, John Stuart Mill, and Thomas Jefferson I began to see universal human rights and human welfare as relative to the culture and/or the particular individual. My own moral commitment or identity made sense within the context of the

social contract, which was the foundation of American constitutional government. Still, I could see that philosophers like Locke and Mill did not agree with each other, and I looked for some principle that would underlie and justify all basic moral discussions. Kant's statement of the basic principle of the categorical imperative, "treat every human being as an end in himself not only as a means," seemed most fundamental. Equal respect for human dignity seemed to me the essence of justice. (1991, p. 13)

In turning to Baldwin and Piaget, Kohlberg formulated a developmental account of an adequate justice-reasoning perspective that would satisfy four requirements.

As I have noted, Kohlberg employed a concept of development that entails the use of a standard toward which developmental change is understood to progress. Each of the six Kohlbergian stages are increasingly fuller realizations of Stage 6, the standard implicit in the description of the sequence as a whole. As the most developmentally advanced stage of moral reasoning, it is that stage most closely approximating or most embodying the ideal of moral reasoning. As I have emphasized, Kohlberg viewed the description of this ideal as a moral philosophic enterprise without which empirical research into moral development cannot begin to orient itself.

If the orienting conception of ideal moral reasoning is sound, and if in fact the phenomena of longitudinally observed moral reasoning can be interpreted through a developmental stage sequence the terminus of which is moral reasoning closely approximating the ideal, then the terminal stage of moral reasoning is the most adequate morally (assuming that ideal moral reasoning is morally adequate). If we admit the additional thesis that moral development occurs as an adaptive response to the stimuli encountered in one's sociomoral environment, then the terminal stage of moral reasoning is the most adequate psychologically or cognitively, qua most adaptive, as well as being the most adequate morally.

Given this conception of cognitive-moral development, Kohlberg seems on the face of it committed not only to claiming that preindustrial, pretechnological societies—whether historically antedating or geographically and culturally secluded from industrial, technological modes of production—are morally inferior. They would be inferior, on this view, in virtue of providing less complex sociomoral stimulation to the individual reasoning agent. They insufficiently stimulate movement toward morally autonomous reasoning. But he also seems committed to claiming that no as yet unimagined postindustrial, posttechnological society will arise in respect to which Stage 6 is inadequately adaptive. So inasmuch as Kohlberg claimed that Stage 6 is adequate *simpliciter*, he implied *both* that sociomoral environments structured on individualism and anonymity (e.g., urban North American cities like Boston and Cambridge, Massachusetts) are morally supreme *and* that there is no possible successor to these sociomoral environments in which the postconventional perspective of universal moral principle will cease to resolve the moral dilemmas and problems that arise.

But since Kohlberg was so explicit about his metaethical constructivism, it is not clear that he was thus committed. As a constructivist, he would be able to contend that new adaptively adequate interpretive constructs could be reached through reflection and interaction with others in new, unforeseen types of sociomoral environments. And so perhaps we should read him as claiming that Stage 6 is as adequate as needed thus far. This was not actually what he claimed, but nothing in my argument prevents us from giving him the benefit of the doubt here.

This noted, we can understand Kohlberg's argument for the adequacy of Stage 6 justice reasoning as employing the following four criteria of adequacy:

(1) The principles of justice employed at the most adequate stage of moral reasoning are those principles that are justified by a moral theory embodying the metaethical assumptions I have described, following Kohlberg, Levine, and Hewer (1983).

(2) Individuals reasoning at the most adequate stage of moral reasoning consistently agree about the "right" action in moral dilemma situations.

(3) The most adequate stage of moral reasoning is well adapted, perhaps fully adapted to the stimuli of a complex sociomoral environment in virtue of embodying reflective equilibrium between, on the one hand, moral intuitions and considered judgments and, on the other hand, principles of justice.

(4) And the most adequate stage of moral reasoning embodies the most complete differentiation of moral from nonmoral concepts and most fully integrates the concepts of and differentiations made at previous stages; we can understand the stages as equilibrium points in moral development.

Kohlberg claimed that Stage 6 justice reasoning meets these criteria. Stage 6 employs principles justified by a moral theory embodying Kohlberg's metaethical assumptions, and it produces consistent agreement on moral dilemmas. Stage 6 produces fully reversible judgments and, correlatively, judgments in equilibrium, and it is the most differentiated and integrated stage of justice reasoning.

Moral Adequacy as Formal Adequacy

According to Kohlberg, moral reasoning qua justice reasoning is deontological, not teleological (goal-based) or aretēic (virtue-based). So the most adequate stage of moral reasoning should avoid commitments to ultimate aims, to conceptions of the good life, to particular virtues, and so on (Kohlberg, 1981, p. 169). Such commitments involve many nonmoral considerations, from a strictly deontological point of view, and the most adequate stage of moral reasoning should most fully differentiate the moral from the nonmoral. Hence, Kohlberg stated, "a criterion of adequacy must take account of the fact that morality is a unique, *sui generis* realm. If it is unique, its uniqueness must be defined by general formal criteria, so my metaethical conception is *formalistic*" (Kohlberg, 1981, p. 170). Since the definition of morality is formal, developmental levels of moral judgment should be found increasingly to approximate "the philosopher's moral form." And since the formal criteria that differentiate moral from nonmoral judgments are fully met only at the most mature stages of moral judgment, the mature stages of moral judgment are more moral. In the formalistic sense, they are more morally adequate (1981, p. 170).

The criteria of cognitive adequacy are parallel with criteria of moral adequacy.

I am claiming that developmental theory assumes formalistic criteria of adequacy, the criteria of levels of *differentiation* and *integration*. In the moral domain, these criteria are parallel to formalistic moral philosophy's criteria of *prescriptivity* and *universality.* These two criteria combined represent a formalistic definition of the moral, with each stage representing a successive differentiation of the moral from the nonmoral and more full realization of the moral form. (1981, p. 171, and cf. p. 180)

Kohlbergian developmental theory, then, assumes *formalistic criteria of adequacy.* Adequacy is characterized formally and not in terms of any specific content. There are no issue-based litmus tests. Moral stages that give rise to judgments that are, whatever their content, more prescriptive and universal are more morally adequate, and those that involve, whatever their content, more conceptual differentiation and integration are more cognitively adequate in virtue of being more adaptive. So the "betterness" of stages more advanced developmentally is partly moral and partly cognitive (1981, p. 190f.). The criteria of more or less peculiarly moral adequacy are (1) and (2), mentioned earlier, and the criteria of more or less peculiarly cognitive adequacy are (3) and (4).

Consensus and Corroboration

The further warrant Kohlberg claimed for his metaethical assumptions is twofold. First, this set of assumptions, or some subset of the majority of them, enjoys the consensus of modern moral philosophers in the deontological tradition from Kant to Rawls (see Kohlberg, 1981, p. 191, and 1984, p. 293). Beyond a mere appeal to authority, to the fact that there is at least rough consensus among such eminent thinkers, their arguments can be employed, and Kohlberg did to some extent marshal them in defense of his guiding metaethical conception. Second, Kohlberg's metaethical assumptions are found warranted heuristically to the extent that they are fruitful in directing empirical research. As I stated earlier, if Kohlberg's research results are as he took them to be, his assumptions have proven very fruitful indeed.

Kohlberg claimed that Stage 6 reasoning employs principles of justice justified by a moral theory embodying his metaethical assumptions. He also claimed that people who use Stage 6 reasoning agree consistently on moral dilemmas. Kohlberg found himself in closest agreement during the 1970s with the moral theory of Rawls's *A Theory of Justice* (1971). Rawls's theory embodied Kohlberg's metaethical assumptions, and it justified the principles of justice employed at Stage 6. Rawls calls these the principle of equal liberty (above all else, maximize equality of liberty) and the difference principle (then, accept only those unequal distributions of resources that most favor the least well off in the unequal distribution). How does Rawls's theory justify Stage 6 principles of justice? Rawls shows that Stage 6 principles are the product of the type of reflective equilibrium referred to in Criterion 3.

There is an "isomorphism" (Kohlberg, 1981, p. 194) or "parallel" between Kohlberg's psychological theory and his normative theory. The psychological theory is explanatory and Piagetian; the normative theory is justificatory and Rawlsian (p. 201). It is worth noting why there is not a complete isomorphism. Flanagan made an important point, in a reply to Kohlberg's response to his argument in "Virtue, Sex, and Gender" (Flanagan, 1982a), about the difference between the Piagetian account of cognitive development and the Kohlbergian account of moral development. In a Piagetian account of failure of cognitive development, the physical world is never the cause of failure to develop. It is always and everywhere the same (Flanagan assumes). However, in a Kohlbergian account of failure of moral development, the subject's social world *is* characteristically the cause of failure to develop.

> The social world . . . unlike its physical counterpart, varies in fundamental ways across the earth, not to mention across town. Yet by modeling his theory on Piaget's, Kohlberg is able to appropriate the claims of universality, irreversibility, and increasing adequacy for his moral stage scheme, while diverting our attention from the social world. Yet it is the social world which is the single most important variable for explaining differences in moral conception. (Flanagan, 1982b, p. 530f.)

What is most plausible and surely correct in Kohlberg's claims about moral development is that to a certain extent it presupposes but is not the direct result of Piagetian cognitive development. For example, at a certain point in their development, children do not recognize that their siblings have a sibling and that their neighbors have a neighbor.

Such a recognition that some relationships are reciprocal requires a concept of reciprocity (whether children recognize they have such a concept or not), and that concept is a cognitive achievement. It is not innate. Only when children can recognize the reciprocality of some relationships can they recognize that the demands for fairness that they make of others apply to the others only insofar as they apply also to themselves. So to a certain extent Kohlberg is correct in modeling moral development on Piagetian cognitive development. Some have argued, however, that the Piagetian model ceases to have application beyond something like Kohlberg's Stage 3 or possibly 4—precisely at the point where variability in social environments produces its effects on stage-sequential development (see Gibbs, 1977, discussed later).

Reflective Equilibrium: The Rawls Connection

The principal conception Rawls and Piaget share is that of reflective equilibrium. Kohlberg explained that the notion of reflective equilibrium has three meanings for Rawls, the first two of which are directly relevant here. First, reflective equilibrium is reached through back-and-forth adjustment and revision "between espoused general moral principles and particular judgments about situations."

> We extract or induce principles that seem to lie behind our concrete judgments and try to make new judgments by them. This process continues to lead to revision, sometimes of our principles, sometimes of our intuitions as to what is right in a concrete situation. (Kohlberg, 1981, p. 195)

In respect to this process of back and forth adjustment and revision, Kohlbergian stages are moments of equilibrium holding between principles and intuitions. The terminal stage, which is to say, the most stable equilibrium between principles and intuitions, settles on the principles of justice employed at Stage 6.

Second, the concept of reflective equilibrium applies to Rawls's concept of social contract as "the equilibrium point among a group of rationally egoistic bargaining players" (a.k.a. lonely men of morality; quotation from Kohlberg, 1981, p. 196). In a game-theoretic situation in which one is ignorant of the facts about one's wealth and social status in a legal/political community, i.e., behind the Rawlsian "veil of ignorance," rationally self-interested individuals discuss what principles should govern their polity and the distribution of its economic resources. They reach reflective equilibrium through back-and-forth adjustment and revision between principles of distribution and considerations of (unveiled) self-interest (behind the veil). One outcome of such a discussion behind the "veil of ignorance," according to Rawls, is the principle of distribution called "the difference principle." This is the principle that unequal distribution is justified only when everyone benefits more than if there were equal distribution, in situations of positive-sum gain, and is most justified when the least well off are made better off than in any other distribution. Kohlberg calls this the principle of equity as it is employed at Stage 6.

Reflective equilibrium, then, represents for Rawls both the outcome of a psychological process of the reflective, dialectical formulation of principles of justice and the outcome of game-theoretic bargaining among rationally self-interested individuals. So in respect to the former, Rawls, like Kohlberg, believed that his preferred principles of justice are the outcome of developmental adaptation to one's social environment (see Rawls, 1971, p. 460 n. 6, and secs. 70–72).

In respect to the latter sense of reflective equilibrium, that of the outcome of game-theoretic bargaining, Rawls and Kohlberg concurred on the preconditions of bargaining. Rawls's conception of the original position under the veil of ignorance is parallel to Kohlberg's conception of the postconventional, prior-to-society justice-reasoning perspective. Kohlberg observed that "the 'veil of ignorance' represents a statement of the fundamental formal conditions of the moral point of view, the conditions of impartiality and universalizability" (1981, p. 197). Kohlberg's concept of reversibility is implied by Rawls's conception of the original position. Reversibility is a quality of judgments that are the outcome of what Kohlberg called "ideal role taking" or "moral musical chairs." He presented reversibility as an alternative that he thought is more plausible than Rawls's conception of the original position. It is clear, Kohlberg stated, that Rawls employed

the idea of reversibility as well as universalizability in the idea of "the original position" or the "veil of ignorance," although he does not develop the idea of equilibrium implicit in the reversibility criterion, because he is bent on developing an equilibrium to be found in a bargaining game conception of the social contract. . . .

I claim that such a process of equilibrated and complete use of Golden Rule role taking is formally equivalent to Rawls's idea of decision in an original position of ignorance of one's own identity and the set to maximize the ego's interests. (1981, p. 199)

Equilibrated, ideal role-taking produces fully reversible justice judgments and yields the same principles and judgments as the Rawlsian game-theoretic "original position." And yet it is more intuitively plausible, Kohlberg thought. It does not require anyone to imagine her- or himself ignorant of her or his own identity and conception of the good. It does not require anyone to imagine her- or himself without specific relationships and without a particular more or less well defined aim or project—though it requires something "formally equivalent" to these.

This second reversibility process for reaching fairness as stated by Rawls is, according to Kohlberg, as follows:

The decider is to initially decide from a point of view that ignores his identity (veil of ignorance) under the assumption that decisions are governed by maximizing values from a viewpoint of rational egoism in considering each party's interest.

In the first procedure, the decider is assumed to start with an altruistic empathic or "loving" orientation; in the second case, the decider is assumed to start with an "egoistic" orientation to maximize his own values, canceled out by the veil of ignorance (1981, p. 199f.).

In the case of both reversibility processes, a judgment that is fully reversible is in reflective equilibrium, whether this equilibrium is reflective and adaptive or game-theoretic.

Explicating the parallel (the quasi-isomorphism) between Rawls's concept of reflective equilibrium and Piaget's concept, Kohlberg continued as follows:

Having considered reversibility in Rawls's philosophic theory, we can now relate it to its central meaning in Piaget's theory. In Piaget's equilibrium theory, the fundamental formal condition of equilibrium in logic as well as morality is reversibility. . . . Piaget defines a stage of logic as a group of logical operations; that is, as a group of reversible transformations of ideas, classes, or numbers that maintain certain relations invariant. Moral reasoning or justice in Piaget's theory represents decisions that are not "distorted" or changed as one shifts from one person's point of view or perspective to another's. . . . [M]orality is the "logic" for coordinating the viewpoints of subjects with conflicting interests, as logic is the coordination of points of view on objects or symbols of objects. (1981, p. 200f.)

Moral reasoning in maturity, on Kohlberg's Piagetian account, is not distorted by the reasoner's being anyone in particular just as logical reasoning is not distorted by a reasoner's having any particular vantage.

The more reversible the justice operations of a particular cognitive-developmental stage are, the more they are in equilibrium. The more the justice reasoning of a stage is in equilibrium, the more adaptively preferable it is. The more adaptively preferable a stage of reasoning is, the more cognitively adequate it is. And according to Kohlberg's formalistic metaethic, the more reversible a justice judgment is, the more morally adequate it is. Kohlberg summarized as follows:

1. Moral judgments that are not reversible by the test of original position or moral musical chairs are not in equilibrium.

2. Moral judgments that are not based on the principle of equality or equity (the difference principle) are not reversible and so are not in equilibrium.

3. When people become aware of the lack of reversibility of their judgments, they will change these judgments or principles to reach a more reversible solution.

4. This search for equilibrium is a basis for change to the next stage.

5. Our final stage, Stage 6, is in complete equilibrium; its judgments are fully reversible. This is not true of Stage 5 and even less of lower stages.

6. Because Stage 6 judgments are reversible, all Stage 6 subjects agree, given common understanding of the facts of the case. (1981, p. 211)

Judgments based on the principles of justice justified by a theory embodying Kohlberg's metaethical assumptions are reversible, and hence in equilibrium, and hence morally adequate (Criterion 1). Reasoning based on these principles of justice produces consistent agreement because such reasoning is fully reversible (Criterion 2), and fully reversible reasoning is more adaptively adequate than is less reversible reasoning because it is more in equilibrium (Criterion 3).

Criterion 4 states that the most adequate stage of moral reasoning embodies the most complete differentiation of moral from nonmoral concepts and most fully integrates the concepts of and differentiations made at previous stages. Kohlberg claimed that the formal criterion of reversibility that he stressed "entails other formal criteria in terms of which Stage 6 is best. Two such criteria are differentiation and integration" (1981, p. 214). That is, the greater reversibility of justice judgments involves the greater differentiation and integration of the concepts of a stage of justice reasoning.

> In summary, there are certain categories used by every moral stage structure or every moral theory, such as the categories of rights and duties. Development through the stages indicates a progressive differentiation of categories from one another—for example, of rights from duties—and a progressive integration of them, expressed in the correlativity of rights and duties. This correlativity is not merely a matter of analytic tidiness of an abstract normative or metaethical theory but leads to very different judgments of obligation, judgments that are in better equilibrium with judgments of rights (1981, p. 219).

So the greater differentiation and integration of cognitive-moral concepts leads to reasoning which is in better equilibrium, and hence which is more adequate (Criterion 4).

Flanagan's Response to the Adequacy Thesis

Flanagan (1984, pp. 162–70) characterized Kohlberg's argument that Stage 6 is adequate in a slightly different fashion. He formulated an important critique of the adequacy thesis that sheds light on the question I have raised about whether Kohlberg's structural stage model is a model of "lonely men of morality." Let me discuss now his assessment of Kohlberg's claim to adequacy for his construal of morality, from the early and mid-1980s, and his critique of the structural stage model as a whole, from his 1991 book, *Varieties of Moral Personality.*

Flanagan found four main "strands" in the argument that Kohlberg offered in support of the adequacy thesis. I paraphrase Flanagan's summary as follows. First, the impetus for seeking better equilibrium between, on the one hand, one's moral concepts and principles of justice and, on the other hand, one's moral intuitions and considered judgments—and hence the impetus that leads one toward Stage 6 reasoning—is the natural inclination to adapt cognitively to one's sociomoral environment. Judgments that are more "reversible," that better integrate the perspective of each party involved in a situation of conflicting claims, are more cognitively and more morally adequate. Stage 6 judgments are fully reversible and hence are maximally adequate both cognitively and morally.

Second, each stage in Kohlberg's developmental sequence is "better integrated and differentiated than its predecessor, which it logically absorbs" (Flanagan, 1984, p. 163). Each stage "logically absorbs" the conceptual integrations made at the previous stage while incorporating new conceptual distinctions (differentiations) that separate the moral from the nonmoral considerations that are relevant. Hence, each stage is logically more adequate than the previous stage in virtue of being more refined conceptually.

Third, people in fact prefer the highest stage they comprehend. And finally, "the best philosophical wisdom independently depicts Kohlberg's highest stage as *the* highest stage. Kohlberg claims that his highest stage converges with the moral philosophies of Kant, Hare, Baier, Frankena, and Rawls" (Flanagan, 1984, p. 164). Flanagan quoted Kohlberg's claim that "the philosopher's justification of a higher stage of moral reasoning maps into the psychologist's explanation of movement to that stage and vice versa" (Kohlberg, 1973b, quoted in Flanagan, 1984, p. 164) The moral theory presupposed by Kohlberg's conception of the terminus of moral development is the moral theory defended by the best moral philosophers.

Flanagan offered some minor and some major objections. The minor objections pertain to the first three strands of Kohlberg's argument, as Flanagan interpreted it. First, Flanagan noted that the phenomena accounted for in the adequacy thesis can be explained by an alternative, social learning account of moral development (a reinforcement-based understanding of moral development). The fact that an individual happens to prefer the stage he or she is in over the stages he or she used to occupy (and the fact that individuals understand only the stages they are presently in or once occupied) does not entail that he or she prefers it *because* of its greater adequacy. Perhaps he or she simply prefers the type of moral reasoning for which he or she is most reinforced by his or her peers and environment in general.

Furthermore, the fact that individuals come to reason from a more and more reversible perspective does not entail the greater adequacy of more reversible perspectives. Perhaps individuals come to adopt such perspectives because they are negatively reinforced for selfishness and positively reinforced for doing what they would have others do. Flanagan noted Kohlberg's recognition that the claim to greater adequacy for more reversible perspectives must be supplemented by a philosophic argument for the moral superiority of a fully reversible perspective. If the social learning account of preferences for types of moral reasoning is correct, then the "natural desire" for equilibrium with one's sociomoral environment can be understood simply as an acquired trait of adaptability. One learns to adapt through making the sorts of compromise demanded in particular, variable social settings.

Second, in respect to the second strand of the adequacy thesis, Flanagan argued that better differentiation and integration are alone insufficient for greater adequacy. For surely the perspective of all living things is better integrated and differentiated than the perspective of all human beings inasmuch as the perspective of all human beings is better integrated and differentiated than the perspective of all the members of a particular society. Yet the perspective that demands equal respect for all forms of life, human and nonhuman, is not more adequate morally, since it is unlivable. All living beings sustain themselves at the cost of other living beings. Furthermore, a conception of respect for life on which we can recognize hierarchy and/or sacrificial interdependence among life-forms—giving permission to humans to consume other living beings, say, fruits, grains, and vegetables—would seem to make room for a conception on which we can recognize hierarchy and/or sacrificial interdependence among societies, or say, racial and ethnic groups, something to which we cannot construe Stage 6 reasoning to give permission. In short, Stage 6 seems to put a halt arbitrarily to the greater integration and differentiation of moral concepts, privileging the human species in an unexplained way.

Flanagan's major objections concern the fourth strand of Kohlberg's adequacy thesis. First, he objected that there is more disagreement about the nature of morality than Kohlberg seems to admit, even among the contemporary liberal moral philosophers whom Kohlberg cites. Kohlberg (1982, p. 524) responded to this type of criticism by pointing out that among the philosophers he cited there is rough convergence on the set of metaethical assumptions that characterize "the moral point of view." As Flanagan noted, however, there are "several widely respected contemporary moral philosophers" (Flanagan, 1984, p. 166) who reject both Kantianism and utilitarianism (he mentions A. MacIntyre and B. Williams in a note) and so who cannot be perceived as defending some conception of Stage 5 or 6. But as Flanagan no doubt recognized, from Kohlberg's point of view this shows only that there are some very articulate Stage 3 and 4 reasoners with a substantial pre-postconventional audience of admirers. Of course this would be so. Still, Kohlberg could not claim to be in agreement with *all* prominent contemporary moral philosophers.

Second, Flanagan noted that the concepts of "utility" and "rights" are widely held to be recent conceptual inventions historically associated with the breakdown of traditional communities and the rise of industrialization. Of course, that these concepts have emerged recently is no criticism of them as such, but, as Flanagan was right to suggest, we can wonder whether we should not describe their emergence as part of an attempt to adapt to the breakdown of morally superior social environments. This consideration motivated Flanagan's third major objection.

Kohlberg's "highest" stage is incapable of criticizing the type of social environment that gives rise to the concepts of utility and rights precisely because the "highest" stage *requires* these concepts. It presupposes the moral superiority of industrialized, technological, urban (and, we might add, multicultural) settings that, Flanagan suggested, seem obviously inferior in some respects, for instance, in family and community loyalty and in concern for future generations. But of course Kohlberg could have responded, correctly, that disloyalty and unconcern for future generations *can* be and *ought* to be criticized from the perspective of a morality of utility and/or rights.

Lying behind Flanagan's criticism of Kohlberg's "highest" stage is a concern about the moral adequacy of a perspective that is consistent with and even condones social settings that seem to encourage anonymity and the priority of impersonal considerations in resolving conflicts. Surely there is something morally suspect about a moral theory that fails to prescribe that a mother save her child from drowning when this would prevent her from saving three unfamiliar children who simultaneously face the same fate (Flanagan's canoe counterexamples). The demand for impartiality and/or maximizing utility seems inappropriate in such a case.

However, the virtue of Stages 5 and 6, Flanagan observed, is the importance of impartiality and utilitarian considerations in resolving fairness disputes between parties who lack a familial or communal association on the basis of which to resolve their conflicts. The "postconventional" stages are indeed crucial in settings in which familiarity and close community do not obtain and in societies in which they obtain only in pockets and in limited associations. Flanagan's objection amounted to this. He objected to treating impartiality and utilitarian considerations as overriding in *all* types of conflict, even where they are not strictly speaking necessary, familial and communal contexts included. We might say that Stages 5 and 6 were treated by Kohlberg and many modern moral philosophers (recall Anscombe, 1958) as superior *simpliciter* on the grounds that the contexts of familial and communal breakdown in which they *are* superior, for lack of reasonable alternatives, are more and more pervasive.

Finally, Flanagan objected that "Kohlberg's stages do not give us a comprehensive picture of the moral sphere. Without such a comprehensive picture the claim to have identified the highest stage of moral development is grossly inflated" (Flanagan, 1984, p. 169). Kohlberg's stages concern the resolution of conflicts of justice and have little or nothing to say about the importance of "supererogatory" care and concern for others. What is more, Flanagan noted, Kohlberg's theory of moral development is a theory about moral reasoning as distinct from moral action. Kohlberg's theory lacked researched programmatic attention to the action of moral agents.

Kohlberg responded to this type of criticism, as I have noted, by claiming that all other moral domains presuppose the stages of justice reasoning. Any particular phase in the development of care and concern for others presupposes some stage on Kohlberg's developmental sequence. Furthermore, the more advanced one is along the stage sequence the more inclined and hence the more likely one will be to do the "right" thing.

Kohlberg was in the just community projects expanding his research into the domain of moral action, as I discussed above. But as Flanagan pointed out, Kohlberg had as yet virtually nothing to say about more or less stable characteristics of moral personality that are expressed or embodied in action, e.g., loyalty, reliability, and respectfulness. His neo-Kantian rejection of the account of the virtues offered by "the ancients" and his endorsement of the virtue of adherence to principle were in keeping with his commitment to the deontological tradition.

Flanagan on the Structural Stage Model

More recently, Flanagan (1991) has offered a trenchant critique of the structural stage model as a whole—which he seems to have taken to be the whole of the Kohlbergian project. His objections go to the heart of the model, undermining it, he believes, at all important points.

> Taken together these [five general] objections call into question the foundational assumptions that were first made available by Piaget and that were then eventually made part of [the] stage theory's essential core by Kohlberg. These assumptions are (1) that moral psychology is plausibly typed in terms of holistic, unified, and distinctive general-purpose stages; (2) that all moral responsiveness is routed through these general-purpose judgment schemes; (3) that each developmental stage is normatively more adequate than its predecessor; (4) that speech acts in response to hypothetical dilemmas are revelatory of the deep structure of moral psychology; and (5) that the essence of morality has to do with interpersonal relations governed by rules, obligations, and rights. (Flanagan, 1991, p. 186)

I rely heavily here on Flanagan's (1991) statement of his own objections. However, I recast them and diverge from them at points in order to make maximum use of Flanagan's insightful criticisms in the specific context of my larger argument in this book. I set out six rather than five (dividing the first of Flanagan's criticisms into two objections) and organize them into two groups of three. Objections 1–3 concern aspects of the Kohlbergian research program and its findings. Objections 4–6 concern the assumptions that orient the program, namely, relating to the philosophical superiority and psychosocial adaptive adequacy of the Stage 6 reasoning perspective, the adequacy thesis.

Flanagan's six objections as I will restate them are (1) that only a specific range of the full panoply of moral issues is studied, namely, problems of justice in which there are conflicting claims of rights between persons, set in situations in which there is a dilemma or quandary about what to do or initiate at some moment. (2) This specific range of issues is studied only by studying verbal responses to thinly described, i.e., abstract, hypothetical dilemmas. And (3) even on the reading given by Kohlbergians, the data collected on this range of issues do not yield clear evidence either for holistic stages or for a well defined pattern of development.

Also, (4) the structural stage model assumes that moral maturity requires a more or less fully equilibrated justice-reasoning structure that is a structural whole, a more or less stable unity qua equilibrium point, having coherent moral philosophic justification. But this is based on the questionable notion that only an equilibrated unity would be psychosocially adaptively adequate. Furthermore, (5) the structural stage model presupposes that justice-reasoning structures that integrate the conceptual competencies of developmentally prior stages and make greater differentiation of the moral from the non-moral (conceived deontologically) are thereby moral philosophically superior to prior stages; in short, that development through a temporally and conceptually ordered sequence entails improvement. But this is based on the questionable notion that psychosocial adaptivity entails moral philosophic superiority. Finally, (6) the impartialism of Stage 6 either fails to make sense of the way partiality in some domains seems morally required or makes sense of this but in an implausible way. By grounding the call for partiality in impartial considerations, impartialism implies that our real motive to partiality should be impartialist. In short, the structural stage model rests on the questionable assumption of the homogeneity of the moral.

Objection 1

Flanagan argues that Kohlbergians have studied only a narrow range of problems, problems of justice in which there are conflicting claims or conflicting rights between persons. But there are other types of issues that should count as within the range of the moral. We can imagine cases such as the following: parents might deliberate about the time and financial resources they devote to, and the types of nurture through which they care for, their children. How much time and money is enough? How important is devoting time and resources to one's children when balanced against one's own interests in one's career and personal fulfillment? Is the most important concern how much time one spends with one's children or how one spends that time? Flanagan suggests that we distort the considerations relevant to parental deliberation on these questions if we put them in terms of the impartial discharge of parents' duties. Parents, we might say, have special duties of partiality to their children just to the extent that those children have claims on their biological or adoptive parents, say, through the (possibly implicit) contractual arrangements their parents have made with them but not with other children. But we are required to invoke this sort of distorted reasoning only if all moral problems reduce to (or presuppose) problems of justice and conflicting claims or rights. This is the type of problem raised by Beverly's response to Stephen in the Needy Children Dilemma. What are one's obligations to children not one's own? Given the enormous need for assistance to children worldwide, could one possibly discharge obligations to anonymous needy children sufficiently to justify sending one's own to college or even to the ice-cream store?

Imagine a second example. You have a friend whose good you think will be protected and fostered only if, on a matter of some sensitivity for him, you discuss frankly with him your perceptions of his conduct and attitudes. If you do this you will risk damaging your relationship. If you do not, your friend is in for a damaging personal crisis made all the more imperiling by his blindness to what you perceive is really going on in the circumstances. For instance, your friend feels a vague but acute sense of need for a change of self manifested in (a) dissatisfaction at work and the felt need for a career change, (b) domestic blahs and longings for novel sexual excitements that seem to suggest a change of spouse, and (c) a strongly felt desire to purchase a sports car, a fast red one. You recognize, let us imagine, that these are classic symptoms of male midlife crisis, a phenomenon typically but not exclusively encountered (when it occurs) in mid-career middle-class men in monogamous, capitalist societies. However, your friend is certain beyond a shadow of a doubt that his situation is utterly unique and entirely contingent upon his particular life-circumstances. He reacts testily, even angrily, to the hints you have dropped so far about the possibility that this crisis episode is a fairly typical phenomenon in men of his age in your culture. Your friend needs your perspective. He will in all likelihood cause himself and others dear to him long-lasting harm if you do not intervene. Your friend has been frank with you in the past, and it has helped you a lot. You would fail your friend if you didn't help. And this seems in some important respects to be a moral issue, one of (partialist) responsibility to your friend. But is this a situation in which you are contemplating a conflict of rights or claims to justice?

Imagine a third and final example. You have come to hold certain ideals for yourself because of your particular life-experiences. These ideals require that you hold yourself to more or less rigorous personal disciplines and that you cultivate habits of thinking and acting that should become, but are not yet, second nature to you. Some you feel strongly about. Others you feel obliged to realize but not out of an especially deep conviction or identification. If you are to realize any or all of these ideals for yourself, you will have to exercise self-discipline in cultivating talents importantly related to what you want to become and so to what you will then be able to contribute to the lives of others and your community as a whole. When you deliberate on particular occasions that call for self-discipline, and when you sketch life-goals and plans for accomplishing them, are you thinking first and foremost, let alone exclusively, about duties you have to others or to yourself that somehow conflict with rights to self-gratification in the short term? Do we distort such deliberations by trying to construe them as matters of impartial justice?

Flanagan thought Kohlberg focused on a narrow range of problems, and he argued that there is no good reason to believe that data Kohlberg and his colleagues gathered—on responses to issues of jus-

tice where conflicts of rights are indeed at stake—provide unambiguous evidence about the broader range of issues that are surely
within the domain of the moral. This is because, for example, one
might be just and admirably fair and yet have a great variety of other
moral failings linked in no determinate ways with one's justice reasoning and dispositions to justice. We would have to be very credu-
lous indeed to believe that all people who reason articulately and with
technical philosophical accomplishment about hypothetical dilemmas
of justice and conflicting claims or rights are on the whole and in
every way morally good people, morally mature at any rate. Some
people are good in some respects and bad in others, good, say, to their
associates and to anonymous people in need while neglecting their
family. Some are bad in many ways but exceptionally good in a small
number of ways, Oskar Schindler for one, whom Flanagan discusses
(1991, pp. 8–9). Focusing narrowly on issues of justice does not provide an adequate basis for making a comprehensive assessment of
one's moral maturity or immaturity.

Objection 2

Flanagan notes that Kohlberg and his colleagues examined this
narrow range of problems by studying verbal responses to abstract,
hypothetical dilemmas. Yet there are two grounds for suspicion that
these responses do not reveal any sort of deep structure of a subject's
overall moral personality. First, responses to abstractly described hypothetical dilemmas may not warrant inferences about responses to
dilemmas in concrete cases of more authentic complexity. And second, verbal responses may not correlate in any regular or predictable way with the decisions made and actions taken in actual lived
situations by a wide variety of subjects with all sorts of moral idio-
syncracies. This second ground for suspicion is the notorious "judgment-action problem." Putting it this way evokes recollection of the
principled reasoning of moral pariahs. Such examples unhinge any
overly confident inferences from judgment or reasoning to action or
moral personality. As Flanagan notes, Piaget himself recognized that
respondents' replies to hypothetical dilemma scenarios are "verbal
. . . to the second degree" (Flanagan, 1991, p. 188, quoting Piaget,
1932, p. 119). Not only is the response merely verbal; the scenario is

verbal as well. And with respect to the first ground for suspicion, we might recall that the person who joined Kohlberg's research team in the early 1970s as a postdoctoral research associate and who was assigned the task of moving research on the structural stage model into the domain of real life (rather than hypothetical) dilemmas herself became the best-known critic of the model's comprehensiveness—Carol Gilligan.

Objection 3

Even on the reading given by Kohlbergians, the data collected (from verbal responses to a narrow range of hypothetical dilemmas, ones concerning justice or conflicting rights) do not yield clear evidence either for holistic stages or for a well-defined pattern of development. As Flanagan puts it, "almost no one gives answers all of which can be scored as belonging to one and only one stage" (1991, p. 186). The standard measure is two-thirds response consistency, with most subjects using two modal stages in a roughly two-to-one ratio. Most children give responses scored as mixtures of Stages 2 and 3, and most (affluent Western or Westernized) adults give responses scored as mixtures of Stages 3 and 4, with Stage 5 very infrequently in evidence in any solid way and with Stage 6 almost never in evidence. All things considered, this is marginal evidence for very little developmental change.

Objection 4

The structural stage model assumes that a person who has reached moral maturity has at his or her disposal (a) a more or less fully equilibrated justice-reasoning structure that is a structural whole, a more or less stable unity qua equilibrium point on a continuum of developmental change. This structural whole (b) has a coherent moral philosophic justification. The idea is that only a unified moral reasoning structure could receive a philosophically unified justification, and only a philosophically unified justification is a fully coherent one. And since morally mature people can give unified justifications, a mature moral personality has a unified moral reasoning structure. Kohlberg,

Levine, and Hewer (1983) argued for this model of moral maturity in setting forth Kohlberg's metaethical assumptions.

But notice that this way of stating the assumption of the link between equilibrated structural unity and moral maturity leaves implicit the fact that, in cognitive-developmental theory, maturity amounts essentially to adaptivity. So the notion that maturity entails "overarching equilibrated unity" implies that adaptivity requires such unity. Therefore, the assumption that an adaptively adequate moral or justice-reasoning structure must admit of philosophically unified justification presupposes the idea that the way of life and sociomoral order to which morally mature reasoning is adequate is itself structurally unified, for only this would account for the need for structural unity in comprehending it. Also, such a structurally unified way of life and sociomoral order is the end or terminus of social development (see Shweder, 1982b)—if you will, sociomoral reality *simpliciter* or as such.

But the way of life and social matrix to which one's reasoning needs to be adaptively adequate may itself be a hodgepodge, a pluralistic and multicultural melange, though stable in the circumstances nonetheless—*e pluribus unum*. To put the matter as Flanagan does, there is nothing incoherent in the notion that one might have a "dominant moral psychological style, possibly appropriately depicted [as the abstractly described Kohlbergian Stage 3], but also, and in addition, several (possibly many) special-purpose procedures for perceiving and dealing with unusual cases" not satisfyingly handled through one's dominant moral psychological style (1991, p. 188). This may in fact be what Kohlberg and his colleagues found in the Connecticut prison and labeled "situational regression." Some inmates who tested as Stage 3 reasoners on the standard hypothetical dilemmas tested as Stage 2 reasoners on dilemmas set in the context of the prison. Perhaps they were simply engaged in special-purpose procedures for adaptively maneuvering prison life. Indeed, there is no inconsistency in supposing that one's moral personality might be "constituted by a network of special-purpose capacities, dispositions, and procedures . . . lacking any single dominant style of response . . . so well coordinated with one another that they produce an integrated personality" (1991, p. 188).

A high tolerance for disunity, facility in ad hoc adjustment, and improvisational dexterity in one's sociomoral adaptive strategies may be a considerable accomplishment in particular life-circumstances. In life-circumstances in which there is little if any overarching unity, the drive for "overarching equilibrated unity" in a moral perspective may characterize disciplined theoretical reflection about justice or morality generally—in spite of the fact that such unity is almost never found in theoretically untutored respondents. Or it may betray that foolish consistency Emerson thought a hobgoblin. At any rate, there is very little evidence in Kohlberg's data that "overarching equilibrated unity" characterizes the moral personality of all or even many people at all or any points in their development. And in assuming there is such a drive in all subjects, cognitive-developmental stage theorists may simply have filtered out much of the disequilibrium and disunity (the "noise" in the data) in obtaining even a two-thirds response consistency over two modal stages on a two-to-one ratio. Even that finding may depend on attenuation of the data. As Flanagan puts it, they've assumed holism and consistency; they haven't tested for it.

Objection 5

The structural stage model presupposes that justice-reasoning structures both integrate the conceptual competencies of developmentally prior stages and involve greater differentiation of the moral from the nonmoral. The later structures are thereby more morally adequate than prior stages. Development through a temporally and conceptually ordered sequence entails improvement. But there is no necessity in supposing that greater differentiation and integration entails developmental improvement, even if it entails greater adaptivity. For greater differentiation and integration of one's conceptual apparatus may be required in adapting to a way of life and sociomoral order that either is in decline or is emergent. A way of life in decline can produce an acute sense of unraveling, fracturing, or splintering, yielding considerable sociomoral confusion and conflict. A way of life that is emerging from a melding or conjoining of disparate sources into a composite society may be characterized in various continuing respects and, at certain moments in particular, by sharp and sometimes violent conflict. In the former case, an understanding of what is in the process of unraveling or splintering might well be a prereq-

uisite for understanding the present state of its unraveling or splintering. People would have to integrate their understandings of earlier
circumstances into their understandings of later circumstances and
would have to make new discriminations not earlier required. In the
latter case, an understanding of the disparate sources in their integrity
might well be a prerequisite for understanding the present state of the
sociomoral order in which they are in conflict with each other. People
would again have to integrate earlier understandings into later understanding, making new differentiations.

Indeed, it might be difficult to imagine the complications involved
in a way of life and sociomoral order developing from simultaneous
unraveling/splintering and melding/conjoining if we did not have
very good reasons to believe this is actually the situation of most of
us most of the time in the global entertainment and consumption
economies. Noticing this, of course, does not commit us straightaway
to decrying the postindustrial, urbanized, multicultural social world
characterized in large part by anonymity and impersonality to which
the Kohlbergian postconventional stages do seem in important respects and at important moments more adaptively adequate. However,
noticing this *does* suggest that a Stage 6 perspective would not be in
a position to certify that such a social world is better than its predecessors, since the notion that Stage 6 is more mature than its predecessors in virtue of being more adaptively adequate presupposes that
this social world is an improvement, that adaptation to it somehow
constitutes sociomoral arrival.

Objection 6

Flanagan's final objection is related to his first. I quote it verbatim.
"Stage 6, the telos of development in moral stage theory, yields implausible substantive conclusions if it is interpreted as demanding actual impartiality in all domains, and it yields the right conclusions
implausibly, from an unlikely motivational source, if it allows for partiality (to one's loved ones, one's own projects, and so on) only if such
partiality can pass impartialistic inspection" (1991, p. 194). Some aspects of our lives do seem morally to require impartiality, as when
we evaluate bids for construction projects or applications for admission to professional school, or when we determine to whom political

asylum or research grants should be given. Though partiality in these areas may be common, it is morally objectionable.

Other aspects of our lives, however, seem morally to require partiality, as when we decide which children should receive financial support from us, considering our own among the pool of prospects, and as when we consider how we should spend our time, considering our jobs, families, and friends among possible uses of our time. This moral requirement of partiality does not seem adequately understood as springing from impartial considerations, such as that showing partiality in these circumstances maximizes utility or optimizes use of available resources or satisfies universalizability tests or reversibility procedures. We should tend and care especially for those closest to us with whom we are attached in projects that bind us together and further our mutual and individual good. And this responsibility seems to have little to do with the abstract principles that guide us in our interactions with anyone and everyone, anywhere and everywhere, at any and every time. Alternatively, the requirement of partiality in some contexts (family, friendship) does seem like a genuinely moral requirement and not merely a supplementary one.

Kohlberg might, however, have replied that this is of course how it *would* seem from the perspective of Stage 3 or a mixture of the conventional Stages 3 and 4. One of the basic theses of the account of the structural stage model is that one can only dimly understand the reasoning one stage above one's own, and certainly not two stages above. Kohlbergians would expect a conventional reasoner not to find the impartial, postconventional moral point of view fully plausible as a whole, but they would expect conventional reasoners to find it plausible in part, in some though not all respects, and this is just what Flanagan does, the reply might go. Furthermore, on an adequate differentiation of the moral from the nonmoral, we would see that partialist considerations do have their place, but only in the context of satisfaction of impartialist requirements as secondary or supplemental to them.

But that response presupposes the greater adequacy of a Stage 6 perspective. It does not establish it. What we need are grounds for supposing Stage 6 impartialism adequate that do not presuppose its adequacy, and the assumption of the homogeneity of the moral, qua impartiality, does not accomplish this. Kohlberg's appeals to the best moral wisdom of academic philosophers did not even help much when he made them, and they might help even less now, since the best philosophers agreed and agree on precious little. Such appeals do not establish the adequacy of impartialism. Flanagan states, "morality is mischaracterized when it is treated as a unitary subject matter requiring a unitary set of problem-solving skills. The heterogeneity of the moral is a deep and significant fact" (1991, p. 195).

But the homogeneously particularistic, partialist perspective is no more comprehensive than the homogeneously impartialist, for just as the impartialist is forced to provide impartialist grounds for partiality in certain domains of the moral life, the partialist is forced to provide partialist grounds for impartiality in certain domains, and this puts no less strain on our motivational structures. It makes little sense to say that we should be impartial in awarding construction contracts or research grants, on the grounds that we and ours are best cared for by our taking this position, or that we can empathically identify with the needs of those outside our circle almost as if they were inside it, such that being fair to them is merely an extension of tending our own. It makes no more or less sense to say that we should care for our own children especially and first of all on the grounds that this is better, all things considered, from an impartial perspective. An ethic conceived solely on the basis of experience at coordinating the activities of those with whom one is interdependent is no more or less adequate, by itself, than is an ethic conceived solely on the basis of experience at coordinating the activities of those from whom one is more or less independent. Interacting with others in real life usually involves a mixture of these kinds of experience and requires a balancing of both ethics. (This, I will argue later, is the notion on which in the end Kohlberg and Gilligan completely agreed.)

The point of partiality is that there are some with whom we are bound in special ways. The point of impartiality is that there are many with whom we are not bound in special ways, and many more with whom we are apparently hardly bound at all. The drive to subordinate and reduce either type of consideration to the other betrays the grip of a philosophical fetish for tidiness and homogeneity that bears little or no resemblance to the actual moral psychology of the vast majority of people. "If, as is true of Kohlberg's scheme, the conception of morality is narrow, and competencies are privileged which are not particularly appropriate in certain domains, then there may even be problematic, but unnoticed, trade-offs between acquiring the competencies required by the developmental end point and becoming moral in some broader sense" (Flanagan, 1991, p. 195). In short, "moral maturity" may require moral inadequacy of one sort or another. But this means that there may be circumstances in which a more or less fully equilibrated, unified moral or justice-reasoning structure, one that admits of a philosophically unified justification, is adaptively inadequate—inadequate in virtue of its tendency to insist on a kind of order and coherence everywhere when as a matter of fact such order and coherence is context-bound at best.

One-Size-Fits-All Morality

Kohlberg argued that Stage 6 justice reasoning was adequate to all situations because reasoning from its perspective was more reversible, better integrated, and more finely discriminating than reasoning from other perspectives in the stage sequence. It performs better, that is, by the relevant formalistic criteria of moral adequacy. There are no litmus-test issues. Those judgments are most adequate morally that are most adequate formally *because* genuine morality is formally distinct from less universalistic, more conventional understandings of justice. Morality is not a local matter, though social convention is. Mature moral reasoning is prior-to-society, universalistic reasoning.

In a context characterized by the loosening and fragmentation of family and community bonds and by the urbanization of heterogeneous populations, more and more people interact socially and morally under conditions of anonymity. People face and deal with each other as with strangers, aliens to their particular identities, purposes, and life-projects. In such circumstances we need something that can serve as a basis for getting along, something that can replace a sense of common identity and purpose, something to which we can appeal when we reason with each other about our actions and policies. A workable replacement should be neutral and impartial. It should not give rise to partisan bickering. To maintain reasoned discourse against armed conflict, we need to share the sense that none is being favored by the very terms of the discourse.

Kohlberg's conceptions of ideal role-taking and the criterion of reversibility make extremely good sense here. Reasoned discourse is maintained against armed conflict by adopting a reasoning perspective in which all perspectives are on equal terms. One size fits all. But it is hard to resist the notion that this leaves us with "lonely men of morality, acting alone and relying only on their own inner moral principles to determine which moral action to take." And in that respect, the terms of the discourse privilege some over others, namely, those whose identities and projects can be expressed in liberal individualist terms.

We are "lonely men of morality" here in two senses. Assuming anonymity, we assume an absence of close relationship. We assume a kind of basic and original distance and separation from each other. We assume no binding common identity or shared purpose. We have to imagine that interdependence derives from some sort of act of will, a choice. But also we assume that we are independent from what Kohlberg called "moral atmosphere." That is, we assume that we are to stand free of prejudices and partialities that presuppose collective identities and projects. It is as if one is an organism adapting to and acting in an independent environment—of which one is not a constituent part and which does not partially constitute oneself. We reason as if we are no one in particular, as if we are an anyone. An anyone is not influenced by "moral atmosphere," for the very idea of "moral atmosphere" is particularizing. Kohlberg meant it to help make sense of the way features of particular contexts and circumstances influence reasoning and acting.

But the assumption of original and basic anonymity or independence cannot structure a pluralist democracy in which nonliberal nonindividualists are participants without begging certain important questions against them. It is not just that the moral atmosphere of competitive coexistence draws them from fidelity to their covenants, which it does subtly and powerfully. It is also that in that idiom they are bound to represent their worldviews as options they have chosen and that others might choose as they might choose between print fonts or color schemes. For from the perspective of a liberal individualist worldview, any other representation smacks of authoritarianism, which of course is bad. Such a democracy cannot incorporate nonliberal nonindividualists without begging an important question against them, namely, are their deepest identities and their fundamental projects consistent with the rights of others and the privacy of the others' own consciences. They had better be.

The just community model might however be more hospitable to nonliberal nonindividualists. I suggested that on the terms of the structural stage model, we reason as an anyone. But we reason and act as an anyone by reasoning and acting as if we are an everyone (i.e., through reversible role-taking), and it is in precisely this respect that Kohlberg's structural stage model, Stage 6 in particular, is, but also is not, a perspective of "lonely men of morality." But this takes me ahead of my story. I will return to this point.

On the way to an examination of the just community model it will be helpful to turn first to Kohlberg's sense that his is a Platonic or Socratic conception of morality and moral education. For it is here that we find a most interesting albeit precarious bridge between Kohlberg's two models.

SEVEN

Following Plato
to Just Community

Socratic Dialectic and Kohlberg's Reading of Plato

I have suggested that there is a tension at the heart of the Kohlbergian project and that all the elements of the tension were present in Kohlberg's dissertation (1958). The most important moment in the project, from the point of view of my argument in this book, was the turn toward G. H. Mead and Durkheim in the early 1970s after Kohlberg visited the Youth Aliyah kibbutz in Israel in the summer of 1969 (Kohlberg, 1971b, 1978). Mead and Durkheim had been present in the dissertation as representatives of views to be rejected. The second most important moment involved a thinker not present in the dissertation but who figured in a near equally significant ambivalence. Kohlberg (1970) thought through his relationship to Plato at about the same time that he turned to Durkheim and Mead. "It is surely a paradox that a modern psychologist should claim as his most relevant source not Freud, Skinner, or Piaget but the ancient believer of the ideal form of the good," Kohlberg began an essay in 1970 (reprinted in Kohlberg, 1981, p. 29).

On the revisionist story I am telling, Kohlberg's interpretation of Plato and his response to Plato's dialogues are important for two reasons. First, Kohlberg began thinking about how to extend the structural stage model into moral education by reflecting on the pedagogical method of the Socrates of Plato's "early" dialogues. However, in a way that I think Kohlberg did not himself fully appreciate, I believe he came to have reservations very similar to Plato's about the pedagogical inadequacy of Socratic dialectic that is practiced outside the cooperative activities of a just community. Second, Kohlberg's articulation of his agreements and disagreements with Plato—and hence of his interpretation of Plato—provides me with an excellent narrative device for making the transition from the structural stage model to the just community model. I will suggest, somewhat paradoxically perhaps, that it is in Kohlberg's early misinterpretation of Plato that we can locate the source of the incoherence in the Kohlbergian project.

Extending the structural stage model into the realm of moral education, Kohlberg argued that the aim of moral education should be the stimulation of the student's cognitive-moral development. As I explained earlier, this development consists in the progression through culturally invariant stages of moral reasoning, from less adequate to more adequate reasoning, culminating in reasoning about and from universal moral principles. There is something odd, though, in the next step of the extension. Kohlberg's account of moral development is informed by psychological concepts at first sight so different from Plato's, and it is influenced by moral philosophers whose views are in important respects so at odds with Plato's, that it might be surprising if in his central thesis about moral education we found Kohlberg claiming that its principal method is Socratic dialectic. Yet this is just what he claimed when he began in the late 1960s and early 1970s to extend the structural stage model into the area of moral education.

Kohlberg claimed at that point that the best way to facilitate the student's cognitive-moral development is through Socratic dialectic, as exemplified in the "early" dialogues of Plato, e.g., *Euthyphro* and *Laches*. Using this method, the teacher would confront the student with moral dilemmas that disclose through "Socratic questioning" the inadequacies of her or his present stage of reasoning. Kohlberg endorsed the pedagogical method of the Socrates of the "early" dialogues, most explicitly that of the Socrates of the (late "early period" or early "middle period") *Meno*. However, he rejected the educational program proposed by the Socrates of the *Republic* (a "middle period" dialogue). So either the methods of the Socrates of the "early" dialogues are inconsistent with the proposals of the Socrates of the *Republic*, or Kohlberg's endorsement of the methods and rejection of the proposals is not fully consistent.

I can summarize in three points what is at first sight puzzling about Kohlberg's interpretation and use of Plato's dialogues. First, Kohlberg claimed that, like Socrates in the *Meno*, one must begin thinking about moral education, about how virtue is to be taught, by first inquiring into the nature of virtue, and that, like Socrates in the *Republic*, one is eventually led to "writing a treatise describing moral development in a school and society that to the philosopher seems just" (Kohlberg, 1981, p. xii). Second, Kohlberg argued for what he took to be the Socratic/Platonic view of the nature of virtue, quoted below (Kohlberg, 1970, reprinted in 1981, p. 30). Third, Kohlberg pointed out that he called his view "Socratic" to indicate that it drew on Socrates' views as portrayed in Plato's "early" dialogues. "The *Dialogues* present a view of moral education as democratic and based on dialogue. In later writings of Plato, such as the *Republic* and *Laws,* a more indoctrinative and hierarchical view of moral education is advanced" (1981, p. 29n.), a view which Kohlberg rejected.

So on the one hand, Kohlberg endorsed the pedagogical method of the Socrates of the *Meno.* In that dialogue the character Socrates points out that we must inquire as to what virtue is before we can inquire about how it is to be taught. He teaches students by asking telling questions and drawing out their own dimly lit knowledge rather than by indoctrinating them. And in a manner at first sight reminiscent of the *Republic,* Kohlberg affirmed the need to set moral education in the context of a just school and state and argued for a conception of virtue that is to be found at least in part in the *Republic.* Yet on the other hand, Kohlberg rejected the educational program proposed by the Socrates of the *Republic* on the grounds that Socrates' educational prescriptions are indoctrinative. I think we have to ask whether Kohlberg was being consistent. But my interest ultimately is not in whether Kohlberg accurately interpreted Plato. I am interested in whether Plato recognized something Kohlberg failed to appreciate.

Kohlberg invoked the words of the Socrates of the *Meno* (71a–b) in explaining why the psychologist of moral education must have a moral theory, a conception of virtue. His reference to Socrates is not incidental, however, since he took his conception of virtue to be Socratic. I quote him at length since some of this is so surprising, all things considered, in light of the structural stage model as I have described it. The setting suggests the Cambridge Rindge and Latin High School, a public high school two blocks west of Harvard Yard. Here Kohlberg began discussions with parents that would lead to formation in 1974 of the Cluster School, an alternative school within a school and Kohlberg's first just community school.

When confronted by a group of parents who asked me, "How can we help make our children virtuous?" I had to answer, as did Socrates, "You must think I am very fortunate to know how virtue is acquired. The fact is that, far from knowing whether it can be taught, I have no idea what virtue really is." Like most psychologists, I knew that science could teach me nothing as to what virtue is. Science could speak about causal relations, about the relations of means to ends, but it could not speak about ends or values themselves. If I could not define virtue or the ends of moral education, could I really offer advice as to the means by which virtue should be taught? . . .

It appears, then, that we must either be totally silent about moral education or speak to the nature of virtue. (1981, pp. 29–30)

Kohlberg intentionally parroted the Socrates of the beginning lines of the *Meno* at this point. Continuing, Kohlberg alluded to classic features of the teachings of the Socrates of the *Republic*.

In this chapter I shall throw away my graduate school wisdom about the distinction of fact and value and elaborate a view of the nature of virtue like that of Socrates and Plato. Let me summarize some of the elements of this Platonic view (already noted in the introduction to this volume).

    * *First*, virtue is ultimately one, not many, and it is always the same ideal form regardless of climate or culture.

    * *Second*, the name of this ideal form is justice.

    * *Third*, not only is the good one, but virtue is knowledge of the good. He who knows the good chooses the good.

    * *Fourth*, the kind of knowledge of the good that is virtue is philosophical knowledge or intuition of the ideal form of the good, not correct opinion or acceptance of conventional beliefs.

    * *Fifth*, the good can then be taught, but its teachers must in a certain sense be philosopher-kings.

    * *Sixth*, the reason the good can be taught is because we know it all along dimly or at a low level and its teaching is more a calling out than an instruction.

    * *Seventh*, the reason we think the good cannot be taught is because the same good is known differently at different levels and direct instruction cannot take place across levels.

* *Eighth,* then the teaching of virtue is the asking of questions and the pointing the way, not the giving of answers. Moral education is the leading of people upward, not the putting into the mind of knowledge that was not there before. (Kohlberg, 1981, pp. 29–30)

Three of the claims central to this "Platonic" view of the nature of virtue deserve special attention: first, the claim that there are not several virtues but only one, whatever the historical, cultural setting; second, the claim that virtue is knowledge of the good; and third, the claim that teaching virtue is not a process of instruction but one of drawing out or educing a student's unrefined awareness of the good which the student possesses antecedent to moral education.

I want to address a certain unnecessary and superficial muddle before proceeding. Kohlberg seems to make the following three inconsistent claims: virtue is the ideal form of justice; virtue is knowledge of the ideal form of the good; and the good is justice. However, if the one virtue is justice, and if virtue is knowledge of the good, then justice is the knowledge of the good. But if the good is justice, then justice is the knowledge of justice. This situation is not remedied by altering the third claim from "the good is justice" to "the good is virtue," for then virtue is the knowledge of virtue. In either case we regress ad infinitum by substituting the *definiens* (defining expression) for the *definiendum* (defined expression): justice [or virtue] is the knowledge of "the knowledge of 'the knowledge of. . . . ' " I see no way out of this that faithfully interprets Kohlberg's summary of his "Platonic view."

Nonetheless, I suggest the following interpretation of Kohlberg's summary. There is only one genuine virtue, not many. That virtue is justice. Virtue is knowledge of the ideal form of the good, and the ideal form of the good is universal moral principle. (Where Kohlberg said "the good" read "the fundamental universal moral principle," i.e., the principle of justice.) So the virtue justice is knowledge, rational or well-reasoned knowledge of the universal principle of justice. To possess such knowledge is to possess the virtue justice. Knowledge of universal moral principles can be educed but need not be instructed because we know them all along dimly or at a low level, and teaching them is more a calling out than an instruction. Teaching the virtue justice is an asking of questions and a pointing the way, not the giving of answers.

This interpretation is faithful to Kohlberg's view as I have described it. Whether it renders Kohlberg's view as faithfully Platonic, and whether this is important, I will take up later. Let me now discuss the three claims central to Kohlberg's "Platonic" view.

The Unity of Virtue and Knowledge of the Good

On Kohlberg's view, there is only one virtue because there is only one first principle or type of first principle that is genuinely moral. Recall that on the Kantian/Piagetian conception of virtue, virtue is persistence in adherence to rule or principle, and note the relevance of the distinction between conventional and genuine virtue.

> Because morally mature people are governed by the principle of justice rather than by a set of rules, there are not many moral virtues, but one. Let me restate the argument in Plato's terms. Plato's argument is that what makes a virtuous action virtuous is that it is guided by knowledge of the good. A courageous action based on ignorance of danger is not courageous; a just act based on ignorance of justice is not just; and so on. If virtuous action is action based on knowledge of the good, then virtue is one, because knowledge of the good is one. I have already claimed that knowledge of the good is one because the good is justice. (Kohlberg, 1981, p. 40)

An action that conforms to the principle of justice but that is performed in ignorance of the principle of justice is not an action performed justly, is not a just action. Since there is only one principle or type of principle that is genuinely moral, i.e., universal prescriptive moral principle, knowledge of moral principle is singular. And since there is only one such type of knowledge, action on the basis of this type of knowledge and the virtue characterized by this type of knowledge are singular in type. Justice is the only genuine virtue.

What grounds are there for claiming that there is only one type of principle that is genuinely moral, whatever the historical, cultural setting? The answer lies in the supposed cultural universality of the structural stage sequence.

> Why do I say that existence of culturally universal stages means that knowledge of the good is one? First, because it implies that concepts of the good are culturally universal. Second, because people at a given level are pretty much the same in their thinking regardless of the situation they are presented with and regardless of the particular aspect of morality being tapped. There is a general factor of maturity of moral judgment much like the general factor of intelligence in cognitive tasks. If they know one aspect of the good at a certain level, they know other aspects of the good at that level. Third, because at each stage there is a single principle of the good, which only approaches a moral principle at higher levels. At all levels, for instance, there is some reason for regard for law and some reason for regard for rights. Only at the highest stage, however, is regard for law a regard for universal moral law and regard for rights a regard for universal human rights. At this point, both regard for law and regard for human rights are grounded on a clear criterion of justice that was present in confused and obscure form at earlier stages. (Kohlberg, 1981, p. 40)

So if there is only one type of principle that governs the moral reasoning of all people regardless of culture and regardless of the level of a person's moral reasoning, this is strong empirical evidence for believing that there is only one type of principle that is genuinely moral. Kohlberg found in Plato's *Republic* a metaphor of ascent to the unitary and homogeneous good that he recrafted to his own purposes.

Kohlberg claimed further that virtue is knowledge of the good and that one who knows the good chooses the good. As I suggested, by "the good" Kohlberg had in mind universal moral principle. By "knowledge" Kohlberg meant very much what the Socrates of the "early" dialogues meant: (principally, among other things) the ability to give a reasoned account that survives attempts at refutation. So Kohlberg's claim that virtue is knowledge of the good entails that virtue is the ability to give a justification for one's action or judgment that is phrased in terms of universal moral principle. One who can give a morally principled justification of an action will (very likely at least) perform that action.

> I have claimed that knowledge of the moral good is one. I now will try to show that virtue in action is knowledge of the good, as Plato claimed. I have already said that knowledge of the good in terms of what Plato calls opinion or conventional belief is not virtue. An individual may believe that cheating is very bad but that does not predict that he or she will resist cheating in real life. Espousal of unprejudiced attitudes toward blacks does not predict action to assure civil rights in an atmosphere where others have some prejudice; however, true knowledge, knowledge of principles of justice, does predict virtuous action. (Kohlberg, 1981, p. 44)

It is unclear from this passage whether Kohlberg held the strong (apparently Socratic) view that a Stage 6 knowledge of the principles of justice determines action or whether he held the moderate view that possessing such knowledge is very likely to lead one to act in accord with the dictates of principle. He said that "He who knows the good chooses the good," and yet he also said that "rational moral judgment is necessary but not sufficient for moral conduct" (Kohlberg, 1984, p. 514). As I explained earlier, Kohlberg analyzed moral action into a three-step process, distinguishing the explanation for "deontic choice" from the explanation for moral conduct and claiming that mature moral reasoners act *more consistently* in accord with their judgments than do reasoners at lower stages. I think it is reasonable to assume that when Kohlberg claimed "He who knows the good chooses the good," he was parroting what he took to be a Platonic view rather than actually subscribing to a Platonic or Socratic view of practical reasoning.

Socratic Questioning, Not Indoctrination

Finally, Kohlberg claimed that teaching virtue is not a process of instruction but one of drawing out or educing a student's unrefined awareness of universal moral principle. The student possesses this awareness, however dimly, antecedent to moral education. Kohlberg is playing on the notion of *anamnesis* or recollection articulated in Plato's *Meno* and other "middle period" dialogues, including the *Sym-*

posium but not the *Republic*. On this notion of recollection, the soul already contains all truths. It merely needs to recall them and understand their rational connections. Drawing the student stage by stage toward a Stage 6 justice reasoning perspective is the aim of Kohlbergian Socratic dialectic.

> Having, I hope, shown the validity of the Socratic view of virtue, I will take the little time left to consider the sense in which it may be taught. The Socratic view implies that, in a sense, knowledge of the good is always within but needs to be drawn out like geometric knowledge in Meno's slave. . . . [Kohlberg has a note here: "By simply asking questions, Socrates led Meno's slave to understand the relationship between the area of a square and the area of the square of its diagonal."—DR]
>
> Returning to the teaching of virtue as a drawing out, the child's preference for the next level of thought shows that it is greeted as already familiar, that it is felt to be a more adequate expression of that already within, of that latent in the child's own thought. If the child were responding to fine words and external prestige, he would not pick the next stage continuous with his own, but something else.
>
> Let me now suggest an example used . . . to indicate another sense in which moral teaching must be a drawing out of that already within. . . . The problem is to draw the child's perceptions of justice from the shadows of the cave step by step toward the light of justice as an ideal form. This last example indicates another Platonic truth, which is that children who turn from the dark images of the cave toward the light are at first still convinced that the dark images best represent the truth. Like Meno's slave, children are initially quite confident of their moral knowledge, of the rationality and efficacy of their moral principles. The notion that children feel ignorant and are eager to absorb the wisdom of adult authority in the moral domain is one that teacher or parent will know is nonsense. (Kohlberg, 1981, pp. 46–47)

Kohlberg used the *Republic*'s imagery of ascent from the cave to represent the process of stage development toward Stage 6. He also employed the image of the divided line (cited below), again invoking the Platonic conception of the relation between the good as the genuinely real and the objects of sense perception as the merely imaginary. As

I have explained, Kohlberg held that the conventional and preconventional stages are inadequate versions of the postconventional Stage 6. They are stages of moral reasoning only in virtue of being inadequately differentiated and integrated, and inadequately reversible, versions of Stage 6.

Kohlberg recommends Socratic dialectic as the best method for drawing the student through stage advancement. He recommends the standard Socratic combination of *elenchus* (refutation) and *psuchagōgē* (psyche/soul-leading).

> The first step in teaching virtue, then, is the Socratic step of creating dissatisfaction in students about their knowledge of the good. This we do experimentally by exposing the students to moral conflict situations for which their principles have no ready solution. Second, we expose them to disagreement and argument about these situations with their peers. Our Platonic view holds that if we inspire cognitive conflict in students and point the way to the next step up the divided line, they will tend to see things previously invisible. (Kohlberg, 1981, p. 47)

In the same vein, Kohlberg stated that

> The way to stimulate stage growth is to pose real or hypothetical dilemmas to students in such a way as to arouse disagreement and uncertainty as to what is right. The teacher's primary role is to present such dilemmas and to ask Socratic questions that arouse student reasoning and focus student listening on one another's reasons. (1981, p. 27)

In a typically Socratic fashion, the teacher is to induce student dissatisfaction with his or her stage of justice reasoning by posing dilemmas that the student's stage of reasoning is unequipped to settle satisfactorily. Then the dissatisfied student is to be exposed to the reasoning of students one stage above his or her own. This suggests to the student a manner of more adequately reasoning about the dilemma and will, if repeated often enough, enable him or her to adopt a new, more adequate stage of justice reasoning. Kohlberg noted that preliminary research (Blatt, 1969) showed this method to be successful in promoting stage advance significantly more often than stage advance occurs in control groups (Kohlberg, 1981, p. 48; see Blatt and Kohlberg,

1975). (In fact, I will suggest that it was Blatt's (1969) surprising findings that drew Kohlberg to this reexamination of Socratic dialogue in the 1970 paper I am now discussing.)

Finally, and very importantly on the revisionist story I'm telling, Kohlberg eventually explained that this method is not by itself the most efficient way of stimulating moral development. Socratic method is most effective when it is employed in the context of a school ordered on the model of participatory democracy. Such is a just community school. This involves the students in active participation in democratic institutions and instills in them the importance of respect for others and for the impartial adjudication of conflicting claims among persons. In rearing children into a model state embodying mature principles of justice, a just community school follows the prescription of the Socrates of the *Republic* in placing Socratic discussion in the political context that is to be achieved by its very practice. Students in a just community school learn participatory democracy by engaging in it, and Socratic dialectic enables them eventually to recognize its superiority over other moral and political ways of life.

It is hard to resist noting here that nonindoctrinative Socratic dialectic works best in an environment in which the moral superiority of participatory democracy is indoctrinated. But that again would take me ahead of my story and would risk putting the matter too bluntly. I will return to this point.

Objections to the Republic in *The Republic*

Given the extent to which Kohlberg's theory of moral education is Platonic, why did he reject the educational program proposed by the Socrates of the *Republic?* Earlier I quoted a footnote in which Kohlberg reported that he has come to call his view "Socratic" instead of "Platonic" since the view articulated in the *Republic* and *Laws* is an "indoctrinative and hierarchical view of moral education," whereas the view articulated in the "earlier" more "Socratic" dialogues is "a view of moral education as democratic and based on dialogue" (1981, p. 29n.). Kohlberg also stated that he would "spend little time on my disagreements with Plato except to point out that I conceive of justice as equality instead of Plato's hierarchy" (1981, p. 30f.). Indeed, Kohlberg did not explain what he meant by Plato's "hierarchy" or "hierarchical view of moral education," but we can assume that in rejecting this he was rejecting Plato's segregation of the polity into three occupational groups: the rulers, the warriors, and the producers. These three occupational groups perform different vital functions in the polity, are accorded different respect and honor, and are given different types and levels of education.

Kohlberg rejected this hierarchical conception of the well-ordered polity. He also rejected the related conception of political justice as the proper coordination of the functions of the three groups and the consequent well functioning of the polity as a whole. He rejected this conception of justice in favor of a conception of justice as political equality for all individuals and impartiality in the adjudication of conflicts among persons. All are to be accorded the same respect as moral agents qua ends in themselves, and all are to be afforded equal opportunity for educational achievement.

While Kohlberg spent little time on his criticisms of Plato, he did criticize a strategy of moral education that he attributed to the "middle" and "later" works of Plato. I quote at length Kohlberg's introduction to his criticism of what he calls the "cultural transmission" or "indoctrination" strategy of moral education. Kohlberg was responding to the tradition of virtue education that William Bennett and the Character Education Partnership currently seek to revive.

> A first strategy for dealing with values in education has usually been called "character education." A traditional answer to the question "What is virtue?" is to enumerate a list or "bag" of virtues. . . . The problem with the "bag of virtues" approach is that it equates the teaching of virtue with indoctrination of conventional or social consensus morality. This is a theory of virtue that commends itself to the "common sense" of those whose view of morality is conventional. In more elaborated form, a theory of the virtues usually rests on social relativism, the doctrine that, given the relativity of values, the only objective framework for studying values is relative to the majority values of the group or society in question, an assumption I criticize.
>
> In a sense, the view of moral education as *character education for a set of virtues* never gets a complete fair hearing in this volume. To do so would mean a full statement of a psychological and philosophic tradition that runs from Aristotle to such modern philoso-

pher-psychologists as Richard S. Peters. . . . It is a fair statement of the history of psychological research in the field to say that the study of character as a set of virtues has not been a flourishing or successful research paradigm.

My philosophical critique of the "bag of virtues" approach is mainly a critique of "cultural transmission" or indoctrination strategies of education. In these chapters, I do not present or critique the view of writers such as Peters, who would say that moral education is a two-phase process. According to that view, parents and educators of young children must necessarily first rely on cultural transmission, inculcating a set of virtues before (or at the same time as) stimulating reflective moral development under conditions of free moral discussion. This mixture of indoctrination and reason is the solution of Plato's *Republic*, although it is not part of the original Socratic viewpoint elaborated in Chapter 2. Plato recognized, however, that indoctrinative moral education presupposed a just society, which he conceived to be a utopian community guided by philosopher-kings. (1981, pp. 1–2)

Kohlberg shared this recognition, as I will note later. Although, as he said, he did not give it a complete treatment in print, he rejected "the view of moral education as *character education for a set of virtues*." He criticized this "bag of virtues" approach to moral education by criticizing the "cultural transmission" or "indoctrination" strategies of moral education. He attributed to Plato's *Republic* a strategy that combines the cultural transmission of values through the inculcation of a set of virtues with the Socratic strategy of "stimulating reflective moral development under conditions of free moral discourse." Kohlberg characterized this as a mixture of indoctrination and reason. It is this mixture of indoctrination with Socratic dialectic that motivated his rejection of the educational program presented in the *Republic*.

Although Kohlberg proclaimed in a footnote that he had come to call his view "Socratic" instead of "Platonic," since the term "Platonic" connotes an indoctrinative element present in the program presented in the *Republic* and *Laws*, he did not emend the reprinted essays so as to change what he called his view. He characteristically and most often called his view "Platonic." Hence, it is not entirely clear whether he attributed the "bag of virtues" approach to the *Republic*. The reason for believing that he did is the fact that he attributed what he called the indoctrination strategy to the *Republic*, and he linked the indoctrination strategy with the "bag of virtues" approach to moral education. However, as I noted earlier, he seemed to have held that Plato believed there is only one (primary or fundamental) virtue, justice, not many (primary or fundamental) virtues, and he seemed to link this with the theory of the form of the good, characteristic of the *Republic*.

So it is not completely clear whether he attributed the following conception of virtue, which he took to be Aristotelian, to Plato's *Republic*.

> In speaking of a Platonic view, I am not discarding my basic Deweyism, but I am challenging a brand of common sense first enunciated by Aristotle, with which Dewey partly agrees. According to Aristotle's *Ethics*, "Virtue is of two kinds, intellectual and moral. While intellectual virtue owes its birth and growth to teaching, moral virtue comes about as a result of habit. The moral virtues we get by first exercising them; we become just by doing just acts, temperate by doing temperate acts, brave by doing brave acts."
>
> Aristotle then is claiming that there are two spheres, the moral and the intellectual, and that learning by doing is the only real method in the moral sphere. (1981, p. 31)

According to Kohlberg, then, the Aristotelian "bag of virtues" consists of two types of virtue: moral and intellectual (for his conception of this distinction, see Kohlberg, 1981, pp. 77–84). Did he attribute this distinction between moral and intellectual virtues to the *Republic* in ascribing to it an educational strategy involving a mixture of indoctrination and reason? I do not think so, for Kohlberg did *not* conceive Socratic dialectic as a method of training the virtue of intelligence. However, he perhaps interpreted the indoctrinative element of the educational program of the *Republic* as involving the training for both types of virtue.

Kohlberg *did* seem to make a distinction concerning virtue that is to be found, though not explicitly drawn, in Socrates' discussions in the "early" dialogues: the distinction between conventional virtue and genuine virtue. I quoted the following earlier:

The problem with the "bag of virtues" approach is that it equates the teaching of virtue with indoctrination of conventional or social consensus morality. This is a theory of virtue that commends itself to the "common sense" of those whose view of morality is conventional. (1981, p. 1)

In the *Meno* (93bc–96b), Socrates argues to the conclusion that virtue as it is conventionally conceived cannot be instructed. (Socrates invalidly infers from this the conclusion that virtue per se cannot be taught, and this invalid inference is part of the explanation for the dialogue's aporetic or perplexing conclusion. See Reed, 1986.) Kohlberg referred to this argument about conventional virtue in his summary of his criticism of the "bag of virtues."

> Let me recapitulate my argument so far. I have criticized the "bag of virtues" concept of moral education on the grounds, first, that there are no such things and, second, if there were, they couldn't be taught or at least I don't know how or who could teach them. Like Socrates, I have claimed that ordinary people certainly don't know how to do it, and yet there are no expert teachers of virtue as there are for the other arts. (1981, p. 38)

Kohlberg seems to have claimed that there are many qualities that are falsely called virtues and that justice is the only genuine virtue.

> I am going to argue now, like Plato, that virtue is not many, but one, and its name is *justice*. Let me point out first that justice is not a character trait in the usual sense . . . justice is not a concrete rule of action such as lies behind virtues like honesty.
>
> To be honest means "Don't cheat, don't steal, don't lie." But justice is not a rule or a set of rules, it is a moral principle. By a moral principle, I mean a mode of choosing that is universal, a rule of choosing that we want all people to adopt always in all situations. (p. 39)

I leave to the side my criticism that the virtue of honesty is more like Kohlberg's conception of the virtue of justice than Kohlberg thinks. (Why should honesty any more than justice be compliance to a set of fixed rules?) Kohlberg seems to have made the Socratic/Platonic distinction between conventional virtue and genuine virtue. If he makes this distinction and if it is correct to interpret his arguments as presuming that the "bag of virtues" is coextensive with the set of conventional virtues, then to ascribe to the *Republic* a "bag of virtues" approach to moral education is to claim that the Plato of the *Republic* thought it possible and even important to teach conventional, non-genuine virtues. To deny this is to refuse to ascribe the "bag of virtues" approach to the *Republic,* in which case it is at best unclear what it means to claim that the *Republic* prescribes indoctrination.

I think the former is the correct account of Kohlberg's interpretation of the *Republic,* and if so it provides an explanation for why Kohlberg rejected the educational program of the *Republic* but accepted the Socratic pedagogical method as it is represented in the *Meno.* He rejected the teaching of conventional, nongenuine virtues which he considered indoctrination and which he found prescribed in the *Republic.* (Note an interesting irony in Kohlberg's reading of Plato. How might he have explained Plato's shift in perspective from the Socratic postconventional virtue perspective of the "early" dialogues to the Platonic conventional virtue of the *Republic?*)

Kohlberg was of course not primarily concerned with rendering an interpretation of Plato, and he perhaps did not believe that much for his purposes turned on an explicit and accurate interpretation of the *Republic.* But as I have argued at length elsewhere (Reed, 1986), the *Meno* (along with but more straightforwardly than other "early" dialogues) presents Socratic dialectic as successful in only a limited range of applications and as insufficient in important respects. Socrates' questioning achieves its end with Meno's slave but, conspicuously, not with Meno. Meno has habits and traits that Socrates' questioning cannot correct or overcome. In the *Republic* Plato compensated for the deficiency of Socratic dialectic by supplementing it with preparatory training of the dispositions of character and intelligence. Were Meno raised in the ideal republic, he would not have had the bad habits and traits that led to the failure of the discussion in the *Meno.* Plato and Kohlberg, then, might seem to contradict each other on the issue of the sufficiency of Socratic dialectic for stimulating moral development. Kohlberg's explicit rejection of the strategy of the *Republic* is certainly in keeping with the anti-indoctrinative posture of his initial efforts to extend the structural stage model into moral education. Of great interest, however, and central to my argument in this book, is the way in which Kohlberg's work on the just community model imitated, unwittingly at first perhaps, the strategy of the *Republic*. And so it is to that model that I now turn.

From Moral Psychology to Moral Education

During the decade after the completion of his dissertation, Kohlberg had no clear plan for moving into moral education (see Kohlberg, 1978; Higgins, 1991b). He did not begin careful reflection on how his structural stage model should be employed in moral education until the late 1960s and early 1970s. His mind was on other things in those first ten years, elaborating the model constructed in the dissertation and drawing followers to assist him in his project. However, in 1966 he did publish an essay titled "Moral education in the schools: A developmental view" (Kohlberg, 1966a). In this essay Kohlberg disparaged "prevalent American conceptions of character education" and offered his own cognitive-developmental interpretation of the famous Hartshorne and May studies of character traits (1928–32). As was usual in those years, he contrasted his interpretation not only with the Boy Scouts and "bag of virtues" notions of character education but also with the behaviorist and the psychoanalytic interpretations of Hartshorne and May's results. In 1966, the task was not yet one of defending Kohlbergianism. The task was getting people to pay attention to the cognitive-developmental approach in the first place.

In this 1966 essay Kohlberg also set out "a developmental conception of the aims and nature of moral education." His basic point, as I indicated earlier, was this. Teachers inevitably moralize to their students. They can do it well or poorly but cannot avoid doing it. Teachers may have no explicit or thought-out conception of the aims and methods of moral education and may want to avoid transmitting their moral values to their students. So they may stick to enforcing the behavioral necessities of classroom management, e.g., don't talk when others are speaking, don't leave the room without permission, etc., withholding comment on moral values. This, Kohlberg argued, implies that these behavioral necessities are either more important than or are conflated with moral values. That won't do, for good reason.

On the other hand, teachers may see themselves as agents of the imposition of a state-determined set of values. In such a case,

> [the teacher's influence as a moral educator] rests upon the fact that the teacher systematically uses the peer group as an agent of moral indoctrination and moral sanction. The classroom is divided into co-operating groups in competition with one another. If a member of one of the groups is guilty of misconduct, the teacher downgrades or sanctions the whole group, and the group in turn punishes the individual miscreant. This is, of course, an extremely effective form of social control if not of moral development. (Kohlberg, 1966a, p. 19)

This won't do either. Using group pressure as a method to the end of unreflective conformity to external authority may be an efficient way to control students and citizens, at least in the short run, but it does not foster development of autonomous moral reasoning.

Preferable is the situation in which a teacher aims to stimulate "the development of the individual child's moral judgment and character." (Early on, Kohlberg frequently referred to "character development" but later dropped such talk as he developed more fully his criticisms of the "bag of virtues" approach to moral education.) "The attractiveness of defining the goal of moral education as the stimulation of development rather than as teaching fixed virtues is that it means aiding the child to take the next step in a direction toward which he is already tending, rather than imposing an alien pattern upon him" (1966a, p. 19). The role of the peer group on this model is to encourage group participation in role-playing (here he cites Turiel, 1966) and moral discussion. These aid in the development of the child's own moral principles and so of her or his moral autonomy. Moral discussion and role-playing were, somehow, to lead the child in the direction of moral principles that are universal, inclusive, consistent, and objective or impersonal. On this conception of principles, Kohlberg mentioned Kant, Sidgwick, and Hare (without citing specific works). Kohlberg found in his structural stage model reason for looking to moral discussion and role-playing as methods of fostering moral development. However, he had not thought this through to a plan for educational intervention. Blatt, a student of Kohlberg's at Chicago, did.

Blatt (1969; Blatt and Kohlberg, 1975) conducted discussions of hypothetical moral dilemmas with a group of sixth graders in a Jewish Sunday School. Working from Kohlberg's research and also from that of two of Kohlberg's earliest students, Turiel (1966) and Rest (1968), Blatt hypothesized that exposing his subjects to reasoning one stage above their own in weekly discussions of moral dilemmas was the most natural and quickest way to stimulate stage development. He found at the end of the twelve-week intervention that 64 percent of the sixth graders had advanced one stage. In comparison to Kohlberg's longitudinal data, where there were no such interventions, this was phenomenal.

Attempting to replicate his result, he conducted similar discussions in four classrooms in a "Boston area" public school. He used two sixth-grade and two tenth-grade classes, this time employing peer-led as well as teacher-led discussions to contrast with his control group. By the end of the eighteen-week intervention, one-third of those in the teacher-led group had advanced one stage whereas the others showed almost no change. A year later on a follow-up test the subjects in the teacher-led group maintained their lead over the others.

"Blatt's venture," as Kohlberg later wrote, "launched cognitive-developmental moral education" (Kohlberg, 1978, p. 3). It wasn't the last word, of course. Indeed, while Kohlberg was visiting Blatt's project at the Boston area public school, the school principal raised an objection of the type often heard from Kohlberg's critics.

"Why is Blatt doing his science-fiction dilemma discussion when I need help with real behavior problems in the school?" What the principal wanted was a curriculum for behavior modification, not a curriculum in philosophic discussion. . . . I replied to his request for help with behavior problems by saying, "Helping you would mean dealing with real life dilemmas, that is, school dilemmas. And dealing with behavior means not only asking what's fair or just, but encouraging action to make the school more just. That means trying to promote fairness in teacher and administrative behavior as well as student behavior." . . . Luckily, the principal did not call my bluff, since I had no idea how I would do what I proposed. (Kohlberg, 1978, p. 8, quoted in part in Power, Higgins, and Kohlberg, 1989, p. 35; and quoted more fully in Higgins, 1991b)

From Moral Discussion to Collective Moral Education

That summer, the year Blatt completed his dissertation, Kohlberg visited a left-wing Israeli kibbutz to examine its moral education practices and to conduct his own cognitive-developmental research on its effectiveness. The Boston-area principal's concern fresh in his mind, he examined the collective moral education of the kibbutz. Describing the practice in terms strikingly similar to those in which he had characterized the teacher's imposition of a state-determined set of values just five years earlier (quoted earlier from Kohlberg, 1966a, with which contrast Kohlberg, 1971b, pp. 355–57), he concluded that "Youth Aliyah kibbutz youth group practice seems better than anything we can derive from our theory, and it is not revisions of practice, but revisions of the way of thinking about it, which I am suggesting" (Kohlberg, 1971b, p. 370). Perhaps the apparently complete change of heart about collectivist education suggested itself to Kohlberg not only from the kibbutz visit but also from a prison intervention project he and two of his graduate students, Joseph Hickey and Peter Scharf, conducted at the Cheshire Reformatory in 1970, a punitive-custody youth prison (see Kohlberg, Hickey, and Scharf, 1972, and Kohlberg, Kauffman, Scharf, and Hickey, 1975).

At Cheshire, group discussions three times a week of hypothetical moral dilemmas à la Blatt had led to expected stage advance, though weaker than one third on average. However, it became clear in the discussions that the inmates could and did distinguish between what they believed right or just in response to the standard hypothetical dilemmas, often characteristically in Stage 3 terms by the end of the intervention, and what they regarded as reasonable in the prison context, which they expressed in characteristic Stage 2 terms. This "situational regression" (Hickey and Scharf, 1980; Higgins, 1991b) is perhaps what led Kohlberg to begin thinking about what came to be called "moral atmosphere," the focus of at least three dissertations by Kohlberg students in the next nine years (Scharf, 1973, on correctional institutions; Reimer, 1977, on the kibbutz; and Power, 1979, on the Cluster School in Cambridge, discussed below).

So what appears reasonable in the circumstances may depend on "moral atmosphere." If so, what seems just hypothetically, in Stage 3 terms for instance, might seem unreasonable in a particular context.

In that context what is reasonable might be understood in Stage 2 terms. Perhaps the reverse could be the case. The context could suggest what is reasonable in Stage 4 (or 5 or 6) terms even though a reasoner characteristically conceives justice in Stage 3 terms. That is, perhaps the moral atmosphere of a context of reasoning and action could make appear reasonable what is recognizable as just one or more stages *above* one's justice reasoning perspective (rather than *below,* as in "situational regression"). This is the fundamental insight of the just community projects (see Power and Reimer, 1978; Wasserman and Garrod, 1983, p. 17). An atmosphere that renders justice reasonable enhances not only justice reasoning but also just conduct. Kohlberg had no doubt at least partially formulated this insight by the time he reversed himself and wrote on the practice of collective moral education in the kibbutz (Kohlberg, 1971b). It was certainly central to the first two just community projects, which set moral discussion of "real life" dilemmas in the context of participatory democracy.

These projects were a just community residential cottage at the Niantic State Farm, a minimum-security women's correctional facility in Connecticut, and the just community alternative school called the Cluster School at Cambridge Rindge and Latin High School in Cambridge, Massachusetts. The just community projects mark a second major transition in Kohlberg's formulation of a practice of moral education. In 1969, the "Blatt effect" (Kohlberg, 1978) had inspired Kohlberg to initiate moral discussion interventions, and the principal's challenge and kibbutz visit inspired Kohlberg to reassess Durkheimian collectivist social theory of education. Then in 1970 at Cheshire and 1971 at Niantic hypothetical moral dilemma discussions opened into discussion of "real life" injustices in the prison itself, its rules, regulations, and social relations (Power, Higgins, and Kohlberg, 1989, p. 24). These discussions were to constitute a central element in Kohlberg's development of the practice of democratic community in the first just community school at Cluster, beginning in 1974. At Cluster, Kohlberg worked to integrate moral discussions into participatory democracy more fully than was possible at Niantic.

Power (1988a) relates an interesting anecdote that is relevant in our understanding of how Kohlberg himself saw this second transition. After Power began graduate study at Harvard in 1975, Kohlberg asked him to design a coding manual for evaluating the Cluster

School's community meetings. Power thought all the features of the needed assessment seemed straightforward, given Kohlberg's cognitive-developmental theory, except the "sense of community" variable.

> When I asked Kohlberg how I should assess the community variable, he advised that I consult Peter Scharf's (1973) dissertation on the moral atmosphere of correctional institutions and "the moral atmosphere folder," which consisted largely of Kohlberg's own unpublished notes. Scharf's dissertation was easy to find, but tracking down "the moral atmosphere folder" required a major investigative effort because it had changed hands among a half dozen doctoral students in 2 years. Each one told me that with possession of the folder came Kohlberg's expectation that the caretaker would write a dissertation on moral atmosphere. Although that initially seemed attractive, when they read the folder they discovered that moral atmosphere was an umbrella term for a number of intriguing but vague ideas for integrating a Durkheimian collectivist approach to moral education with cognitive developmental principles. Unwilling to pin their futures on a project with such a shaky foundation, they passed the folder on. (Power, 1988a, pp. 172–73)

Power found the folder and wrote the dissertation on moral atmosphere (Power, 1979). He is also the chief spokesperson among Kohlbergians for a Durkheimian understanding of the just community projects. He has written about "The Sociological Turn in Kohlbergian Research" (Power, 1988a) and has emphasized that "Although [the just community approach] retains many concepts from cognitive developmental psychology and Kantian moral philosophy, it relies quite heavily upon Durkheimian sociology and Roycean philosophy" (Power, 1988b). Power makes quite explicit that the just community projects embody "communitarian" assumptions about the moral life (Power, 1988b; Power, Higgins, and Kohlberg, 1989).

Kohlberg saw that adequately incorporating what rendered kibbutz collectivist moral education so successful into his cognitive-developmental paradigm required reassessing Durkheim and G. H. Mead. His graduate students, and presumably he too, saw that this might make for a "shaky foundation." In keeping with the essentially collectivist, research-team style of the Kohlbergian research program, Kohlberg often relied on his graduate students to advance the Kohlbergian project in their dissertations. Power certainly did not disappoint. Power and Higgins edited two of the three projected volumes of his collected papers finally published by Harper and Row in 1981 (edited by Power and Higgins) and 1984 (edited by Higgins) and brought to publication after his death what seems in some respects to have been intended initially to be the third volume (Power, Higgins, and Kohlberg, 1989).

Development of the Just Community Model

The decade from Kohlberg's kibbutz visit in 1969 to the closing of the just community project at the Cluster School in 1979 was a time of intense experimentation. The theory developed behind the practice in these years (Kohlberg, 1985, p. 27). In beginning the first two just community projects (in 1971 and 1974), Kohlberg was doing what he had earlier said he would do:

> We could conclude that total immersion through adolescence in the kibbutz is a much more powerful moral education environment than Blatt's limited discussion procedures . . . it makes sense that this should be the case. Our own plans for a program of moral education which is broader than simple discussion involves running our own "kibbutz" in the United States for purposes of moral education, a kibbutz which will combine the principles of moral discussion we have listed with some of the psychological principles of collective education. (Kohlberg, 1971b, p. 369)

Kohlberg eventually stressed that "the [just community] approach assumes a much different relationship between theory and practice than did our first efforts in moral education, i.e., classroom hypothetical dilemma discussion" (Kohlberg, 1985, p. 27). Higgins and Power (Higgins, 1991b, and Power, Higgins, and Kohlberg, 1989; see also Kohlberg, 1985, and Kohlberg and Higgins, 1987) have described the evolution of the just community model, and they have given a full account of its rationale along with accounts of three of the first just community schools, the Cluster School already mentioned, the Scarsdale Alternative School in Scarsdale, New York, and the School-Within-a-School in Brookline, Massachusetts (Power, Higgins, and Kohlberg, 1989). There is no need to repeat their accounts here, but

I can help show how far Kohlberg did in fact go in creating "our own 'kibbutz' in the United States for the purposes of moral education" by offering a brief discussion of the eventual structure and operation of the first just community school, the Cluster School (1974–79).

Elsa Wasserman (Wasserman and Garrod, 1983, an expanded version of Wasserman, 1976), a counselor at Cluster from its beginning in 1974, described the structure of the just community school as including five components: community meetings, small-group sessions, advisor groups, the discipline committee, and the staff-student-consultant meetings (Wasserman and Garrod, 1983, p. 22).

> Concern for responsible moral action (as opposed to the former concern for advancement in moral reasoning stage) stimulated Kohlberg and his associates in the second phase of their educational research, the "Just Community Approach" to moral education. The hypothesis was that by building collective norms and ideas of community at a stage higher than that of many of the members of the group, more responsible student action would be promoted. Participatory democracy was the vehicle selected because, first, it was hoped that putting sociomoral decisions equally in the hands of both students and staff, as members of the school community, would give them a greater sense of responsibility for governance of the school, and, secondly, it was anticipated that participatory democracy would create a sense of the school as a caring community. Kohlberg's thinking in this area (Kohlberg, Wasserman, and Richardson, 1975) was influenced by Dewey, Mead and Piaget, as well as by the group theories of Durkheim (1961), [and] Israeli Collective Education (Kohlberg, 1971c; Lewin, 1936). (Wasserman and Garrod, 1983, p. 17)

The small groups were no larger than fifteen students, and the enrollment in the school, including grades 9–12, ranged in size from fifty to seventy-five. So up to eighty-five or ninety might have been present at some community meetings. They tried to maintain a student-staff ratio of 10:1. These numbers were optimal, they found, for keeping Cluster's participatory democracy functional. In outline, it was as follows:

> Central issues and the agenda for each weekly community meeting were carefully thought through in advance by staff and some stu-

dents in a weekly meeting with Kohlberg and some associates. Issues coming before the community meeting were usually discussed in small groups the day before the meeting. At the community meeting, a representative from each small group presented the group's position on a particular issue and a general discussion followed that typically involved a comparison of various proposals. At this time, members of the small group were called upon to defend their positions. (p. 23)

From the beginning the rule was one person, one vote. Teaching staff, students, and a small number of "consultants" (Kohlberg, Higgins, Power, and other select colleagues) all stood on equal ground in the weekly community meetings. Participants settled all major rules and policy decisions in the community meetings. The participants were unequal in their advocacy skills, of course, but this inequality did not alter the fact that each individual had to reach her or his own decisions in discussion and voting.

Two types of discussion preceded the community meetings, one among consultants, teachers, and interested students one evening each week, and the other among the small student groups the day before the community meeting. At the former, participants discussed among other things the progress of the developing just community, the previous week's community meeting, and the agenda for the coming week. Teachers prepared in these meetings to lead their small groups in discussion of the issue to be raised in the upcoming community meeting. Two such issues the Cluster community addressed were how to deal with an internal theft and whether to use openings for admission to move in the direction of racial balance in the community, passing over white students on the waiting list to do so.

It was here also where the teachers, all regular Cambridge High School teachers who volunteered for duty in the alternative school, learned the theory behind the just community model. Initially, all the volunteer teachers maintained half-time duties in the larger high school, though eventually four became full-time at Cluster. But they were not only putting this model into practice. They participated themselves both in formulating the model and in extending and articulating the theory. The democracy was participatory, and so was the theory- and model-construction. Students gained a sense of ownership in the community, and teachers and research colleagues gained a sense of ownership in the research program.

The students were enrolled in an English/social studies core in Cluster as well as electives in both Cluster and the traditional high school. In the small-group meetings the students held their own mini-community meetings. They were to develop a group position on the issue to be discussed at the upcoming community meeting and were to be prepared to defend their position in that larger meeting. This meant that even those who would not be likely to speak up in a gathering of seventy or more people would be expected to voice and defend their own positions and that as a result many more would develop a sense of ownership in the decisions of the group. All would be heard, and all would be responsible for the final decision. It also meant, of course, that everyone had been involved in a focused discussion of the sometimes very complex community issue before they would gather perhaps ninety-strong to resolve it.

Much work went into making Cluster governance democratic. This was no evasion of responsibility by teachers and administrators. Students were not simply asked to make important decisions. They were guided in a carefully worked out process of participatory democratic (school) life. And yet this was no mere scheme to gain student compliance either. One person, one vote, come what may—within the bounds of law and some of the requirements of the traditional high school. The point was not to make schooling easier. It was to make rational, public, moral discourse in a participatory democracy possible—during and after school in "real life."

Wasserman and Garrod (1983) explain what they think distinguished the just community model as embodied at Cluster from other democratic alternative schools at the time.

Kohlberg's research and experience with participatory democracy in correctional institutions and kibbutzim suggested reasons why the "Just Community" School might succeed where others failed. First, participatory democracy had sometimes failed because it was not perceived as a central educational goal, but as one of several important and sometimes conflicting school goals. Democracy as moral education provided that central commitment. Second, democracy in alternative schools often failed because it bored students. Students preferred to let teachers make decisions about staff, courses, and schedules rather than attending lengthy, complicated meetings. Kohlberg's research, however, suggested that school democracy should focus on issues of morality and fairness. Issues concerning drug use, theft, disruptive behavior, class cutting and grading were rarely boring, if handled as issues of fairness. Third, democracy sometimes failed because of the extreme difficulty of making policy in a large student and staff meeting. Experience suggested the community needed to be small enough to allow all members direct access to participation in community meetings. (Wasserman and Garrod, 1983, p. 21)

This direct access was provided in the community meetings and was facilitated more fully by the preceding small-group sessions.

The advisor groups provided opportunities for students to raise issues of a more personal nature, for instance, how one was being treated at home. Teachers had student advisees and assumed some individual advising and counseling duties under supervision by a school counselor on the staff. In addition, students themselves received training in peer counseling. These groups expanded the mutual support offered by the students to each other in the school, giving them occasions to take and give personal advice and help, and they deepened the sense of community among the students. In the process individual students came more to identify with the welfare of others in the community, with their academic and also their personal well-being.

The discipline committee provided an avenue for appeal of rules and sanctions when these seemed to anyone unfair in individual cases. The committee consisted of one student from each advisor group, chosen by lot on a rotating basis, and one staff member. This was essentially the way jurors were chosen from the districts or "demes" (the "demo" in democracy) of ancient Athens. Jury duty was a duty of citizenship. At Cluster, however, any decision of the discipline committee could be appealed to the community as a whole, and so the community as a whole was ultimately directly accountable not only for rules and policies but also for individual cases.

Commenting on the individual and group development that were the collective result of the practice of democratic community at Cluster, Wasserman and Garrod summarized the results of the just community intervention.

> The consideration of moral issues in the community meetings showed a gradual shift from the preconventional to conventional thinking during the first two years of the Cluster School. Concurrent with this was the growth of a community consciousness in the individual thinking of students and staff, a state which was also evidenced by statements in the public meetings. The evolving community meeting process reflected a development of moral concerns and a higher expression of these concerns through the introduction of student-centered issues that produced significant cognitive conflict. In addition, the community meeting process demonstrated the development of a sense of the school as a moral community. There was increased reference by students to the point of view of the school as a whole and greater effort to speak for and represent that community point of view. In sum, these changes can be seen as the progress of the school toward providing the conditions for moral growth. (Wasserman and Garrod, 1983, p. 27f.)

Kohlberg and his colleagues had come to identify the conditions for moral growth in terms much more like those of the *Republic* than like those Kohlberg had taken to be presupposed in Plato's "early" dialogues. They located moral development in a community and in the cooperative pursuit of common goods. In this respect, Socratic discussion alone was insufficient. Students and other participants had to acquire democratic habits of thinking and acting. They had to be habituated for participatory democracy.

EIGHT

Just Community:
Collectivism vs. Individualism

Local and Postconventional

The abstract "Kohlbergian" theory of justice—which I have argued is inconsistent with the construal of morality that informs the just community model—was at Cluster realized, in part, in a particular setting. The universal was made concrete in this setting in some ways that are replicable and in others that are simply unique to Cluster itself. Before this point, in his response to his 1969 kibbutz visit, Kohlberg had articulated an understanding of the relation of abstract, universal principles to concrete contexts.

> Universal ethical principles with rational grounding . . . may, however, have a distinctive and rich coloring in terms of one's local community and tradition. Developmental moral education does not deny the relevance of community and tradition but sees such community as a particular way of embodying principles for the young. (Kohlberg, 1971b, p. 366)

The basic ideologies of Israel represent universal human principles, principles of justice, but embody them in very concrete ways of life. When we talk about an ideology, we are usually speaking about something which has an element of moral principle; it is not just the conventional morality of an ideological group. The individual's own commitment to moral principles is mediated by his joining the group or sharing this ideology of the group. But the adolescent must make or remake ideologies for himself to really arrive at moral principles. Or to put it differently, to reach full maturity he must differentiate the kibbutz ideology or way of life from the basic universal moral principles on which that way of life rests. In short, any thoughtful approach to moral education which attempts to escape the charge of relativity and arbitrariness will end with goals similar to ours, goals

> of stimulating the development of a principled level of judgment and
> of action in accordance with such judgment. (Kohlberg, 1971b,
> p. 367)

It is worth attending carefully to the language of Kohlberg's account
here.

I am interested in discerning what Kohlberg thought was the status
or standing of universal principles. What do Kohlberg's expressions
imply? Local communities and traditions *embody* universal ethical
principles in distinctive and richly colored ways. An ideology of universal human principles can be *embodied* in a very concrete way of
life. I want to ask, can they be, or be embodied, or exist at all in any
other way? An individual's commitment to universal moral principles
can be *mediated* by his or her joining the group or sharing the group
ideology. I ask, can commitment to them be mediated in any *other*
way?

Moral maturity requires an ability to *differentiate* an ideology or way
of life from the basic moral principles on which it rests. I want to ask,
in order to differentiate the principles from the ideology or way of life,
must it be possible not only to articulate the universal moral principles independently of their kibbutz embodiment but also to articulate
them independently of any social embodiment whatsoever? Or are *all*
principles of justice based in and formative of the traditions of particular communities? (Are they all tradition-constitutive and tradition-constituted? See MacIntyre, 1988) Is it sufficient to be able to
identify alternate concrete just ideologies and ways of life, say, by way
of their relevant similarities or family resemblances to a paradigm
("textbook") case?

The question of tradition is the heart of the matter. Are principles
of justice available to us in reflection independently of their actual or
conceivable social embodiments? (I say "conceivable" here to mark a
distinction from a social embodiment that is possible but not from
our present point of view conceivable, an embodiment that would be
possible per se but inconceivable *for us,* given our present conceptual
resources.) If principles are *not* available to us independently of their
embodiments, then in an important respect all justice reasoning is
conventional reasoning. All principles in this case are available in our

reasoning only as the conventions of an actual or conceivable way of life, say, in a concrete just community. Postconventional principles would on this understanding be available (though perhaps not universally apprehended) as the "conventions" of postconventional societies. But if principles *are* available independently of social embodiment, where are they? What is their standing? What is their unembodied form if not as the conventions of some actual or conceivable society? They might be transcendent statutes in some sort of natural law, for example. And how do we get at them? By some act of disembodiment? We can imagine a Kohlbergian response: "Principles are interpretive constructs, not externally subsisting laws of nature or God. If they were such laws, we might be thought to have to locate them somehow. But they are not, and so we don't." However, the problem is not gotten rid of so easily. The question remains: does our rational (re)construction of principles as heuristic devices require either actual, possible, or conceivable embodiment in social life? If it does, in what sense is justice reasoning ever genuinely postconventional?

Kohlberg and all Kantian moral philosophers need a distinction between the conventions of particular societies and ways of life, on the one hand, and the principles that transcend all such concrete contexts, on the other. They need this distinction because there is no defeating relativism without it, given the parameters of their construal of morality. The categorical imperative is supposed to be entirely content neutral, indifferent to local customs and conventions. Some have even held that no knowledge of local custom or convention is required to employ the categorical imperative (see Flanagan and Adler, 1983, esp. p. 582, for a criticism of this view). Kohlberg had to insist that there really are postconventional stages of justice reasoning, even if the data are not what one might expect. If there is no such reasoning, there is no moving beyond arbitrary conventions, he thought, and so there is no universal, rational ground of justice. Postconventional reasoning cannot simply be more mature conventional reasoning.

The argument is something like this. Conventions are always more or less local. Local conventions are not universal. Their content is more or less arbitrary and relative, coming into existence through historical contingencies not replicated in other contexts, say, the threat of active volcanoes, or frequent confrontations with cunning nonhuman predators, or the dominance of mechanized agriculture and industrialized production, or universal access to chemical and genetic medicine. Genuine, objective critique of local convention requires transcendence to the rational ground of the conventions. This rational ground is embedded in the deep *structure* of the local way of life and may itself be more or less adequate morally, occupying some point in the structural stage sequence. So the principles embodied are nonhistorical, noncultural, and noncontextual because they are deep structural. They are not the historical, cultural *content* of the particular way of life in question. They are, instead, transcendent.

The point of the just community schools, on this argument, is to *embody* principles of justice in a moral atmosphere adaptation to which will promote moral development. The individual makes or remakes for her- or himself, in such an environment, the ideology of the society. In cognitively, sociomorally adapting, she or he *differentiates* and rationally reconstructs in her or his own reasoning the principles that the moral practice of the community embodies. One formulates for oneself the logically consistent rules governing the practice of community in which one is learning to adapt through judgment and action (Sullivan, 1986). One does this stage-sequentially, of course, not skipping directly to advanced, postconventional reasoning. Yet only if this leads her or him to universal, postconventional principles does she or he transcend the arbitrariness of the specific context in which she or he learns them. And of course only if the way of life actually embodies postconventional principles does her or his moral environment facilitate rather than frustrate development to full moral maturity.

In short, according to this line of thinking, a just community in Kohlberg's sense is a nonrelativist democracy or, alternatively, the social embodiment of maximally nonrepressive principles of justice. A moral agent's rational reconstruction of the principles of justice embodied in this type of society leads to postconventional justice reasoning. Two things should be separated here, nonrelativism and democratic polity. I will discuss them separately so that I may touch once again on the tension in the Kohlbergian project. Pursuing these two will enable me better to pick back up the strand of my story concerning the nonlocal or translocal standing of universal principles.

Indoctrinating Democracy

Democratic polity can be liberal individualist or communitarian (and of course there are other possibilities as well). The difference between these two forms of democracy is crucial. Kohlberg acknowledged explicitly at one point that "the moral educator . . . must be a socializer, teaching value content and behavior, not merely a Socratic facilitator of development . . . the teacher moves into 'indoctrination' . . . " (Kohlberg, 1978, p. 84). He asserted, though, that indoctrination in democracy does not violate the child's rights (1978, p. 85, see Kohlberg, 1980a). So he had not, he believed, moved away from the spirit of his original anti-indoctrination stance. But how can this be?

Suppose, on the rules-based construal of morality, that the aim of *democratic* polity, in contrast to other types, is protection of the rights of individuals and the maximization of their liberty. The development of moral autonomy and self-determination is central. A minimally hegemonic polity in a society of independent individuals could maximize individual choice and responsibility. People would choose their own values, beliefs, and conceptions of the good. The state would impose only a minimum value structure, namely, just what is necessary to preserve the rights and liberty of persons (Kohlberg, 1981, p. 296). Indoctrinating children into such an ideology or strongly advocating it in open, egalitarian discussion would not violate their rights because the ideology is specifically designed to defend and preserve such rights. In fact, their liberty would be both safeguarded and maximized (though of course not their liberty to choose an illiberal upbringing). This form of polity would optimize pursuit of rational self-interest consistent with the liberty of each from the tyranny of others.

However, though this account fits with the structural stage model and the construal of morality that underwrites it, what Kohlberg and others working on the just community projects kept emphasizing does not fit here.

> In addition to individual responsibility, then, *collective responsibility* is stressed. The individual is responsible for the welfare of the group. The group is also responsible to and for the individual, to give support and constructive discipline if necessary, and to recognize when the group has failed that individual. . . . According to the theory, if a group is organized on a basis of fairness, and if reasoning at higher

stages is listened to and supported by staff members and inmates, the group will naturally move in a more moral direction. The whole moral development program may be seen as a process in which the group as a whole moves from one stage to the next. . . . Eventually, the group reaches a Stage 4 level of making fair rules and maintaining them as a whole, setting its welfare above their own and above the welfare of individuals to whom they are close. (Kohlberg, Kauffman, Scharf, and Hickey, 1975, pp. 258–59)

The moral atmosphere research, which commenced in 1975, helped to clarify that the norms that were developed in the just community programs reflected a concern for the common good that went beyond the demands of justice. . . . Collective responsibility entails that members of a group are accountable not only for their own actions but also those of their fellows. Cluster members demonstrated collective responsibility by agreeing to make restitution when money was stolen by an unidentified thief. . . . The whole moral discussion approach focuses on the development of individual moral reasoning, but the just community approach focuses on the development of a collective or shared consciousness of norms and values. (Power, 1988b, p. 199, and 203)

A just community democracy is a maximally participatory community of collective interdependence. It optimizes pursuit of common flourishing by fostering those habits and excellences (virtues) that promote such flourishing. The just community school and reformatory foster group identification through participation in cooperative community. In this group identification, selves are knit together in their very constitution. They begin to reason and act as members of a unified group rather than as independent individuals. And this is the whole point.

So the type of democratic polity into which children could be indoctrinated without violation of their rights (as conceived on the rules-based, rights-centered construal of morality) is quite different from the type of democratic polity into which people are being indoctrinated in Kohlbergian just community projects. Indeed, in just community democracy, independence, individual rights, and personal liberty are displaced or at least decenterd by interdependence, collective responsibilities, and attachment in the common project. We are back to the basic incoherence in the Kohlbergian project—liberal individualism vs. communitarianism—the one that Kohlberg's students found when they got hold of the folder and learned what Kohlberg meant by "moral atmosphere."

Rival Anthropological Myths

Notice that the critique I have just offered may capture what is so plausible in criticisms directed at the separation- and disconnection-based anthropology of the rights theory on which Kohlberg's individualist psychological stage theory rests (esp. Gilligan, 1982). Beginning before his first just community project, created in a residential cottage in a women's prison in Niantic, Connecticut, in 1971, he tried to redescribe what even on his own terms were the successes of kibbutz collective education. He attempted to make sense of them in the idiom of a liberal individualist moral psychology (recall Kohlberg, 1971b, pp. 369–70, quoted earlier). One of my theses in this book is that though he may not initially have understood he was attempting something like alchemy, he eventually may have realized this. To change metaphors, he held in the end a mixture, not a solution. He confronted not a synthesis but a choice between the structural stage model and the just community model.

But abandoning the structural stage model would not have required Kohlberg to abandon his antirelativism. The rational ground for nonrelativism supplied by his liberal individualist psychology could be summarized (abbreviated) as follows: the basic social unit is the free, rationally self-interested individual. Presupposing limited availability of primary goods, the conditions of the possibility of civil society and hence of individual survival and self-interest are universal because species-based. Humans, being what they are, engage in strategic, rationally self-interested competition for what they want. Reflecting on their predicaments, they recognize ("prior-to-society" as it were) the strategic value of mutual constraints on their naturally ruthless desires to accumulate and consume. Human attachments of care presuppose the mutual constraints of just institutions—which make it possible for people to let their guards down and become attached to each other. The deep structural principles of justice embodied in all varieties of such local, tradition-bound just institutions are universal—humans being what they are. Furthermore, the political necessity for just institutions obtains not just locally but now, at *least* as a contingent historical fact, globally. Free, rational self-interest now requires global institutions of justice.

Notice that this sort of account of the rational ground of nonrelativism presupposes a type of philosophical anthropology that rests on a certain archetypal myth. The anthropology is separation- and disconnection-based. The central idea is the free, rationally self-interested individual. The myth is of an original "state of nature" (whether real or hypothetical) in which no human community existed. All individuals were independent of each other. (We might, in the spirit of Locke, admit original community among members of nuclear families, but the slope from this through extended families, tribal societies, and multiclan communities is slippery indeed, and all stops along the way are marked ethnocentrically.) Community or at least civil society had been constituted by an artifice which was practically rational from the point of view of all or sufficiently many such separate, independent individuals. Free, rational self-interest leads us into society with others. The rational ground of community remains individualist, and so what is constituted out of the state of nature is a society of minimal community among independent individuals. The paradigms are offered by Plato's Glaucon in the *Republic* and by Hobbes in the *Leviathan*.

On the other hand, the rational ground of a communitarian nonrelativism might be summarized (abbreviated) as follows: the minimal conditions of common flourishing are species-based, consistent with great cultural diversity. Humans being what they are, a certain level of community is necessary for common flourishing, and so certain sorts of convention are required for maintaining community. Members of our species are prepotentiated for certain types of satisfaction and fulfillment, and these require certain conditions to be realized. Though the chances of realizing our full potential for common welfare depend a great deal on local and historical contingencies, the importance of community and cooperation for our good as humans is species-based and universal.

This account also presupposes an anthropology that rests on an archetypal myth. The anthropology is attachment- and connection-based. The central idea is the community cooperating for its common welfare. The myth is of an original community of humans that disintegrates, resulting in rationally self-interested individualism. Restoration of original human community is to be achieved by reconciliation to common interdependence. The task on this account is not one of constituting civil society out of an original state of nature in which no community existed. It is a task of reconstituting human community from its dissolution, mythically represented in stories such as the stories of Eden, Babel, and diaspora.

Both the communitarian and the liberal individualist anthropologies rest on archetypal myths, and we can add the account of the original position to that of the state of nature, as myths, without offending Rawls's current position on its function in his account of justice as fairness. But of course the account of the origin of the cosmos in some primordial big bang is just as much a myth. Myth inevitably occupies the horizon of our rational understanding—no less for the fact that the horizon often recedes as inquiry advances, reason flat-earthers to the contrary notwithstanding.

Now, one might claim that original liberty is natural and that being embedded in civil society is contrived. Or one might claim that being embedded in human community is natural and the ideal of independent liberty is derivative by disintegration. But the plausibility of each of these claims is socially constructed. We find plausible what we do because of the ways of life in terms of which we understand things. Liberty and embeddedness are principles of ways of life from each of which people interpret the practice of social life in their own idioms. The differences between the two are worth pursuing, but there may be no ultimate rational adjudication between these understandings. Yet even if there is no ultimate rational adjudication between these two very different ideology types, and even if this seems to imply precisely the sort of relativism Kohlberg spent his career combating, still we may be able to construct rational strategies for community-building and for communication between different and even antagonistic communities. This, so my account goes, is what is so important about what Kohlberg was doing in the just community projects.

I have also promised to pick up again a strand in my story concerning the nonlocal or translocal standing of universal principles. I have suggested this is not a problem for the just community model but is one for the structural stage model. If universal principles are always conceived in the idiom of particular actual or conceivable social embodiments, then are not postconventional principles really just the conventions of postconventional societies and so not in reality postconventional qua structurally universal at all? Or perhaps it is a problem for one but not another interpretation of the structural stage model. I want to suggest that the problem can be solved in part by reinterpreting the structural stage model. Let me begin formulating this suggestion by drawing together and reviewing some of the various parts of my revisionist story about the development of the Kohlbergian project.

Brief Review of the History of the Kohlbergian Project

Kohlberg's understanding of his project developed substantially from the initial stage theorizing begun in the 1958 Chicago dissertation. In the early 1960s Kohlberg attempted to elaborate and gain a hearing in the literature for the version of the structural stage model he constructed in his dissertation. In the late 1960s, before or soon after moving to the Harvard Graduate School of Education, Kohlberg discovered what he came to call the "Blatt effect" and also visited an Israeli kibbutz, two episodes that he worked to incorporate into his understanding of how to extend his psychological theory into educational practice. He worked in Connecticut reformatories in the early 1970s and in school just community projects beginning at Cluster in 1974. As I draw together my review of the development of the Kohlbergian project, I will use the following narrative device: I will tell a story of a succession of three problems that occupied Kohlberg's primary attention at different points. His focus on solving in turn these three problems defined the nature of the earlier and later Kohlberg, an earlier and later Kohlberg that I associate with the original, formulation-phase work on the structural stage model and then on the just community model, respectively.

Initially, in his University of Chicago days as an undergraduate in the college, then as a graduate student, and later as an assistant and associate professor in the psychology department at Chicago, Kohlberg addressed the problem that would motivate his project for the next thirty years. The problem requiring a solution was the problem of relativism. Kohlberg may have been convinced relativism and/or parochial conventionalism provided the backdrop to international hesitation in the face of Nazism, a hesitation leading to unspeakable consequences during the first two decades of Kohlberg's life. Kohlberg responded to Nazism, relativism, and parochial conventionalism by constructing an antirelativist research project, a project thoroughly Kantian, more "Kantian" even than Kant (see Flanagan, 1991, p. 181) and perhaps more "Piagetian" even than Piaget (see Lapsley, 1996). Against the current of behaviorism in social science and of emotivism in moral philosophy, both auxiliaries of positivism, and in the same year that Elizabeth Anscombe (1958) called moral philosophers to discontinue moral philosophy until we could arrive at a satisfactory moral psychology on the basis of which to proceed (Anscombe, 1958; Flanagan and Jackson, 1987), Kohlberg offered both a critique and a program in the tradition of Kantian liberalism (Kohlberg, 1958).

But by 1968, exactly two decades after completing his work smuggling refugees and beginning his one-year bachelor's degree by examination at Chicago, and one decade after finishing his dissertation, he had moved to the Harvard Graduate School of Education. At this point, the problem that required solution had become, how does this Kantian moral psychology inform our understanding of educating for moral life? Kohlberg's solution began with Blatt's dissertation work (1969; Blatt and Kohlberg, 1975), work wholly consistent with the liberal individualism of Kohlberg's (1958) dissertation stage theory. Blatt's moral-discussion findings indicated that students could be stimulated through Socratic questioning about hypothetical dilemmas to advance in the stage sequence. But Kohlberg's reckoning with Blatt's work was soon followed by and informed significantly by his encounter with kibbutz collectivism. In the summer of 1969, Kohlberg visited the Youth Aliyah kibbutz in Israel for a study of its educational practices. This encounter inspired a reassessment of Durkheim and G. H. Mead, moralists he had criticized in his dissertation.

By the time he and Blatt published Blatt's findings in 1975, Kohlberg had done an about-face on the collectivism he had criticized so sharply in 1966 (Kohlberg, 1966). He took a completely different view of the collectivism to which he had contrasted his Kantian liberalism. Indeed, he had begun the turnabout four years earlier when he published his report on the kibbutz study (Kohlberg, 1971b). Kohlberg was by 1975 thinking about "moral atmosphere" and was recruiting graduate students to do dissertations on it (Scharf, 1973; Reimer, 1977; Power, 1979). Kohlberg had supervised two prison interventions in 1970 and 1971 (see Power, Higgins, and Kohlberg, 1989). The one in 1971 at the Niantic Women's Reformatory in Connecticut had begun the construction of what came to be called "the just community approach to moral education." He began the Cluster School just community in Cambridge in 1974. By this time, the problem that required solution (the third in the succession of three) had become the problem of building community in ways that were democratic, not authoritarian, to the end of a group sense of collective responsibility and common good. The problem of relativism (the first of the three) was still for Kohlberg *the* problem, but I think he may have been convinced it was at least in outline solved, insofar as this is possible theoretically. However, his Kantian individualist response to relativism (and parochial conventionalism) was in a holding pattern trying to maintain altitude. On the front edge of the development of the Kohlbergian project, Kohlberg gave his energies to a collectivist approach to the Deweyan practice of democratic community. The individualism Gilligan would criticize to such popular response in 1982 (Gilligan, 1977, 1982) had actually receded from the front edge of progress on the Kohlbergian project well before it came to dominate and even define "Kohlbergianism" in the public mind.

Indeed, prior to the publication of Gilligan's famous critique, Kohlberg was already refocusing his attention in ways that took account of some of the most pressing worries Gilligan would articulate. Working on the judgment-action problem led Kohlberg and his colleagues in a direction the "different voice" criticisms failed to acknowledge. By this I don't just mean that Kohlberg had long since begun to include women colleagues on his research team and women subjects in their studies, which he certainly had done. I mean that the sequence of justice-reasoning stages Gilligan has all along taken to be more or less typical of men's development had itself come into tension with the work in the just community projects. But this is overlooked not only by Gilligan (esp. 1977, 1982) and her colleagues (see Gilligan, Ward, and Taylor, 1988) and, for example, by Flanagan (esp. 1982a, 1982b, 1984, 1991, Flanagan and Jackson, 1987). It is also overlooked by many who think about moral development in Kohlbergian ways. I am not sure it was not overlooked by Kohlberg himself. He continued throughout to attempt to measure progress in the terms of the structural stage model as well as by other measures.

This abbreviated history of the development of the Kohlbergian project suggests two things. First, some of the best-known critics of the project, including Shweder (1982a, 1982b; Shweder and Bourne, 1982; Shweder, Mahapatra, and Miller, 1987; Shweder and Miller, 1985; Shweder and Much, 1987) along with Gilligan and Flanagan, have missed one of its most important features by attending only to the structural stage model and not to the just community model. Their criticisms of the early formulation(s) of the structural stage model have been decisive in important ways. And indeed, their omission is certainly understandable on my account, since Kohlberg never articulated the just community model as fully as he had the structural stage model—and since, at any rate, Kohlberg (1985) continued to suggest that the just community model extended and depended upon the structural stage model. Still, Kohlberg and his colleagues have been publishing results from the just community work since the mid-1970s (e.g., Kohlberg, Kauffman, Scharf, and Hickey, 1975; Kohlberg, Wasserman, and Richardson, 1975; and see Kohlberg, 1978, 1980a, and 1980b), in which they have described the aims of their work in terms of collective identity and responsibility. But furthermore, and second, even some of the defenders of the Kohlbergian project (and perhaps Kohlberg himself) seem on the whole not to have come to a full appreciation of the significance of Kohlberg's understanding of the just community model. That is, some continue to hold to the idiom of the liberal individualism of the structural stage model and—if they pay attention to the just community work at all—attempt to articulate in that idiom the collectivism of the just community model.

This occurs in one way as Power and Higgins (Power, Higgins, and Kohlberg, 1989) contend that the group norms or collective norms cultivated in the just community schools are supererogatory and not fundamentally in tension with the individual norms of postconventional reasoning. This is striking, since Power has been the one among Kohlberg's colleagues most insistent about our attending to Kohlberg's reassessment of Durkheimian collectivism and since he and Higgins have called our attention to the communitarian nature of the just community projects (Power, 1988a, 1988b; Power, Higgins, and Kohlberg, 1989). Furthermore, no one has been or continues to be closer to the work in the just community projects than Higgins. And so since I might most expect Power and Higgins to share my view about the departure of the collectivism of the just community model from the individualism of the structural stage model, I should give their case special attention. They address the relation between the two models by articulating the collectivism in the idiom of this individualism. On their account, the collectivism supplements the individualism and presupposes it. In this, they are consistent with the rules- and principles-based, rights-centered construal of morality that informs the structural stage model. I will propose resolving what I take to be the problem about the relation between the individualism and collectivism of the two models in just the reverse fashion, by articulating the individualism in the idiom of the collectivism. In this I will follow the relationship-based, goods-centered construal of morality that I have suggested informs the just community model. But first I will restate why I think there is even an apparent incoherence and why the resolution offered by Power and Higgins will not do.

Just Community Collectivism as Supererogatory Liberal Individualism

Since I have been over this before, I will abbreviate my account of the contrast I claim between the individualism of the structural stage model and the collectivism of the just community model. Stage 6 postconventional justice reasoning focuses on universal human rights and respect for the dignity of all persons. To claim a right to something is to take a posture toward the person to whom or against whom the claim is made that presupposes that the relationship between the two has broken down. What do I mean? At the very least, claiming a right to something against someone else's conflicting claim presupposes that matters have reached such a point that an appeal to an external authority like the law (positive, natural, moral, divine) is the most congenial way in which the conversation can proceed. We're not going to be able to come to terms without such an appeal, and of course maybe not even then. Appealing to rights against the claims of others forestalls our coming to blows and it also keeps us talking, at least for the moment.

So the conception of morality in which rights claims are not just possible but central is a conception that regards morality as essentially a matter of conflict resolution, conflict resolution between people who are not in close community with each other. This notion of conflict resolution is ubiquitous in discussions of Kohlbergian moral dilemmas. Rights-centered arguments regard us as separate and disconnected beings needing to appeal to external authority in making claims against each other. Such a notion of morality seems almost designed for just the sort of circumstances in which Kohlberg found himself when as a twenty-year-old he read Kant perhaps for the first time during the year he spent in the college of the University of Chicago after returning from his work on the *Paducah* (see Kohlberg, 1991, p. 13). In such circumstances, when community appears simply to have disintegrated, and in urban settings characterized by anonymity and impersonality, a conflict-resolution model of morality, consisting of universalizable, reversible, and prescriptive general ethical principles (Kohlberg, 1984, p. 636), has strong claim to being the most adaptively adequate.

But if this model of morality makes sense in settings in which close community does not obtain, it may be out of place in settings in which community is being nurtured and sustained and also in settings in which community is being constructed as if from scratch. This constructing, nurturing, and sustaining of community out of conditions of anonymity and impersonality was the task of the just community projects. Kohlberg and his colleagues worked to foster not autonomous independence but rather interdependence, not competition in conditions of conflict but rather cooperation in conditions of building consensus. They strove for a "sense of community" or collective identity, for collective or group norms, and for collective responsibility, upholding trust and unity in the group (see esp. Power, Higgins, and

Figure 8.1

Structural Stage Model	Just Community Model
Autonomy/Independence	Interdependence
Liberal Individualism	Collectivism
personal identity	collective identity
autonomous norms	collective norms
individual responsibility	collective responsibility
Conflict/Competition	Consensus/Cooperation
Rival Purposes	Common Good

Kohlberg, 1989). In short, they worked to construct and nurture precisely the conditions in which a rights-centered morality could be seen as a last resort and not the order of the day (see fig. 8.1).

But if this is right, the account Power and Higgins (Power, Higgins, and Kohblerg, 1989) give is puzzling. They worked closely with Kohlberg in the just community project at Cluster (1974–79), administering and scoring MJIs to measure individual development but also developing coding schemes for measuring development of a collective "sense of community." Whereas I have described the rights-centered morality of conflict resolution as a last resort in situations of community breakdown, they describe it as being supplemented by and presupposed by the collective morality of a close community. They assert that

> communal justifications presuppose but go beyond justifications involving concerns for individual rights and welfare. This means that the members of a community commit themselves to supererogatory acts, such as care and collective responsibility, which do not violate but go beyond the minimal dictates of a morality, based either on utility or fairness. (1989, p. 129)

Now, this is certainly consistent with Kohlberg's published responses to Gilligan's critique. The justice perspective is presupposed by the care perspective, as the structural stage model of morality is presupposed by the just community model of collective responsibility. In both cases, the latter supplements the former and presupposes it. It is already built in, somehow.

The story, then, is this. Liberal individualism is a presupposed minimum, and communitarian collectivism is supererogatory. There are two problems with this. I will mention them only briefly. The first is that Power and Higgins themselves talk sometimes about conventional norms being "moralized" to communal norms, sometimes about "typically moral norms" being "further developed" to communal norms. This suggests a transformation of norms of substantive justice and order into norms of community rather than a mere supplementation of the former by the latter (Power, Higgins, and Kohlberg, 1989, p. 129). I want to affirm this as an understanding of the move from the conventional morality of Stages 3 and 4 to the postconventional morality of Stages 5 and 6, but that will require me to explain how Stage 6 can be interpreted as communal or collective rather than as individualist. I will address this shortly.

There is a second problem with the supererogation account, the account that suggests that the collectivism of the just community model is an extension of and not an alternative to the individualism of the structural stage model. Acts of supererogation by their very nature go beyond what is morally required, where moral requirements are conceived as minimal standards. For example, we might think of ourselves as morally required to refrain from harming others but not as morally required to benefit them in positive ways. Doing others a benefit would be laudable or praiseworthy, we might think, but not required. If you come upon a motorist having car trouble on a remote stretch of state highway, you are morally obliged to avoid hitting him or her with your car, but you are not obliged to stop and help. Helping would be laudable, but not morally required. It would, in this sense, be supererogatory. Or we might think of ourselves as morally required to benefit others but not to incur great sacrifice in doing so, selling everything we have to give to the poor, and so on. If you have a CB radio or a cellular phone in your car and can call for help for the motorist without stopping, you should, but you are not morally required to make yourself late for a job interview or to cut short a visit with a friend in the process—let alone to risk the possibility that the "motorist" is actually a clever and cunning thief preying on naive motorists who might stop to help. But this means that the rationale for the minimal requirement is insufficient to justify requiring the supererogatory acts. The reasons you should call for help on your CB or cellular phone do not entail that you should miss your interview or cut short your visit by stopping to help. So in being called to acts of supererogation such as those characteristic of just community collectivism, we will need to know not only why to be moral but also why to go even further. What is more, we will need to know how supererogatory collectivism goes further than respecting rights, further *in the same direction*. That is, in what sense is just community collectivism super-moral, whereas Stage 6 reversible role-taking leading to equilibrated justice judgments suggests actions that are minimally moral? (Recall that on Stage 6 terms, total strangers are duty-bound to steal the drug for Heinz's wife.) Alternatively, in what sense is just community collectivism more moral and not simply minimally moral plus different in certain nonmoral ways, morally neither here nor there—where the differentiation of moral from non-moral is conceived on supposedly fully cognitively and morally adequate Stage 6 terms? I think this is a grave problem with the supererogation account, but I shall leave it at this.

My suggestion, then, is that we need to reinterpret just community collectivism. I am arguing that it should be seen as an alternative to, rather than an extension of, the liberal individualism of the structural stage model. I believe that the comment of Power and Reimer (1978, p. 107) that I have quoted hints at this alternative account, and I think that comment is echoed by Kohlberg himself. When shifting in their discussion of "The Current Formulation of the Theory" from the elaboration of the stage definitions to the sociomoral atmosphere research, Kohlberg, Levine, and Hewer state,

> So far we have discussed moral action as if it were something de-
> termined solely by internal psychological factors in the subject. This
> is not the case, for moral action usually takes place in a social or
> group context, and that context usually has a profound influence on
> the moral decision making of individuals. (Kohlberg, 1984, p. 263)

We can discuss the structural stage model "as if [moral action] were something determined solely by internal psychological factors," but the moral atmosphere research in the just community projects suggests something quite different.

The clear aim of Kohlberg's just community prison and school interventions was the development of group norms and group consciousness, a sense of collective responsibility and a priority of collective welfare over individual self-interest. From many and diverse ethnic backgrounds and socioeconomic circumstances, many and di-

verse self-understandings and conceptions of what makes life meaningful and worthwhile, they crafted—at least in the context of the
prison or school—a common identity and a common good. (*E pluribus
unum.*) In settings in which we might expect to find selves as idiosyncratic as anywhere in our culture, Kohlberg and his colleagues
worked at the construction of conditions of commensurability.

The stories of the just community model in the literature frequently
make reference to episodes in which a theft of money became the
subject of debate at a school community meeting (see Wasserman and
Garrod, 1983; Kohlberg, 1985; Kohlberg and Higgins, 1987; and
Power, Higgins, and Kohlberg, 1989, pp. 113–15, for an extended account of one of the instances). The question was whether and how
the victim should be compensated, given the strict rules concerning
theft adopted in a "just community" community meeting. The stories
tell about a point at which one and then several begin to see this as
a problem not of the individual victim alone but of the group as a
whole, as a collective. Eventually the group decides that everyone will
contribute a small amount so that the victim's money can be restored.
Their reasons are clear. This theft was an offense not against the victim alone but against the solidarity of the community. The whole
community had been violated in the violation of the community's
agreement about stealing and in the violation of the trust that agreement might have inspired, and the whole community would take responsibility together to restore the stolen money.

Those who have told this story have emphasized the ways in which
this shows the development of group consciousness and collective responsibility. The students began to reason about this problem not as
separate individuals but as members of a group. They began to conceive their responsibility in the situation not as unaffected individuals
who happen to go to the same school, even participate in the same
"experiment," but as members of a body the whole of which has been
affected by the offense to a part.

Here is my suggestion. Individuals who began in this situation to
articulate their concerns not in the idiom of individual rights but
rather in an idiom of collective responsibility began not so much to
move from reflecting in their own thinking what others would think
(Stages 3 and 4) to thinking for themselves (Stages 5 and 6). They
began rather to think as for the group. We might say that they began

to think and articulate their concerns *as* members of the group. But I want to suggest a description one step even further separated from individualism. They did begin to reason as members of the group, but in a way they began to reason *as the group*. They moved from a heteronomous reasoning in which they conceived themselves as subjects of an external authority, an authority other than themselves, to an autonomous, cooperative reasoning. But their notion was not of ruling themselves as individuals subject to their own authority. It was of ruling themselves as a community would rule itself. The individuals began to reason as a self-ruling community. They began to reason intersubjectively.

Piaget had noticed that children move from heteronomy to autonomy in playing the game of marbles precisely when they realize that the authority of the rules of the game depends on mutual consent and cooperation (Piaget, 1932; see Power, Higgins, and Kohlberg, 1989, p. 28). Indeed, he had called the second type of morality a morality of autonomy and cooperation, not a morality of autonomy and independence. Working with colleagues and Rindge and Latin High School teachers and counselors, Kohlberg coordinated construction of a school community in which students would make just this move. They would come to see the community's rules as valid cooperative schemes to the aim of just community, not as impositions from an external authority. The idea of reversibility, wherein individuals were to imagine a moral dilemma from the point of view of each party involved, was transformed into an ideal of intersubjective, collective justice-reasoning. Each individual was to understand the issues with which the community dealt as if she or he were the coordinated mind of the community as a whole.

Integrating the Earlier and Later Kohlberg

As we might notice, this notion of intersubjectivity is in one way quite at odds with a Stage 6 prior-to-society conception of universal justice. Intersubjective reasoning, reasoning by a community of people who are of one mind, is in an obvious way not prior to society. But there is another angle as well. The aim of Stage 6 reversible role-taking is in one respect and at second glance an intersubjective point of view—the view from everywhere (in contrast to the "view from nowhere"

[Nagel, 1986]). That justice judgment is valid which is fully reversible, which is acceptable from the point of view of every individual involved. A Stage 6 justice reasoner comes to reason in one way as an anyone, as no one in particular. In another way, she or he comes to reason as an everyone, as an intersubjective being constituted in the convergence of the perspectives of all individuals involved.

Applying the criterion of reversibility in the Heinz Dilemma, we have seen, involves determining what judgment would result from the consensus among participants who imaginatively or hypothetically adopted the perspective of each participant in the dilemma situation. Each participant would consider the question whether Heinz should steal the drug from the point of view of every other participant. For this reason, role-playing and role-taking opportunities help one develop the cognitive skills necessary for forming reversible judgments. Kohlberg contended that in the Heinz dilemma, consensus would settle on stealing the drug, because even the druggist would see that were he either Heinz or Heinz's wife he would recognize that the right to (or value of) life outweighs the right to (or value of) property. The druggist's right to realize a profit on, or simply recover his investment in, the cancer drug pales in comparison to Heinz's wife's right to life (and to life-sustaining medical care). And even the druggist will recognize this if only he will consider how the matter must be evident from the perspectives of Heinz and his wife as well as from his own.

An intersubjectivist rendering of Stage 6 would sound very much like this, with an important difference. On such a rendering, the ideal convergence of perspectives would be cooperative, not individual, and actual, not merely virtual. On an individualist rendering of Stage 6, individuals who reason in Stage 6 fashion perform a type of deliberative reflection that would naturally be done alone, even though it might be done cooperatively. Heinz's wife, the druggist, and Heinz would each reach, on their own, reversible judgments and then compare notes if they wished. But on an intersubjectivist rendering, the three—and others in their community as well—would approach reflection on Heinz's dilemma, first and foremost, as a quandary they face as a community and not as one Heinz faces on his own. Heinz and his wife's situation is a problem for the whole community, not just for Heinz and his wife. This is the way the Cluster community approached the theft from the girl's purse when they decided they should all pitch in to recompense her loss (Power, Higgins, and Kohlberg, 1989, pp. 113–15). Although when discussions of the theft began in community meetings, students argued that this was the girl's problem, not everyone's ("she shouldn't have been so stupid to leave her purse unguarded"), they eventually understood the theft as a violation of their community agreement to make Cluster a trusting environment, safe from stealing. This is also the way the Cluster community approached the issue of race-based preferences in admissions. The issue became one of fostering a certain kind of community in the midst of hostile race relations in the larger school, not simply one of those who deserved or had a right to, didn't deserve or have a right to, admission, in abstraction from what they would add to the community.

Second, those involved would approach the Heinz Dilemma as a problem they will not have resolved fully until they are of one mind as to its resolution. The aim is not simply a fully reversible judgment, with Heinz acting on that judgment. The aim is community consensus. This is essentially the way Kohlberg, Boyd, and Levine (1986, 1990) stated the matter in their final revision of the definition of Stage 6 (which I will discuss later). They emphasized "dialogue," "mutually acceptable agreement," "agreement-seeking through dialogue," and "ideal consensus" (Kohlberg, Boyd, and Levine, 1990, pp. 158–63). The "prior-to-society" rendering of Stage 6 was transformed into an ideal for cooperative community. And equally important, moral dilemmas in the just communities became, in the context of consensus-seeking, occasions for work on the life of ongoing community. In this, Kohlberg, Boyd, and Levine were both indebted to and allied with Habermas (1990b; see also Habermas, 1990a and 1993).

This understanding of Stage 6, however, raises three types of problem that suggest the attractiveness of an individualist (or perhaps narrowly individualist) understanding of Stage 6, in the present circumstances in the liberal democracies in the West. First, if we consider the Needy Children Dilemma on the intersubjectivist rendering, Stephen's concern for hungry, diseased, and dying children the world over raises a problem global in scope. All those children need help. But how would *global* consensus-seeking proceed?

By comparison, the Heinz Dilemma appears local, and ideal consensus-seeking poses a hypothetically local problem. Admittedly however, Kohlberg contended that even a stranger should steal the drug to help Heinz's wife. His idea was that, from a Stage 6 perspective, the right to (or value of) life outweighs the right to (or value of) property whether one is directly related to or associated with the person whose life is at stake or not. This, we should note, is not a narrowly individualist understanding of the Heinz Dilemma. It means that if Heinz didn't steal the drug, anyone and everyone else should, including total strangers. Even you and I, given means and opportunity, should steal the drug, or spend our own money, in order to save the life of Heinz's wife, however distant from us she might be. For were we to seek a reversible judgment about whether stealing the drug is the right thing to do, reasoning in Stage 6 fashion, we would on Kohlberg's view realize it is. And if we generalize from Heinz's wife's situation to all relevantly similar cases in which indigent persons need life-sustaining medical care (or nutrition, or environmental protection, etc.)—which is to say, if we apply Kohlberg's understanding of the principle of universalizability—that is, if we consider the Heinz Dilemma as an instance of a problem of large-scale social policy concerning poverty, and not as an isolated case, the Heinz Dilemma itself implies a problem global in scope. Thus, Kohlberg's own reasoning on the Heinz Dilemma implies that anyone and everyone with means and opportunity is morally obliged to steal (or to spend down their savings, or to sell their belongings), in order to save the lives of desperately ill persons in poverty, or desperately undernourished people, or environmentally endangered people. This is a matter of (impartial) justice.

In the Needy Children Dilemma, the global scope of the problem of responding to poverty is explicit. For though Stephen and Beverly are making a decision for their family and not for social policy, the problem of needy children as Stephen poses it is a problem that on the intersubjectivist rendering must be addressed by communities wherever and whenever there are needy children, namely, the world over and all the time. And think of what "agreement-seeking through dialogue" leading to "mutually acceptable agreement" or "ideal consensus" on such global problems entails, even hypothetically. Everyone must engage in such consensus-seeking dialogue about problems global in scope, on the intersubjectivist rendering. We need hardly look any farther for adaptive problems for the intersubjectivist rendering, given the tendency to suggest on the (narrowly) individualist rendering that individual and/or local autonomy are preferable to large-scale solutions to social problems.

There is a second type of problem. If we consider the Disposable Hook-Up Dilemma on an intersubjectivist rendering, we raise issues that from an individualist rendering appear to be serious violations of privacy. Consider whether Julie should file a formal complaint of sexual harassment against Brad and his three fraternity brothers on behalf of Reanna. On an individualist rendering, Julie needs to reach a reversible judgment, and this she would do naturally on her own. She would engage the perspectives of all others involved in the dilemma situation, but she would do this virtually, not actually. On an intersubjectivist rendering, however, the problem of sexual harassment and the problem of how to address sexual harassment are community problems to be addressed by each community as a whole (however we might individuate or identify individual communities). Julie and we cannot proceed with "agreement-seeking through dialogue" leading to "mutually acceptable agreement" or "ideal consensus" unless she and we foreclose the possibility that Reanna be allowed to endure her ordeal in private. There was no way for the Cluster community fully to discuss remedying the theft from the girl's purse without disclosure of the victim's identity, because her standing as a particular member of the Cluster community was an important feature of the case. And there was no way for the Cluster community to address the question of race-based preferences in admissions without possibly raising racial tensions within Cluster that would be expressed occasionally in personal terms. The right to privacy has a different standing on an intersubjectivist rendering of Stage 6 than it does on an individualist rendering, because the criterion of reversibility has been transformed into a call for an actual and not merely virtual cooperative consensus in moral judgment.

A third problem has to do with the discretion families, kinship groups, and interpersonal associations (such as religious organizations) have over the care of their own. It also has to do with how we identify the relevant community for the purpose of seeking "ideal consensus." In the Elderly Parent Dilemma, Tarissa, Willard, and Jerry have to decide whether and how they will cooperate in insuring

Tarissa's well-being in her new circumstances of disability. On an individualist rendering of Stage 6, each must reach a reversible judgment about the right thing to do. Tarissa needs to appreciate the matter from Jerry's point of view as well as from Willard's, and Jerry from Tarissa's, and so on. And since if Tarissa does not receive adequate care now, she will, before long, inevitably or in all likelihood be in a situation analogous to that of Heinz's wife, we should consider the Elderly Parent Dilemma as no less a moral dilemma than is the Heinz Dilemma. And yet, if we follow Kohlberg in thinking that anyone and everyone is just as obliged as Willard and Jerry to help Tarissa *insofar* as this is a question of justice, then we would hold that any special obligation Willard and Jerry have is not a moral obligation. That is, if they are required to go beyond others outside the family in assisting Tarissa, they are not *morally* required to do so. As a corollary, insofar as justice is concerned, Tarissa is not obliged to accept any solution to her predicament that she does not herself autonomously choose. She may not have any special *moral* claim on Willard's and Jerry's assistance, but neither is she *morally* bound to accept their judgments about her care.

On an intersubjectivist rendering of Stage 6, however, these two matters are different. Any one person's decision on what should be done is to be not only fully reversible but also the decision the relevant community would make were it to be of one mind. To the extent that determining Tarissa's care is a community concern requiring "mutually acceptable agreement," and so on, both among the three persons and among a larger community—say, their extended family, including Willard's nieces and nephew and Willard's cousins, or their synagogue, or perhaps their local community or state—two things follow. First, Tarissa does not have full discretion on what assistance she should accept. In fact, to this extent, the three together do not have full discretion. If, for example, contrary to fact, Tarissa, Willard, and Jerry were Jehovah's Witnesses, they would not be free to approve blood transfusions as any part of Tarissa's medical treatment. Second, any special obligations Willard and Jerry (or anyone else for that matter) have in assisting Tarissa are moral obligations. For they are what the relevant community would hold their obligations to be if it were of one mind.

To what extent is Tarissa's care a community concern, on an intersubjectivist rendering? The main problem raised by this question is the problem of defining the relevant community. In an individualist culture, this is not possible without some arbitrariness. For among the natural options (immediate family, extended family, synagogue, neighborhood, local community, municipality, state, etc.), it is not clear that any one is clearly preferable when we do not automatically assume an individualist rendering of Stage 6. There is no obvious answer to this question in cultures in which individualism is the default rendering. And so this is yet another way in which the individualist rendering of Stage 6 seems more attractive in the circumstances, prior to the realization of just community (prior-to-society, as it were).

On the intersubjectivist rendering, then, the "ideal conditions of reversibility" become transformed into the conditions of intersubjective, cooperative consensus. Indeed, the stage sequence as a whole admits an interpretation on which the progression is toward greater and greater intersubjectivity, where the reasoning perspectives are not so much those of individuals as of increasingly intersubjective practical rationality. Sandel (1982) has made a similar observation about the conditions of Rawls's hypothetical original position (see Sandel, 1982, p. 132). It would not be all that surprising, then, though it would be interesting, if the Kantian link between Kohlberg and Rawls were at the heart of this similarity. I think it is.

The famous Kantian categorical imperative also admits an intersubjectivist reading, one Kant himself seems not to have had in mind. The categorical imperative is supposed to be the minimal consistency condition of practical rationality, as the laws of logic are the minimal consistency conditions of intelligible communication. Our speech has to be minimally consistent to be intelligible. We cannot communicate intelligibly with one another, say, about Abby, unless we can assume in our reports about her that Abby cannot be both a resident and a nonresident of New York in the same respect, at the same time, that she has to be one or the other, and that Abby is herself and is not someone else even when she is "not herself." If we could not assume these things about Abby—and if we could not assume speech about her is minimally consistent—we could not interpret what each other says about Abby and would not know what to think about her ourselves. And if it seems bizarre even to mention these assumptions explicitly, this only shows how fundamental they are for us. Kant thought the categorical imperative was equally fundamental—Kohlberg would say, equally structurally basic—as a principle of practical rationality.

To be practically rational, Kant thought, rational in one's actions, one must act on maxims or precepts (statements of the "rule" of one's actions) on which one could will all others to act as well, in similar circumstances. But when reasoning so that the maxim or precept of one's actions could be a universal law of nature or universally accepted as determining action in relevantly similar situations, one aims at more than consistency. For one could be perfectly *consistent* in action while violating the categorical imperative right and left—or at least while violating what Kant meant by it, given the examples he gave to illustrate its application (Kant, 1983 [1785]). There is no inconsistency in my willing exceptions for myself as long as I am both consistent in what types of exception I will and careful to explain how my own case is unique. For instance, I might reason that theft of academic and personal papers from an archive would be permissible whenever these papers bear materially on the biographical research one is conducting on a person concerning whose project of moral development and moral education one has already published a philosophical treatise. There would be no inconsistency in willing this to be a universal law of nature or universally determinative of action. However, if it were a universal practice to steal from archives, whatever the nature of one's research, archivists could not afford to make these papers accessible. In that case I would be in no position to steal some of Kohlberg's papers. An unqualified maxim concerning stealing from archive papers therefore involves practical inconsistency, whereas a more carefully crafted one does not.

But the categorical imperative requires consistency not simply in the judgment and action of an individual. It requires consistency in the judgment and action of all rational people considered together. On this interpretation of the categorical imperative, for instance, I could not write exceptions for myself as Kohlberg's biographer into the maxims or precepts of my actions. For on this interpretation, I formulate maxims not only as and for myself or even for all who find themselves in "relevantly similar" circumstances. I formulate them *as* the community of all rational beings were it to be of one mind about a particular practical situation. My actions, or rather the precepts on which I act, have to be consistent, Kant thought, with the precepts on which all other beings who act from precept act. But what Kant did not say is that a person applying the categorical imperative reasons for or as all rational beings—not simply for or as him- or herself, but for or as every rational being, some of whom might find themselves in "relevantly similar" circumstances. The Kantian categorical imperative is the minimal consistency condition of practical rationality not for an individual—who could consistently will exceptions for him- or herself—but for all moral agents as an intersubjective unity, a community of one mind.

My suggestion is this. Just community efforts toward constructing collective consciousness and collective responsibility aim toward intersubjective, socially constructed justice. And in one way, the aim of Stage 6 reversible role-taking is an intersubjectivity of collective moral imagination. But the actual convergence of perspectives into an intersubjective justice reasoning is the result of radically contingent historical and cultural processes. In a culture and times in which idiosyncratic selves with idiosyncratic final vocabularies (Rorty, 1989) are the norm and in which hearty commensurability of identity and purpose seems all too distant a possibility, something like Kohlberg's just community model appears to be needed, and on a much grander scale than Kohlberg and others have accomplished or attempted in schools and reformatories.

I began by suggesting that the emphasis in the just community model on collective norms, collective identity, and collective responsibility is in tension with the structural stage model emphasis on autonomy—unless Stage 6 reasoning can be understood as collective or intersubjective reasoning. On the account I have given, Stage 6 autonomous reasoning, which I have suggested Kohlberg originally conceived as in the tradition of Kantian liberal individualism, can be reinterpreted as intersubjective reasoning (though not without raising the three problems I described). We can understand the individualism of the structural stage model in the idiom of the collectivism of the just community model. This reinterpretation of Stage 6 shares an advantage with the supererogation account offered by Power and Higgins (Power, Higgins, and Kohlberg, 1989). It removes any apparent inconsistency between the structural stage model and the just community model. However, reunderstanding the individualism in the idiom of the collectivism rather than understanding the collectivism as supererogatory individualism has an additional advantage. It helps us see what some of Kohlberg's best-known critics have missed. For on this alternative reading of Stage 6, its assumption of separateness and disconnection disappears. An intersubjectivist interpretation of Stage 6 presupposes essential connection and a normative ideal (if not accomplishment in every case) of consensus. The work of the just community projects then can be seen as work at the practice of democratic community aimed at overcoming precisely the separation and disconnection that have so worried many of Kohlberg's critics.

I now return to a question I have postponed answering. Did Kohlberg fail to recognize something Plato appreciated? At first, yes; but eventually they agreed in significant and crucial respects. We can read Plato's *Republic* as a deliberately overstated reaction to the faults of the democracy of Athens early in the fourth century B.C.E.—an overstatement designed dialectically to promote the mean by calling for an erring in the direction of the opposite extreme (see Gadamer, 1986, pp. 70–72). In short, people cared too little for wisdom and too much for power, too little for cooperation and too much for personal advancement. Plato expressed his response through the character of Socrates in Socrates' retelling of a conversation with stock characters of fourth-century Athenian democracy, including the brash and articulate sophist Thrasymachus. If ambitious politicians like Glaucon and Adeimantus—Plato's older brothers whom he made characters in the dialogue—were not to become more wisdom-loving (philosophical) and more cooperative in their understanding of polity, Athens would surely end up ruled by tyrants who had gone to school with sophists like Thrasymachus. In the dialogue, Thrasymachus described the relation of ruler to ruled on analogy with the relation of shepherd to sheep, where the object of good shepherding is not the care of the sheep but preparation for the bounty from their slaughter. In the end, Kohlberg articulated an understanding of the practice of democratic community that was both wisdom-loving and cooperative. Constructing and reconstructing for oneself the moral law became, in the Kohlbergian program, a process of becoming more and more oriented toward cooperative consensus—something the character Socrates aimed at but for various reasons failed to achieve in the *Republic*. Both Plato and Kohlberg (by 1975) came to the conclusion that the proper context both for learning and for doing justice was the cooperative community. Yet it was not until struggling with the import of Gilligan's critique of the structural stage model that Kohlberg began to articulate the importance of cooperative community in his formulation of that model as well as in his formulation of the just community model.

NINE

Gilligan's Counterpoint

A Family Disagreement

The so-called "Kohlberg-Gilligan debate" has been much discussed (e.g., in the philosophy literature, see Flanagan, 1982a; Benhabib, 1987; Flanagan and Jackson, 1987; Blum, 1988; Adler, 1989; in the psychology literature, beyond the work of Gilligan and her colleagues discussed in this chapter, see e.g., Walker, 1984; Baumrind, 1986; Walker, 1986 and 1991). In fact, many people now know Kohlberg first through Gilligan's accounts and criticisms of his views. Gilligan's *In a Different Voice* (1982) extended the argument of an earlier *Harvard Educational Review* essay by the same title (Gilligan, 1977) and touched chords in many both inside and outside the academy. It sold and continues to sell like few university press books ever do. That book made her the best-known critic of the Kohlbergian project, ironically, and also one of the most widely read proponents of central Kohlbergian assumptions. The irony is not in the fact that Gilligan holds or held Kohlbergian cognitive-developmentalist assumptions. Rather the irony is in the fact that she would ever have come to be known as Kohlberg's nemesis.

The truth is, Gilligan is neither Kohlberg's harshest nor his most fundamental critic. She continues to accept a good many cognitive-developmentalist assumptions and sees (at least, saw) her work as correcting and supplementing rather than overturning the Kohlbergian project. Indeed, Gilligan is scarcely interested in overturning the fundamentals of Kohlberg's theory. Her project was and continues to be that of moving beyond the limitations of current cognitive-developmental theory in two important respects.

First, she aims to break thoroughly with long-held tradition both within and outside cognitive-developmental psychology by including the voices of girls and women in the construction (not just the corroboration) of theories of human development. Gilligan does this as a thoroughgoing cognitive-developmentalist. Second, she aims to expand the methodological repertoire of human development studies from the standard methods of empirical investigation in psychology (which she practices with her own improvisations) to include especially the insights into human life and development of literature and literary criticism, history and historiography, and anthropology and ethnography (see Gilligan, 1982, p. 1, and her Prologue in Gilligan, Ward, and Taylor, 1988, pp. xiv-xv, and also pp. 289–90 in the Afterword to that volume). Worries about methodological problems with Gilligan's work often spring from her innovations on this front, and critics sometimes fail to recognize that she is not being untidy but rather is openly challenging what she takes to be the narrow and exclusive practices of a long male-dominated social science tradition. She is in this respect as well a thoroughgoing cognitive-developmentalist, extending and advancing the research tradition within which she works. Because work toward the first aim focuses on girls and women and work toward the second is deliberately multi- and interdisciplinary, Gilligan's project is perhaps more accurately understood not as standard academic psychology but rather as a theme within Women's Studies, and this is how Gilligan herself understands it (see her Preface to Gilligan, Lyons, and Hanmer, 1990, esp. p. 6 and p. 24f.).

In her research on girls and women in theory construction (not just corroboration) and in her employment of an interdisciplinary methodological repertoire, Gilligan is with Kohlberg, for all intents and purposes, a cognitive-developmentalist collaborator. While Kohlberg was more intent on connections with moral philosophy and Gilligan on connections with literature and the narrative social science disciplines, they share a commitment to interdisciplinary approaches to the study of human development. And if Kohlberg was slow to accept the philosophical import of Gilligan's recommended corrections, he nonetheless ended up moving through a series of theory modifications and adjustments to a position very similar (for all practical purposes identical) to Gilligan's suggested two-voice model of moral maturity (see Kohlberg, Boyd, and Levine, 1990).

Gilligan earned a B.A. in literature at Swarthmore College and a Ph.D. in Psychology and Social Relations at Harvard and came to the Harvard Graduate School of Education on a research fellowship to work with Kohlberg. She conducted research to determine how people navigate real-life moral dilemmas. This was the very work that led to Gilligan's discovery of "a different voice" (see Gilligan, 1977, and 1982, esp. p. 1). Joining Kohlberg's new research team soon after he came to Harvard in 1968, Gilligan was a colleague, collaborator, and coauthor (see Kohlberg and Gilligan, 1971; Gilligan, Kohlberg, Lerner, and Belenky, 1971; Gilligan and Kohlberg, 1977 [1973]). As a collaborator, she worked with the early versions of the present MJI interview and scoring instrument (Colby and Kohlberg, 1987a and 1987b). And since Gilligan was a member of the research team on whose work Kohlberg's claims to empirical support stood, Kohlberg himself was committed to affirming that she understood the finer points of Kohlbergian theory.

It *should* come as a surprise, then, that she is the best-known critic of the Kohlbergian project. She should have accepted the theory and preferred Stage 6 reasoning, given the no-regression thesis and the thesis that everyone is supposed to embrace the highest stage perspective they understand.

It is crucial, then, that we hear her criticisms as she has made them. I will perhaps err on the side of quoting Gilligan too extensively. I believe this is important in order to hear the extent to which the "Kohlberg-Gilligan debate" is a family disagreement and not, what might be more tantalizing, intercontinental ballistic gender warfare.

Hearing the Contrapuntal Theme of the Same Movement

Gilligan's criticism of the Kohlbergian project is primarily that Kohlberg did not incorporate women's experiences and voices in the construction (in contrast to the corroboration) of his theory. Because Kohlberg followed Piaget and many other predecessors by working, in the initial theory-construction phases of his research, with an all-male sample (Kohlberg, 1958), he became blind to women's development (deaf to women's moral voices) and to the moral saliencies noticed characteristically by women. This is not, however, to say that Gilligan thinks the Kohlbergian structural stage model does not more or less accurately represent one line of development arising from one type of experience. And it is not to say that she rejects the cognitive-developmental approach to moral development. Indeed, she with Attanucci holds that "Kohlberg's stages describe the development of justice reasoning. We have described different ways women think about care and traced changes over time in care reasoning" (Gilligan and Attanucci, 1988, p. 84).

> The quarrel with Kohlberg's stage scoring does not pertain to the structural differentiation of his levels but rather to questions of stage and sequence. Kohlberg's stages begin with an obedience and punishment orientation (Stage One), and go from there in an invariant order to instrumental hedonism (Stage Two), interpersonal concordance (Stage Three), law and order (Stage Four), social contract (Stage Five), and universal ethical principles (Stage Six).
>
> The bias that Haan and Holstein question in this scoring system has to do with the subordination of the interpersonal to the societal definition of the good in the transition from Stage Three to Stage Four. This is the transition that has repeatedly been found to be problematic for women. [Gilligan, 1977, p. 489; Gilligan cites Haan (1971) and Holstein (1976) as finding evidence of divergence between the sexes in moral development, and cites evidence for a similar conclusion in the findings of three Kohlbergian studies: Kohlberg and Kramer, 1969; Turiel, 1973; and Gilligan, Kohlberg, Lerner, and Belenky, 1971.]

The question for Gilligan in 1977 was not whether moral development can be charted along structurally differentiated levels. It was whether Kohlberg had quite captured the stages and their sequence in the cognitive-moral development of all people.

If Gilligan has not always been careful to remind us of the intended scope of her claims about the different voice she has found and describes (or perhaps has not always been careful to stick to this intention herself), she does state her intention clearly, and too many interpreters of Gilligan's argument have simply ignored this stated intention.

> The different voice I describe is characterized not by gender but theme. Its association with women is an empirical observation, and it is primarily through women's voices that I trace its development. But this association is not absolute, and the contrasts between male and female voices are presented here to highlight a distinction between two modes of thought and to focus a problem of interpretation

rather than to represent a generalization about either sex. In tracing development, I point to the interplay of these voices within each sex and suggest that their convergence marks times of crisis and change. (Gilligan, 1982, p. 2)

The different voice is a structural pattern of thought (cognition) the development of which can be traced. It happens to be found in her research primarily in women's thought, but there is nothing necessary about this. In fact, she continues,

No claims are made about the origins of the differences described or their distribution in a wider population, across cultures, or through time. Clearly, these differences arise in a social context where factors of social status and power combine with reproductive biology to shape the experience of males and females and the relations between the sexes. My interest lies in the interaction of experience and thought, in different voices and the dialogues to which they give rise, in the way we listen to ourselves and to others, in the stories we tell about our lives. (1982, p. 2; compare, e.g., p. 8f. and p. 156; and see Gilligan and Wiggins, 1987, p. 286)

The difference is not hardwired, in other words. Gilligan is not an essentialist about gender and the themes she finds associated with gender (or perhaps we should say Gilligan is not an essentialist about sex in relation to gender, if we define gender by these themes). The predominance of these voices in different sexes as well as "the interplay of these voices *within each sex*" (emphasis added) are contingent facts, explicable by reference to contextual factors influencing the combination of social status and power (the variable part) with reproductive biology (the hardwired part).

Continuing, Gilligan states the "central assumption of [her] research," completing in summary a statement of her adoption of the most basic Kohlbergian presuppositions.

Three studies are referred to throughout this book and reflect the central assumption of my research: that the way people talk about their lives is of significance, that the language they use and the connections they make reveal the world that they see and in which they act. All of the studies relied on interviews and included the same set of questions—about conceptions of self and morality, about experi-

ences of conflict and choice. The method of interviewing was to follow the language and the logic of the person's thought, with the in-
terviewer asking further questions in order to clarify the meaning of
a particular response. (1982, p. 2)

Gilligan is interested in (A) the development of two [or at least of very
few] thought structures (B) actively constructed (not passively received and internalized) by people in their everyday lives in their interaction with their environments. These cognitive structures concern conceptions of self and morality and their relation. (C) They and
their culturally variable conceptual contents more or less exhaust
the available cognitive resources for conceiving and thinking about
self and morality. (D) Furthermore, Gilligan takes what people say
about their conceptions, in response to interview questions and in-
terviewer probes for clarification, as reliable evidence of those underlying cognitive structures. Finally, (E) morality is at play exclusively
or primarily—but at the very least, in all its essentials—in situations
in which a conflict has arisen over which a choice must be made (see
also, e.g., tables 1, 2, and 4 in Lyons, 1990). That is, she adopts a
conflict-resolution model of morality. We saw in Flanagan's criticisms
of the Kohlbergian project that it is about these five elements (at least
about A, C, D, and E) of Kohlberg's theoretical presuppositions that
Flanagan is concerned, *not about what distinguishes Kohlberg from Gilligan*. Nonetheless, there are, obviously, differences.

Gilligan and her colleagues have found a way of understanding self
and of thinking about morality to which Kohlberg was deaf, at least
initially. The justice voice, according to their research (e.g., Gilligan
and Wiggins, 1987; Gilligan and Attanucci, 1988, and other essays
in Gilligan, Ward, and Taylor, 1988), is dominant—when it is dominant—primarily in men, while the care voice is dominant—when it
is dominant—primarily in women. (One voice is considered dominant if 75 percent or more of an individual's responses are codable as
justice responses or as care responses). Still, only 31 percent of subjects in three small studies (25 out of 80 total subjects, discussed together in Gilligan and Attanucci, 1988) exhibited an exclusive use of
one voice or the other, with 25 percent giving exclusively justice responses and 6 percent giving exclusively care responses.

The three studies involved as subjects thirty-four women and forty-six men, ages fifteen to seventy-seven. Respondents were asked a series of open-ended questions about their experience of "a situation of moral conflict where you have had to make a decision but weren't sure what was the right thing to do" (Gilligan and Attanucci, 1988, p. 78). Each of the interviews, which were taped and later transcribed for blind scoring, lasted about two hours. Twelve women and one man (16 percent of the 80) gave either exclusively or dominantly care responses, and ten women and thirty men (50 percent) gave either exclusively or dominantly justice responses. Twenty-seven of the subjects (roughly a third of the women (12) and a third of the men (15), 34 percent of the total, gave responses less than 75 percent codable as one of the two voices and so which were more or less mixed.

Clearly, (1) the justice voice was heard in men and women combined far more often than the care voice (even correcting for the larger number of men than women in the study); (2) the care voice was spoken by a substantial number of the subjects (50 percent gave responses at least 25 percent of which were codable as care-based); and (3) those who spoke primarily in a care voice were overwhelmingly women.

If the results of these three small studies are anywhere near representative, it is clear that talking only to boys and men would naturally lend support to the assumption that justice is the single structural core of morality in the thinking of theoretically untutored subjects. This would especially be true if one embarked on research already expecting to hear justice voices, as Kohlberg, following Piaget following Kant, did. Indeed, since 84 percent of the subjects in these three small studies gave responses at the very least 25 percent of which were justice-based, and 50 percent of the subjects (roughly a third of the women and two-thirds of the men) gave responses 75 percent+ justice-based, it is possible that one would come to this conclusion (that justice is the single structural core of morality in the thinking of theoretically untutored subjects) even if one started with *both* men and women subjects, especially if one already expected to find this conclusion. But if one started with boys aged ten to sixteen and followed them longitudinally into adulthood, and then added girls and women only after the stage theory was already constructed, and especially if one had more or less completely formulated one's notion of moral maturity (whether or not the whole stage sequence itself) in terms of justice, before one talked to any subjects at all, then it is easy to see how one would come to the conclusion that all people think about self and morality in ways based in one or another structurally whole conception of justice.

At any rate, on Gilligan's view, Kohlberg had heard only half of the story (or only three-quarters, depending on how we count). Or to change metaphors, he heard only half of the notes in the contrapuntal movement of human development, its point-counterpoint thematic (see Gilligan, 1982, e.g., p. 1 and p. 151; and see especially Gilligan, Rogers, and Brown, 1990). The half he did hear, he heard as accurately as possible in the circumstances. Yet—and this is a crucial point of Gilligan's critique—the justice voice does not develop independently of dialogue with the care voice, either interpersonally or intrapersonally. When we hear only one voice or theme in a contrapuntal movement, we do so only in ways distorted by the theme's abstraction from the whole movement. Hearing only half of the movement composing human development distorts our interpretation not only of the whole but also of the half we hear.

> Since this dialogue [between "male and female voices" speaking out of different experiences of attachment and separation in adolescence] contains the dialectic that creates the tension of human development, the silence of women in the narrative of adult development distorts the conception of its stages and sequence. Thus, I want to restore in part the missing text of women's development, as they describe their conceptions of self and morality in the early adult years. In focusing primarily on the differences between the accounts of women and men, my aim is to enlarge developmental understanding by including the perspectives of both of the sexes. While the judgments considered come from a small and highly educated sample, they elucidate a contrast and make it possible to recognize not only what is missing in women's development but also what is there. (Gilligan, 1982, p. 156)

Gilligan was in the earlier book interested more in spelling out the contrast between the two different cognitive structures than she was in being precise about exactly what are their empirically delineable loci. The important thing, from her perspective at that point, was noticing that there *is* a contrapuntal movement in human development.

Kohlberg's failure to hear the whole movement was Gilligan's central and, in important respects, her only point of contention. They were listening to the same piece. Kohlberg, as if tone deaf, just wasn't hearing all she was hearing.

The Real Issue

Some might suggest that Gilligan's beginning theory construction with "a small and highly educated sample" of predominantly middle and upper-middle class, young, white women living in the northeastern United States is not entirely unlike what she finds Kohlberg at fault for having done. This would not be quite fair. The abortion study on which the 1977 article was based involved "twenty-nine women, diverse in age, race, and social class . . . referred by abortion and pregnancy counseling services [in a large metropolitan area (Gilligan, 1982, p. 3)] and [who] participated in the study for a variety of reasons" after becoming pregnant for a variety of reasons (which Gilligan summarizes, Gilligan, 1977, p. 491). They ranged in age from fifteen to thirty-nine; some were single and some married (Gilligan, 1982, p. 3). This was in important respects not a homogeneous group, even if they were all women, which was in one way the whole point of the new inquiry.

This study along with two others formed the basis for the argument of the 1982 book. The first of the other two studies included "twenty-five students, selected at random from a group who had chosen as sophomores to take a course on moral and political choice [and who were interviewed as seniors and then five years after graduation]," along with the sixteen women of the twenty women and men who dropped the course and who were later interviewed as seniors (Gilligan, 1982, p. 2). The second of the other two studies was based on "the hypotheses generated by [the earlier two studies] . . . [which were] further explored and refined" in the third study. The third study included "a sample of males and females matched for age, intelligence, education, occupation, and social class at nine points across the life cycle: ages 6–9, 11, 15, 19, 22, 25–27, 35, 45, and 60," with "a total sample of 144 (8 males and 8 females at each age), including a more intensively interviewed subsample of 36 (2 males and 2 females at each age)" (1982, p. 3).

On the most generous interpretation we can give of the total sample on which the argument of *In a Different Voice* was based, we have 29 + 25 + 16 + 144 = 214 subjects or respondents, all of whom were living in the northeastern United States, approximately 120 (56 percent) of whom were either in elite colleges or were college age or younger at the point when they entered the studies in question, and approximately 130 (61 percent) of whom were women. Seventy-two of the approximately 85 men (85 percent of them) from the 214 total came from a single study that occurred after the other two were completed, the hypotheses for which were derived from the earlier two. The 80 of the 144 from the third study who were not college age or younger at the time of the third study made up 84 percent of the approximately 95 non-college-age-or-younger subjects in the 214 total. On a less generous interpretation, then, of the total sample on the basis of which the theory articulated in *In a Different Voice* was constructed (i.e., eliminating the third study), at the very least 41 of the 70 subjects (59 percent) were students at an elite, expensive, private northeastern university, probably three-quarters or more of whom were middle- and upper-middle-class whites, and 57 of the 70 subjects (81 percent) were women.

But the theory construction from which *In a Different Voice* proceeded began at the very least five years earlier. If "The Development of Women's Moral Judgment" (section 2 of the 1977 article) was illustrated through interviews and longitudinal follow-up interviews with twenty-nine ethnically and economically diverse women subjects in the abortion study, the "Characteristics of the Feminine Voice" (section 1 of the 1977 article) were illustrated with "examples drawn from interviews with women in and around a university community" (Gilligan, 1977, p. 482), in fact, undergraduate women at Radcliffe. Gilligan quotes from four to seven respondents, depending on how she uses the expression "other Radcliffe students," in the 1977 article. These Radcliffe students had taken part in a pilot study Gilligan conducted in 1970 on undergraduate moral development. She quotes from interviews with two other women, "a thirty-one-year-old Wellesley graduate" and "a divorced middle-aged woman, mother of adolescent daughters, resident of a sophisticated university community" (Gilligan, 1977, p. 486 and p. 487).

On the least charitable interpretation we can give, then, the subject pool on the basis of which Gilligan constructed her "different voice" theory consisted of four to seven middle and upper-middle-class, mostly (or exclusively) white women attending an elite, expensive private university in Massachusetts plus one thirty-year-old middle- or upper-middle-class (probably white) woman alumna of another Massachusetts college and a forty-something divorced middle- or upper-middle-class (probably white) woman living in Cambridge, possibly an alumna of one or the other of these elite, expensive, private Massachusetts colleges or universities. Gilligan apparently believes that, on the basis of this sample, supplementing the work she had been doing with Kohlberg interviewing people about real-life moral dilemmas, she has become able to hear all the themes in the contrapuntal movement of human development.

This, however, is grossly unfair. I have very badly misrepresented what Gilligan did, at the very least by the implications I have made. She surely began to hear themes, perhaps especially from women subjects she was interviewing as a member of Kohlberg's research team that "[fell] through the sieve of Kohlberg's scoring system" (Gilligan, 1982, p. 31), that simply didn't fit the Kohlbergian justice categories but that were common in recognizable ways. She probably began to hear unified themes in these difficult or impossible to score voices and began then to form hypotheses about what would come to be so well known as "a different voice." She began perhaps as early as 1970 (but probably two to four years later) deliberately to look for these themes and to contrast them with what the early Kohlbergian scoring manual led her and her Kohlbergian colleagues to look for. She then constructed her own studies on the basis of these hypotheses, modifying the theory she was constructing as the data she gathered indicated she should. And she has continued to this day to expand her sample base and to refine and modify her theory to accommodate apparently anomalous data (see, e.g., Bardige, Ward, Gilligan, Taylor, and Cohen, 1988).

Even if she began with what in some respects was an extremely small, very homogeneous sample, she has moved far afield from that narrow base, finding corroboration in quite heterogeneous samples of subjects, more and more locating and specifying the variables that influence the development of the two voices in a much wider variety of subjects. But this, it is now possible to see, is exactly what Kohlberg and his colleagues did, and it is with this very modus operandi that Gilligan has so famously found fault in Kohlberg. The underlying question of research methodology may be, at what point in the early stages of working with initial samples does theory construction cease and theory refinement and corroboration begin? This is simply not one of those questions to which there is an unambiguous answer. And since early pilot studies are almost always conducted before researchers fully understand what variables will in the end prove relevant, it would not be surprising if most interesting, theoretically innovative research programs in psychology were vulnerable to precisely the critique of Kohlberg which I have tried to show can be turned back on Gilligan. The point is not that both are equally guilty of some avoidable offense. It is that the charge is misdirected. It presupposes a false dichotomy between theory construction and theory corroboration.

I have set up this comparison between Gilligan's movement from her original sample and Kohlberg's movement from his original sample not out of any this-for-that, eye-for-an-eye wish for revenge. Rather I think this comparison may help us to focus on the real issue. The real issue between Gilligan and Kohlberg is not finally sex-bias or gender-bias or class-bias or race-bias or geographic-region-bias in one's initial research methodology. The real issue is rather the adequacy of one's eventual, refined definition and operationalization of moral maturity. On this point, Gilligan et al. and Kohlberg et al. (in their final statement of Stage 6) are almost indistinguishable. And this is surely at least in part because Gilligan and her colleagues made her one primary criticism of the Kohlbergian project so effectively and because Kohlberg and his colleagues, even if slowly and cautiously at first, have heard that message and taken it to heart.

In fact, responses to Gilligan's charges of sex-bias and, furthermore, occurrences of the word "care" and cognate concerns began to appear in publications issuing from the Kohlbergian research team as early as 1978, where they had been absent before. See, e.g., Colby (1978) for a response to the sex-bias charge (from the person on Kohlberg's research team chiefly responsible for managing the revision and distribution of the MJI interview and scoring manual). See also Power and Reimer (1978) for an extended discussion of the development of attitudes of mutual care and trust in the Cluster just community (from two of the people on the team most closely involved with the just community work, Power at Cluster and Reimer in the interface with the kibbutz model of community). Also, recall the final sentence in Kohlberg's (1978) introduction to the issue of *New Directions for Child Development* in which the Colby and the Power and Reimer pieces appeared. "It is my hope that these chapters will illustrate, as well as encourage, the movement of moral development research beyond either a cultist focus on moral judgment stages or a countercultist critique of them to an examination of the enduring problems of moral development and moral education" (p. 86). This was four years before the publication of *In a Different Voice*.

The Point-Counterpoint of Moral Development: Justice in a Fugue

All this leaves me with three questions to which I will attempt to provide answers in my discussion of Gilligan's criticism of the Kohlbergian project. First (recalling the last-quoted passage from Gilligan, 1982, p. 156), how are we to understand the contrapuntal dialogue between the different experiences of boys and girls and the tensions this dialogue creates in their adolescence such that we understand more fully why failing to attend to the care voice distorts our conception of human development? Second, what is Gilligan's conception of the relation between the justice and care voices in moral maturity? And, third, how is this different from Kohlberg's final formulation of Stage 6?

Gilligan and Attanucci (1988, esp. p. 73f.) explain why we find "two voices and . . . two interweaving lines of development" (Gilligan, 1988b, p. 144; see also Gilligan, 1988a, pp. xviii–xix, 4–5, 149). The care orientation, with its focus on responsiveness to the particular needs, fears, and joys of particular others, develops out of the universal experiences of attachment, dependency, and abandonment. The justice orientation, with its focus on even-handedness and respect for the integrity of all humans, develops out of the universal experiences of inequality, separation, and oppression. And all members of our species experience all of these to greater and lesser degrees in all human relationships, but especially and originally in the relationship between child and parent or guardian. We respond by actively constructing cognitive schemata that help us make sense of our experiences and orient ourselves actionally in adaptation to our environments. And because the experiences are universally similar, structurally, the cognitive schemata are structurally similar universally. Yet because of utterly contingent social constructions of gender and distributions of gender role expectations and duties, and because of the influence these happen to have on parenting and also on a society's childrearing and educational practices outside the bounds of kinship structures, girls tend to experience attachment-dependency-abandonment and inequality-separation-oppression differently from boys. (For another concise summary of this account, see Brown, Debold, Tappan, and Gilligan, 1991, pp. 28–29, and for a more elaborate version, see Gilligan and Wiggins, 1987.) But there is nothing necessary or in all likelihood universal about the way things are in this regard here now.

> At present, the question of sex differences marks a chasm between psychological theory and social reality. In many ways the lives of girls and women differ from the lives of boys and men in contemporary North American society. It would be surprising if such differences— in early childhood relationships, in adolescent experience, and in adult social and economic status—had no psychological ramifications. (Gilligan, Ward, and Taylor, 1988, Afterword, p. 291)

If this account of the circumstances in which all members of our species construct adaptive cognitive schemata were true, it would explain why there are at the very least two voices. It would also explain why, given that experiences and constructive adaptational responses vary from society to society and from relationship to relationship and from individual to individual, members of our species in all cultures, societies, and kinship groups speak and/or understand both voices in all varieties of combination. And in a society in which individualist political, legal, and commercial institutions so dominate people's lives and ways of thinking and relating, it would explain why the care voice would be relatively contained to a variety of small close-knit communities and interpersonal relationships and why the justice voice would be so audible in so many respondents, both women and men, presented with so many different interview probes. And there would be no reason, on this account, why different members of our species might not respond to identical or relevantly similar interview or real-life situations from all manner of different, idiosyncratically learned, context-sensitive combinations of the two orientations. In short, the two and only two voices Gilligan hears in the contrapuntal movement of human development might be responsible for an absolutely enormous variety for cognitive-moral personalities (compare Flanagan, 1991, pp. 209–12).

At the very least, some of this variety would be inaudible were we to fail to attend to the care-based themes in the vast repertoire of movements in the sometimes disharmonious or atonal, often polyphonic symphonies of human development. Indeed, what we could hear we would fail to interpret accurately, for the idiosyncratic but nonetheless structurally related voices we could hear would be heard without the dialogue. We would not hear the dialectic between, on the one hand, what we could understand as arising from the concern that we preserve respect for the integrity of all humans and, on the other, what we would fail to hear as arising from the concern for the needs, fears, and joys of particular others in contingent, concrete relationships with their own peculiar histories and meanings. It would be as if we were listening to one end of a complex, give-and-take phone conversation from another room, without recognizing it was actually only one end of a conversation.

Gilligan objects both to the strategy of denying anything genuinely distinct from the justice orientation and to the strategy of subsuming the care orientation within the justice orientation. Perhaps she means to reject not only the exclusion of voices heard primarily from women. She may also mean to reject the tendency to muffle variety, to reduce the complexity even at the apparent gain of avoiding what sounds (to the untrained ear?) to be relativism (see Gilligan, 1988, p. xxvii).

> The description of care concerns as the focus of a coherent moral perspective rather than as a sign of deficiency in women's moral reasoning (or a subordinate set of moral concerns within an overarching justice framework, such as concerns about special obligations or personal dilemmas) recasts the moral domain as one comprising *at least* two moral orientations. Moral maturity then presumably entails an ability to see in *at least* two ways and to speak *at least* two languages,

and the relationship between justice and care perspectives or voices becomes a key question for investigation. (Gilligan, 1988b, p. xx; emphasis added)

And so Gilligan and Attanucci assert a two-voice model of moral maturity and address the question, what is the relation between the two voices? Both voices are coherent moral perspectives or languages intertwined in dialogue with each other, which is not to say they are adequate in isolation from each other.

> The distinction made here between a justice and a care orientation pertains to the ways in which moral problems are conceived and reflects different dimensions of human relationships that give rise to moral concern. A justice perspective draws attention to problems of inequality and oppression and holds up an ideal of reciprocity and equal respect. A care perspective draws attention to problems of detachment or abandonment and holds up an ideal of attention and response to need. The two moral injunctions—not to treat others unfairly and not to turn away from someone in need—capture these different concerns. (Gilligan and Attanucci, 1988, p. 73)

Both concerns are valid and both types of injunction and orientation are necessary for a mature moral orientation.

> Our analysis of care and justice as distinct moral orientations that address different moral concerns leads us to consider both perspectives as constitutive of mature moral thinking. . . . Care Focus and Justice Focus reasoning [i.e., 75 percent+ dominant in either voice] suggest a tendency to lose sight of one perspective in reaching moral decision. The fact that the focus phenomenon was demonstrated by two-thirds of both men and women in our study suggests that *this liability is shared by both sexes*. . . . The evidence of orientation as an observable characteristic of moral judgment does not justify the conclusion that focus is a desirable attribute of moral decision. . . . it is also possible that such studies might find and elucidate further an ability to sustain two moral perspectives—an ability which according to the present data seems equally characteristic of women and men. . . . If moral maturity consists of the ability to sustain concerns about justice and care, and if the focus phenomenon indicates a tendency to lose sight of one set of concerns, then the encounter with

orientation difference can tend to offset errors in moral perception. (Gilligan and Attanucci, 1988, pp. 82–85; emphasis added)

Speaking or responding in either voice to the exclusion of the other, or in one or the other dominantly, whether justice or care, is a liability and displays a deficiency.

> The current research on moral voice documents a tendency for people to silence one voice or lose sight of one set of moral concerns when describing moral conflicts. . . . The concepts of moral voice and moral orientation which are key to the current mapping of the moral domain provide a way of representing differences which avoids simplistic views of women or men as well as the presumption of a neutral standpoint (a voiceless position) from which to make male-female comparisons. (Gilligan, Ward, and Taylor, 1988, Afterword, pp. 290–91)

It would be simplistic to think the care voice is (and incorrect to think it should be) the exclusive or even typical women's voice, and it would be simplistic to think the justice voice is (and incorrect to think it should be) the exclusive or even typical men's voice. Furthermore, it would be simplistic to think there is a neutral standpoint from which to compare men and women morally or moral developmentally. Further still, it would be simplistic to think there is a neutral control booth from which we might flip voice switches, turning on now justice and now care, as the situation or problem dictates. For the choice of which voice is appropriate, or better still, of what combination and orchestration of the two voices together sounds most appropriate, in the circumstances, cannot be made voicelessly.

Mature Orchestration

How then shall we understand how these two coherent but (in some respects) independently inadequate moral voices relate in mature orchestration? Gilligan once used the Gestalt image (e.g., duck/rabbit, faces/vase, young woman/old woman, background/foreground in a drawing of a transparent cube) as a metaphor for the relation between the justice and care perspectives (see Gilligan, 1987, and Gilligan and Wiggins, 1987; see Flanagan and Jackson, 1987). In the case of images of this type, the machinery of perceptual organization is such that we cannot see both images at once but can know both are "there," since we can vacillate, and it is such that seeing one may be more appropriate for some purposes and the other for others, in respect to *the same lines on the page*. At that point she thought of the two voices as independently adequate but for different purposes in the same context, or in different contexts, in response to different protocols of one sort or another. (Note, again, that this implies she thought of the justice perspective as adequate in its own way for its own particular purposes.) They simply cannot be integrated into a single voice, she thought, though they are not opposites anymore than men are the opposite of women.

She has changed her tune about their relative adequacy and has adopted a different metaphor to represent her new key.

> Soundings has many meanings: measuring the depth or examining the bottom of a body of water, making or giving forth sound, and sound that is resonant, sonorous. In all these senses of the word, we are taking soundings into psychological development. And we are arranging these soundings in musical terms, because by drawing a language for psychology from music rather than from the visual arts, the idea of development enters time. Psyche, or self, rather than being placed at stages, steps, or positions and marked off by borders and boundaries, can be represented as *in* relationship—relationships that exist in the medium of time or change. The experience of self can then be compared with the unity of a musical composition, where meaning at any one moment is indeterminate, since it can only be apprehended in time. Then, in speaking about development, one can speak about themes that develop, change key, recur, drop out; of discrete movements characterized by changes in rhythm and tempo; of harmonic sequences that change the sound of individual notes and intervals; of leitmotifs that convey character and dramatize the ways in which people affect or move one another. In addition, the shift away from a visual imagery that depicts Psyche or self as fixed, still, stopped in time and from positional metaphors to a musical language makes it possible to speak about differences in terms other than hierarchical arrangements or invidious comparison. (Gilligan, Rogers, and Brown, 1990)

One of the implications of changing metaphors like this, and of calling attention to the visual metaphors used typically to imagine our positions and to represent our perspectives, is that doing so implies that the visual metaphors are metaphors, that inspecting and seeing may not be somehow the very nature of knowledge acquisition and possession, that our models are models, useful for some purposes and meaningful in some respects, but in the end constructed and adopted for purposes that may have been abandoned and with intentions that may have changed. Changing metaphors can be a political act, an act of moving beyond existing or outdated arrangements that previous metaphors had been used to underwrite. Gilligan, Rogers, and Brown (1990) make their political intentions explicit. They want to make it "possible to speak about differences in terms other than hierarchical arrangements or invidious comparison" (see also Gilligan and Wiggins, 1987, p. 279).

Two things bear remembering as I explicate the musical metaphor for the relation between the justice and care voices, two things relevant to my suggestion that Gilligan's and Kohlberg's accounts of moral maturity are ultimately compatible, indeed almost indistinguishable. First, Kohlberg thought of the stages in his theory as equilibrium points in processes of constant change. The structural stage model does not require they be anything other than ideal types (see Kohlberg, Levine, and Hewer, 1983, in Kohlberg, 1984, p. 242f.), useful for charting one's progress like landmarks on a winding, nonstop journey. Second, there is no inconsistency between the political intentions of Gilligan, Rogers, and Brown and the political intentions of the practice of democratic community enacted in the Kohlbergian just community projects, beginning in 1971. These were projects whose conductor was the rumpled Harvard professor who insisted everyone, including the students at Cluster, call him "Larry."

Reflecting on Gilligan's previous work and earlier theory, and on the stage theory in contrast to which she initially defined her project, Gilligan, Rogers, and Brown reiterate their reason for proposing the musical metaphor.

> Attention to this confusion—to the tension between psychological theories of human development and the experience and situation of women—suggested that what had been represented as steps in a de-

velopmental progression might be better conceived as an interplay
of voices, creating "a contrapuntal theme, woven into the cycle of life
and recurring in varying forms in people's judgments, fantasies and
thoughts" (Gilligan, 1982, 1). This interplay of voices seemed particularly intense in the lives of both women and men at times of crisis
and change. Thus insights gained by studying women's conceptions
of self, relationship, and morality taken together with the recurrent
problems psychologists had encountered in understanding or interpreting women's experience raised the question of whether there was
a need for new language—a shift from a visual imagery of stages,
steps, positions, levels to a musical language of counterpoint and
theme. (Gilligan, Rogers, and Brown, 1990, p. 318)

Gilligan, Rogers, and Brown announce the change of metaphors in
consort with a move away from Kohlberg's Piagetian stage criteria,
and their point applies as well to Gilligan's own previous non-
Piagetian stages (see Gilligan, 1977 and 1982; also Gilligan and Murphy, 1979, and Murphy and Gilligan, 1980).

The meaning of development in its musical sense, of altering or expanding a basic melody, picking up different voices and a recurrent
contrapuntal theme, suggests the musical form of the fugue, or of a
double fugue. The OED tells us that a fugue (from the Latin *fuga,*
flight) is "a polyphonic composition on one or more short subjects
or themes, which are harmonized according to the laws of counterpoint and introduced from time to time with various contrapuntal
devices" (Stainer and Barrett 1880). Other dictionaries describe a
fugue as a musical form or composition design for a definite number
of instruments or voices in which a subject is announced in one voice
and then developed contrapuntally by each of the other voices. A
double fugue is the common term for a fugue on two subjects or
themes, in which the two begin together. This musical form is sensitive to development in its many meanings, and in a plurality of
voices. . . . The fugue, then, offers a way to listen to many voices, as
themes and variations on themes. . . . (Gilligan, Rogers, and Brown,
1990, p. 320)

They then describe the separation of themes of care and of justice
from each other in terms of plainsong melodies that are not in con-

trapuntal relation. Care Focus and Justice Focus are the plainsong of care and the plainsong of justice (pp. 321–22).

The justice and care voices, then, are related but independent melodies, capable of resonance on their own as plainsong voices but also of accompanying each other (in the musical sense of accompaniment) to form a harmonic whole. Such accompaniment in the orchestration of these two voices is a sign of moral maturity. Moral maturity "consists in the ability to sustain concerns about justice and care" but not necessarily by some predetermined measure of balance or mix. And this (I take Gilligan, Rogers, and Brown to mean) implies that a mature independence of the voices is not ruled out as appropriate on occasion, as the circumstances indicate. There is no single algorithm or set of equations that enables us to determine in abstraction from particular contexts what moral maturity will call for.

This, by the way, is not to say that determinations cannot be made objectively within their contexts. If we have here something appropriately called "contextual relativism," it is nonetheless not inconsistent with a Kohlbergian view that abstract principles inform well the reasoning of particular people in particular contexts only when people understand fully enough how the features of the context invoke those principles. Both Gilligan et al. and Kohlberg et al. hold that moral maturity requires good judgment by particular people in particular contexts. And neither requires us to imagine that judgments can be well-made out of context. On these points their accounts are indistinguishable. If Kohlberg's dilemmas were abstract and oversimplified, relative to "real life," it was not necessarily because he thought dilemmas in "real life" are uncomplicated. It could simply have been because he needed a measurement instrument that would not unnecessarily overcomplicate the measurement task—though this is a judgment call of no little consequence.

Is the MJI Sex-Biased?

Such is the account of the relation between the care and justice voices in Gilligan's two-voice model of moral maturity. I am suggesting that this account is, for all practical purposes, indistinguishable from Kohlberg's final account of Stage 6 moral maturity. This suggestion is, I concede, curious. The so-called "Kohlberg-Gilligan debate" has raged, and there has been no apparent rapprochement (see, e.g., Baumrind, 1986, and Walker, 1986).

Gilligan had articulated their disagreement originally in terms of a two-part charge of sex-bias (Gilligan, 1977, 1982). First, Kohlberg had constructed his stage theory and conception of moral maturity on the basis of an all-male sample of research subjects. This had led him to hear in the voices of boys and men the moral saliencies boys and men in contemporary Western and Westernized cultures characteristically notice, but it had prevented him from giving sufficient attention in his theory construction to the moral saliencies girls and women characteristically notice. Second, this had led to sex-bias or gender-bias in the MJI interview and scoring manual itself, and evidence for this was the way girls and women scored consistently lower than boys and men on the stage scale, apparently arresting at Stage 3.

Gilligan's (1982) account of the "different voice" in which girls and women characteristically (on her account) construct their moral awareness bore similarities to Stage 3 but traced a developmental sequence parallel to and independent of Kohlberg's justice stages. It showed that what could be seen on Kohlberg's scoring scale as arrested development could also be seen as an independent sequence of development toward a different type of moral maturity. Women and men, on this earlier account, tend to have different experiences out of which they construct different conceptions of self and relationship. (For the clearest [exaggerated] statement of this gender-difference claim, see Lyons, 1983, reprinted in Gilligan, Ward, and Taylor, 1988, and Lyons' 1982 dissertation. Though Gilligan's introduction to *In a Different Voice*, as quoted earlier, had underplayed this gender difference, stating that her interest in the book was in differences of theme contingently associated in her examples with gender and not in gender differences themselves, almost everyone interpreted the rest of the book as about gender differences and not differences of theme indeterminately associated with gender. In this reading we were not missing anything obvious.)

The responses to this sex- or gender-bias charge came as early as 1978 (as noted earlier), from, e.g., Colby, (1978). But the most decisive response came from Lawrence Walker (1984) who reviewed the MJI research and found, consistent with earlier statements by

Kohlberg and others, that there are no statistically significant differences between the scores of women and men on the MJI *when educational level and professional status are taken into account.* (An earlier version of Walker's 1984 article had been presented at the June 1982 meeting of the Canadian Psychological Association, and was quoted extensively by Kohlberg, Levine, and Hewer, 1983, in their response to Gilligan's *In a Different Voice.* See Kohlberg and Kramer, 1969; also Lyons, 1983; although not a response to Gilligan's charge, it was cited by her in the charge's formulation and discusses sex differences along with class differences on scores on the early MJI.) That is, when samples of men and women subjects are stratified according to education and profession, they score no differently on the Kohlbergian moral development measure (see also Walker, 1986, 1987, 1991).

Since the publication of Walker's studies, Gilligan has dropped (or ceased repeating) the sex- or gender-bias claim about the MJI. She and her colleagues continue to remind us, however, of the fact that Kohlberg's initial theory-construction-phase sample was all male. About this they are certainly right to remind us. And their different-voice critique is unaffected by Walker's findings. For even if women and men score identically on the MJI, that measuring instrument may still rely on an incomplete and so distorted theory of moral maturity, a theory in which only half the contrapuntal movement of human development is heard. Also, therefore, even if there are no genuine sex-based differences in scores on the MJI, that instrument may fail to measure contingent sex differences in moral development, including the development of moral reasoning. If we can empirically verify sex differences in moral orientation focus-phenomenon (and the work of Gilligan et al. at the very least goes some way in this direction), the MJI will be insensitive to these differences to the extent it fails to recognize Care Focus on its own terms. So even if the MJI is not sex-biased, it may fail to detect contingent sex differences in moral development—since differences in care reasoning may in fact show contingent sex differences even if there are no such significant differences in justice reasoning.

As I have noted, Kohlberg's own published response to the charge of bias in the theory has taken basically two forms since Gilligan's 1977 article, leading up to and including the final formulation of

Stage 6 (Kohlberg, Levine, and Hewer, 1983, and Kohlberg, Boyd, and Levine, 1990, from a paper originally presented in 1984). And though Kohlberg rejected the thesis that either his theory or his measurement instrument is sex-biased, he has conceded the importance of Gilligan's call to attend more carefully than he had at first to considerations of care and responsiveness in particular relationships (Kohlberg, Levine, and Hewer, 1983, quoted later).

Indeed, if education and professional status but not sex are significant variables affecting MJI stage scores, and if the care voice is not peculiarly or even typically feminine but is a theme arising from experiences in relationship of both men and women, it is not clear how the charge of sex-bias could be substantiated, given the current account of the origins of these voices. For imagine that empirical investigation seemed to show the care voice to be typically female but that this derived from the contingent fact that more women than men experienced attachment, dependency, and abandonment, on the one hand, and inequality, separation, and oppression, on the other, in ways that led to adaptive development in women of a dominant care voice rather than either a dominant justice voice or a more or less equal mix of the two voices. And imagine this happened because of, say, local social constructions of gender and the effects these constructs have on childrearing. This situation might not be different in kind from a situation in which men but not women typically achieved the educational and professional status associated with higher stage scores. Both of these situations involve sex-bias. But the bias in these situations is not in the test. It is in the society.

It would still be possible to argue that the test is biased for the reason that it leaves unquestioned and in fact even appears to endorse or condone existing social arrangements that yield such results. Imagine a society in which, by and large, men more often than women achieve the educational and professional status associated with higher-stage scores and in which, by and large, the effect of socially constructed gender roles and educational and childrearing practices deriving from these is that men tend to develop Justice Focus and women Care Focus. And imagine we could determine that both the local gender constructs and the educational and professional barriers to women's advancement are oppressive to women.

Would not a conception of moral maturity focusing exclusively or near exclusively on justice reasoning—and hence on reasoning typi-cal of men but not of women—endorse or condone this status quo? Would not it in effect fail to call these oppressive arrangements into question by failing to attend sufficiently to the adaptive responses of women (Care Focus) to their oppressive effects? No. In fact, quite the contrary. This hypothetical situation, which is not different enough from our own present actual situation in North America, is unfair to women. It is precisely this sort of unfairness that the justice voice recognizes as salient quite independently of the personal relationships fostered or damaged by the unfairness. And it is in adaptive response to experiences of precisely this sort of oppression that the justice voice develops in the first place, on Gilligan's own present account.

The care orientation is especially well attuned to how these social arrangements lead to harm to particular individuals in concrete cir-cumstances of attachment. The justice orientation is better equipped to address these arrangements on a society-wide scale and with re-spect to individuals with whom one is not in relationships of attach-ment. That is, the justice voice, even uncomplemented by the care voice, far from endorsing social arrangements oppressive to women, is more able to address and call into question such society-wide arrangements than is the care voice. But in fact both Gilligan and Kohlberg (before his death) adopted a model of moral maturity that requires both voices, both justice and care as equal participants in mature conversation.

TEN

The Final Description
of Moral Maturity

Kohlberg's Penultimate Response to Gilligan

Kohlberg initially held that the care orientation expands beyond the justice orientation and presupposes it, entailing "a broader ethic or valuing process" (Kohlberg and Power, 1979, reprinted in Kohlberg, 1981, see p. 354). I quote here at length from a 1983 statement by Kohlberg, Levine, and Hewer which echoes this view but also foreshadows the one that replaced it (emphases in the original, as reprinted in Kohlberg, 1984).

> In the classic studies of moral development by Hartshorne and May (1928–30), morality was defined by a narrow conception of justice as honesty and altruism, and care as "service." Modern formalist philosophers such as Frankena (1973) and Peters (1971), however, recognize at least two virtues or two principles: the principle of justice and the principle of benevolence. . . . While both of these principles are focused upon in our theory and scoring system, we admit that the "principle" of altruism, care, or responsible love has not been adequately represented in our work. This point has been made forcefully by Gilligan (1977, 1982). . . .
>
> We have come to understand Gilligan's (1982) claim as the claim that our moral dilemmas and scoring system were limited in the sense that they did not deal with dilemmas (or orientations to those dilemmas) of *special relationships and obligations.* Special relationships include relations to family, friends, and to groups of which the self is a member. We do believe that dilemma situations involving such special relationships can be handled by a universalistic justice ethic of respect for persons or rules and with the concepts of reciprocity and contract. However, we also believe that such [dilemma] situations [involving special relationships] can also be handled by a morality of *particularistic* relations which differentiate such special rela-

tionships from universalistic relationships handled by justice reasoning. Central to the ethic of particularistic relationships are affectively tinged ideas and attitudes of *caring, love, loyalty, and responsibility.* . . .

Carol Gilligan had the acuity to hear a moral orientation framed to situations or relations of particularistic care "intruding" into the responses to her dilemma about abortion, and both she and we have found this orientation sometimes "intruding" into our standard justice dilemmas. (Kohlberg, Levine, and Hewer, 1983, in Kohlberg, 1984, pp. 227–28)

The care orientation is able to handle dilemmas of special relationships, but so is the justice orientation. The justice orientation is able to handle dilemmas of competing or conflicting rights of individuals, but the care orientation is not—not adequately anyway. Even still, Kohlberg et al. have not to this point—on their own account—attended enough to "the 'principle' of altruism, care, or responsible love." Further, the care voice, the "moral orientation framed to situations or relations of particularistic care," "intrudes" into discussions of dilemmas of competing or conflicting rights. (Kohlberg, Levine, and Hewer do not explain what this shows or suggests. I think the different view articulated by Kohlberg, Boyd, and Levine (1990), discussed shortly, moves far in the direction of making sense of this "intrusion" by attending more fully to "benevolence.") However,

This and other material does *not* indicate to us that there are two separate general moralities, one morality of justice and generalized fairness and another completely separate or opposed morality of care. In our view, special obligations of care presuppose, but go beyond, the general duties of justice, which are necessary but not sufficient for them. Thus, special relationship dilemmas may elicit care responses which supplement and deepen the sense of generalized obligations of justice. In our standard dilemmas considerations of special relationship are in some sense supplementary, since they go beyond the duties owed to another on the basis of a person's rights. These considerations, however, need not be seen as being in conflict with a justice ethic; in our example, Heinz's care for his wife deepened his sense of obligation to respect her right to life. Thus, those responses to our justice dilemmas which articulate these special considerations use them as supplements to, rather than alternatives for, justice solutions to the problems posed. We believe that what Gilligan calls an ethic of care is, in and of itself, not well adapted to resolve justice problems, problems which require principles to resolve conflicting claims among persons, all of whom in some sense should be cared about. . . .

Thus, we argue that it is the different kind of dilemmas noted above that invoke different types of moral considerations. (Kohlberg, Levine, and Hewer, 1983, in Kohlberg, 1984, pp. 229–31)

So, as I have noted, on the account offered by Kohlberg, Levine, and Hewer, the care voice does not conflict with the justice voice. It presupposes and goes beyond it. Justice is a moral minimum. Care supplements the minimum. It is supererogatory. The idea is that even our "relations to family, friends, and to groups of which the self is a member" presuppose a framework of rights possessed by all individuals of the species, irrespective of our particular relations to them. A "moral orientation framed to situations or relations of particularistic care" presupposes this framework outlining minimum rights and implied duties and goes beyond it by focusing on conditions in which supplemental responsibilities can be acquired.

Citing the research by Higgins, Power, and Kohlberg (1984) in the just community setting, Kohlberg, Levine, and Hewer expand on their claim that different types of dilemmas in different settings evoke different types of consideration.

In summary, this study suggests that both considerations are used by both sexes and that preferential orientation is largely a function of the type of moral problem defined and of the sociomoral atmosphere of the environment in which the dilemma is located. Dilemmas located within a "community" or "family" context are likely to invoke caring and response considerations, so too do dilemmas of responsibility and caring that go beyond duty (i.e., supererogatory dilemmas and dilemmas of special obligation to friends and kin). In brief, choice of orientation seems to be primarily a function of setting and dilemma, not sex. (Kohlberg, Levine, and Hewer, 1983, in Kohlberg, 1984, p. 350)

As I have suggested, Gilligan et al. came to adopt more or less this account (see esp. Johnston, 1988, and Gilligan and Attanucci, 1988).

The reason we find people using the justice voice at some times and the care voice at others is that different types of dilemma situations evoke different types of response. Some are set in situations of supplemental responsibility, as in the just community settings where attitudes of mutual care and trust and of collective identity and responsibility are deliberately fostered. Some dilemmas are not set in situations of supplemental responsibility. And there is all manner of variety in the type and extent of supplemental responsibility.

Kohlberg, Levine, and Hewer concede that this was not Kohlberg's earliest understanding of the matter.

> We do agree that our justice dilemmas do not pull for the care and response orientation, and we do agree that our scoring manual does not lead to a full assessment of this aspect of moral thinking. We do not agree, however, that the justice reasoning dilemmas and stages lead to an unfair, biased downscoring of girls' and women's reasoning, as Holstein [cited in the passage quoted earlier from Gilligan (1977)] suggests, because it measures them using a stage sequence and scoring manual developed on a sample of males.
>
> The charge of sex bias in the test may have been partially true of the original (Kohlberg, 1958) method for stage scoring. (Kohlberg, Levine, and Hewer, 1983, in Kohlberg, 1984, p. 343; see also pp. 252–53)

But changes in that scoring system, distinguishing response content from underlying response rationale, have eliminated the earlier tendency to score references to norms of caring and affiliation automatically as Stage 3 responses. Changes in the theory have also integrated the care orientation into the Kohlbergian understanding of moral maturity, though (as I will show) not as fully in the account now under consideration as in the final Kohlbergian account of Stage 6 offered by Kohlberg, Boyd, and Levine (1990).

So Kohlberg, Levine, and Hewer partially accept the charge of sex-bias but only for an earlier, erroneous scoring scheme, one long since corrected. They seem to deny Gilligan's (1982, 1988) and Lyons' (1982) accounts of the experiences leading to gender-related differences in moral orientation or voice (though it is not clear they need to if they were to accept my earlier analysis). And they refer to work in the just community projects as showing how the relevant types of experience can be integrated into a single just and caring environment.

> We do not think that the experiences that lead to development on the justice side of moral judgment are distinctly different from those experiences that lead to the development of the caring side of morality. The educational approach of our colleagues to stimulating moral judgment development is called the "just community" approach. Their work indicates that experiences of democratically resolving issues of conflicting rights are interwoven with considerations of community and considerations of caring and responsibility for the group and for each of its members. In our philosophic end point of moral reasoning, the hypothetical sixth stage, there occurs, we believe, an integration of justice and care that forms a single moral principle. (Kohlberg, Levine, and Hewer, 1983, in Kohlberg, 1984, pp. 343f.; see also p. 356)

But while this notion of a single moral principle integrating justice and care is explained by Kohlberg, Boyd, and Levine (1990) as the principle of respect for persons, entailing co-integral considerations of justice and benevolence or care, Kohlberg, Levine, and Hewer (1983) hold to their account of the presupposition of the justice orientation by the distinct but not independent care orientation.

This important essay by Kohlberg, Levine, and Hewer (1983) summarized at the time of its writing the principal features of the current formulation of the stage theory and offered synopses and replies to prominent critics of the theory. This essay is at a final transition point between an initial view when care considerations were thought either not even moral considerations at all, since "justice" and morality were identified, or supererogatory moral considerations, and a final view that justice and care are co-integral parts of respect for persons, the new understanding of the core of Stage 6.

Rapprochement, Almost

Kohlberg, Boyd, and Levine (1990), in a paper first presented in 1984 at the Max Planck Institute, published in German as Kohlberg, Boyd, and Levine (1986), reintroduce Stage 6. As late as when Kohlberg, Levine, and Hewer (1983) summarized the current stage theory and responded to critics, Stage 6 had been considered "hypothetical." But after being eliminated from the theory as not adequately receiving empirical confirmation, Stage 6 is reintroduced, albeit in revised form, as the terminus of the Kohlbergian stage sequence. In reintroducing Stage 6, Kohlberg, Boyd, and Levine drop the notion that the care orientation presupposes the justice orientation. The core of Stage 6, on their account, is no longer justice but respect for persons. Or perhaps, it is no longer respect for persons defined as justice.

> The core idea that has always been the integrating factor in Kohlberg's conception of Stage 6 is that of respect for persons. In the past, discussions of the idea of respect for persons have focused primarily on a conception of justice as an essential part of this idea. Thus these discussions have emphasized the components of Stage 6 that are appropriately articulated in terms of such notions as rights, reciprocity, and equality. As Boyd (1980) has pointed out, however, an equally essential part of the idea of respect for persons is oriented toward some notion of benevolence, or "active sympathy" for others. Thus we begin our discussion of Stage 6 with our understanding of respect for persons as necessitating the awareness that justice and benevolence concerns are both necessary dimensions of moral relationships and that a coordination of these concerns must be sought in resolving moral conflicts. (Kohlberg, Boyd, and Levine, 1990, p. 153)

Care considerations are no longer thought of as supererogatory. Both types of consideration are necessary to mature moral understanding. Benevolence or "active sympathy" for others is "an equally essential part of the idea of respect for persons."

Curiously, Kohlberg, Boyd, and Levine do not once identify benevolence with care, as had Kohlberg, Levine, and Hewer (1983). (The word "care" does not occur in the 1990 essay.) They do not once mention Gilligan's work, as had Kohlberg, Levine, and Hewer. It is nonetheless clear that the final formulation of the reintroduced Stage 6 incorporates her insights. One way in which this is apparent is in their distinction of justice from benevolence in terms of a difference in the way in which separation rather than connection is assumed in the concept of self and relationship characteristic of justice considerations.

> From a Stage 6 standpoint the autonomous moral actor has to consciously coordinate the two attitudes of justice and benevolence in

dealing with real moral problems in order to maintain respect for persons. The way of regarding the other that we are calling benevolence views the other and human interaction through the lens of intending to promote good and prevent harm to the other. It is an attitude that presupposes and expresses one's *identification and empathic connection with others. . . .* Thus, as a mode of interaction between self and others that manifests a Stage 6 conception of respect for persons, benevolence is logically and psychologically prior to what we are calling justice. On the other hand, justice views the other and human interaction through the lens of intending to adjudicate interests, that is, of intending to resolve conflicts of differing and incompatible claims among individuals. Given this adjudicatory lens, justice presupposes a momentary *separation of individual wills* and cognitively organizes this separation in the service of achieving a fair adjudication through a recognition of equality and reciprocal role-taking. Thus, these two attitudes of benevolence and justice may be experienced in potential tension with each other. (Kohlberg, Boyd, and Levine, 1990, p. 157; emphasis added)

Though the language Kohlberg, Boyd, and Levine use to describe the justice-benevolence relation is different from that used by Gilligan, Rogers, and Brown (1990), this difference has little or no practical import. Justice-thinking and care- or benevolence-thinking are equally necessary for moral maturity, which requires a conscious coordination of these attitudes potentially but not necessarily in tension. Kohlberg, Boyd, and Levine might even accept the fugue metaphor developed by Gilligan, Rogers, and Brown, stating their account in terms of a contrapuntal movement. The following could easily be rewritten along those lines.

We wish to emphasize that although these attitudes are in tension with each other, they are at the same time mutually supportive and coordinated within a Stage 6 conception of respect for persons. This coordination can be summarized thus: benevolence constrains the momentary concern for justice to remain consistent with the promotion of good for all, while justice constrains benevolence not to be inconsistent with promoting respect for the rights of individuals conceived as autonomous agents. In other words, the aim of the autonomous Stage 6 moral agent is to seek resolution of moral problems in such a way that promoting good for some does not fail to respect the rights of others, and respecting the rights of individuals does not fail to seek promotion of the best for all. (Kohlberg, Boyd, and Levine, 1990, pp. 157–58)

Justice has come to be conceived as a "momentary concern" involving a "momentary separation of individual wills," autonomous wills normally better construed as selves whose identities are constituted collectively and by relationships of attachment, at least in large part. Kohlberg here may be integrating his just community model with his understanding of moral maturity as it might be articulated in the structural stage model.

Still, Kohlberg, Boyd, and Levine employ an idiom of moral principle that may not seem fully compatible with the idiom of the musical metaphor offered by Gilligan, Rogers, and Brown. Respect for persons takes a principled form at Stage 6.

As we have utilized this notion in previous discussions (Kohlberg, 1981, ch. 5; Boyd, 1978, 1984), a principle is a generalized prescriptive proposition that guides individuals in making moral judgments about situations in which there are conflicts between otherwise acceptable rules or norms. The two cases we have just quoted exemplify this understanding by articulating respect for persons as a principle of equal consideration of the dignity or worth of all persons, which, as we can see, they use to guide their specific moral decisions and generalize from one dilemma to another. (Kohlberg, Boyd, and Levine, 1990, p. 158)

But this hardly seems to be aimed at fostering "hierarchical arrangements or invidious comparison." The role of the idiom of moral principle is here what it has perhaps always been in Kohlberg's work, a counterpoint to necessary attention to the so-called "contextually relative" considerations on which difficult moral dilemmas turn. Kohlberg has never denied that good moral judgments have to be made in context. Even though he may not always have fully enough appreciated what this entails, he never denied this. What Kohlberg asserted from the beginning, though, is that a good judgment in context is equally good in every relevantly similar context. The same is the case for bad judgments. This is the real import of the criterion of universalizability.

An idiom of universal moral principle is perfectly compatible with attention to utterly unique features of particular situations arising in special relationships, as I have argued. We have to attend to the considerations most salient in such a case if we are to make a good judgment in that case. The idiom of universal moral principle employed by Kohlberg, Boyd, and Levine simply requires that were there ever to arise an identical or relevantly similar case, the same considerations would be most salient. What is most significant about the account offered by Kohlberg, Boyd, and Levine is that they now make it so explicit that considerations of special relationship are co-integral with (and apparently less "momentary" than) considerations of impersonal justice.

For even if Kohlberg, Boyd, and Levine describe benevolence and sympathy in an idiom that at points sounds abstract, it is also clear at other moments that they mean the same thing, for all practical purposes, that Gilligan has all along meant by "care." Thus, "sympathy at this stage understands that one's perception of persons and their construction [and reconstruction over time] of [their] interests in terms of [their] life plans are not independent of contingencies such as psychological, social, structural, historical, and cultural factors" (Kohlberg, Boyd, and Levine, 1990, p. 166). And "as we have interpreted the operation of sympathy, it is not simply some vague empathic connection to others, but it is what Joan [an interview respondent] calls the 'recognition of the dignity and integrity' of others as 'unique special beings.' Thus it entails an active understanding of the other in terms of his or her *own* interpretation of personal uniqueness" (Kohlberg, Boyd, and Levine, 1990, p. 170). In moral maturity, others are understood empathically, on their own terms, i.e., in terms of their own interests based on their own life plans in their own contingent psychological, social, structural, historical and cultural contexts. (Contrast the quite different understanding of what Kohlberg's view entails given by Gilligan and Wiggins, 1987, p. 291.)

My contention is that Gilligan and Kohlberg and their colleagues now offer conceptions of moral maturity that are for all practical purposes indistinguishable. That contention amounts to this. First, their accounts of moral maturity now seem isomorphic. Second, it is simply not possible to move to a concrete situation from what Kohlberg, Boyd, and Levine describe at an abstract level as respect for persons and arrive at a response both (1) demonstrably entailed by "respect for persons" and also (2) distinguishable from what the voice of care as in contrapuntal dialogue with the voice of justice would arrive at. Both the deep structures and the practical imports of moral maturity on their accounts appear to have converged completely.

This is not to say that they understand moral development itself in similar ways. Gilligan has abandoned the idea of cognitive-developmental Piagetian stage sequence. She never asserted such a model for the care orientation, and she seems at times to abjure any sort of pre-orchestrated developmental sequence. Kohlberg (1985) retained the structural stage model even in his discussion of the just community model, though it is unclear exactly how "benevolence" figures into the justice stage sequence, something he never worked out in print. But their conceptions of the terminus of development, and their adoption of basic cognitive-developmentalist assumptions about morality, render whatever disagreements remain family matters, in-house disputes.

In light of this account of the final state of the Gilligan-Kohlberg dialogue concerning moral maturity, let me spell out one of Puka's (1991b) insights (see also Puka, 1982, 1990, 1991a). Kohlberg and his colleagues have tended to emphasize what was new at each stage in the developmental sequence. They underscored the large-scale social-institutional perspective that emerges late in the stage sequence. They emphasized this perspective beginning at Stage 4 but most fully and clearly at Stages 5 and 6—as a "society-creating" rather than "society-maintaining" perspective—because it is given distinctive form in the postconventional stages. However, accentuating what is new late led Kohlberg and his colleagues to underemphasize what is carried forward and enriched, the perspective of concrete interpersonal relationships. In a way, this is finally what both Gilligan and Kohlberg came to hold. Care and justice, justice and benevolence, must be understood as two co-integral valences in morally mature understanding and responsiveness. Kohlberg's error had been in failing to continue to stress the importance of the kind of responsiveness distinctive of Stage 3. Though he had long contended that the stages are increasingly integrative and differentiating, he had emphasized new differentiations without making salient the types of responsiveness integrated into the new cognitive circuitry of the postconventional stages.

Gibbs (1977, 1979, 1991) has made a similar or related point as he has pointed out the morally mature features of some types of conventional reasoning. Stages 3B and 4B are both interpersonal and autonomous. When Snarey (1985; Snarey and Keljo, 1991) and Edwards (1981; see also Edwards, 1974, 1975, 1978, 1982, 1985, 1986a 1986b, 1987; Edwards and Whiting, 1980, and Whiting and Edwards, 1988) emphasize the way different societies accentuate filiality and collectivist interdependence, on the one hand, or justice and autonomous independence, on the other hand, they suggest equally important ways of articulating the same point. In the end, no one need deny that filiality, interdependence, care, and benevolence, on the one hand, and justice and autonomous independence, on the other hand, are universal features of mature moral understanding and responsiveness. There is of course the interesting ethnographic question about the extent to which different societies and subcultures orchestrate or accentuate these.

Conclusion

My argument, then, comes down to this. The structural stage model was underwritten by a construal of morality (via metaethical assumptions) deeply at odds with the construal of morality Kohlberg and his colleagues articulated in their work developing the just community model. In this respect—in spite of the fact that Kohlberg may have intended the just community model as an application or extension of the structural stage model—the unfinished theoretical program that combined the two models was incoherent. If Kohlberg ever imagined integrating the two models through something similar to the intersubjectivist understanding of Stage 6 (or perhaps 3B and 4B) which I described earlier, he never worked it out in print.

Furthermore, though Kohlberg and his colleagues revised the scoring categories and criteria of the MJI measurement instrument more or less continuously from the late 1960s on, the structural stage model was in all its essentials in place in the 1958 dissertation. Once

Kohlberg gained a substantial audience for his cognitive-developmental account of moral development by the late 1960s, he began to devote his creative energies to the construction of the just community model of moral education and of the practice of democratic community. His work on the MJI and the structural stage model after moving to Harvard in 1968 was mainly troubleshooting and damage control. His heart was in the just community work.

Thus, the prominent criticisms of the structural stage model published in the late 1970s and early and middle 1980s failed to deflate the project as a whole. These criticisms did partly succeed in dressing down some magnificent claims made on behalf of the structural stage model (such as that Kohlberg had finally made a science of morality, that he had empirically and theoretically captured the structural bases of all moral development in all people of all cultures for all time). But the critics did not thereby succeed in addressing, let alone devastating, the vital force of the Kohlbergian project. In fact, Kohlberg and his associates had by the late 1970s already moved the just community model to a position from which they would have been able to provide a response to some of the most damaging criticisms of the structural stage model. If Kohlberg's research team failed to meet these criticisms, it was because they continued to try to articulate the construal of morality that underwrote the just community model in the idiom of the construal that underwrote the structural stage model.

The rest of the story, the details of which are beyond the scope of the present essay, might begin as follows. Stages 1–3 are valid as the cross-cultural data indicate, insofar as the measurement instrument measures what it purports to measure (Gibbs, 1991; Snarey, 1985; Edwards, 1981, 1982, 1986a, 1986b, and 1987). However, we find Stage 4 almost exclusively in settings with complex social institutions, like a formal legal system or an administrative hierarchy (see Shweder, 1982a; Shweder and Bourne, 1982; and Shweder, Mahapatra, and Miller, 1987), and we see Stage 4 substantially in evidence there only in individuals who actively engage in activities prefigured by those institutions. Such institutions are not found in all cultural and subcultural regions of the world and are not in every case lacking where they are absent. Also, Stages 5 and 6 in their individualist form can be understood as (and, vis-à-vis substages 3B and 4B, coded as) variations on Stages 3 and 4 in "postconventional" societies (see Gibbs, 1991). Communitarian variations on Stages 3 and 4 are equally adequate in some cultural and subcultural regions—in which individualist variations are not necessarily lacking where they are absent (Snarey and Keljo, 1991).

Stage-based responses to interview-prompts may articulate the rationales for judgments and judgment tendencies only at a time lag and subsequent to those tendencies coming fully online in respondents' lives. Piaget (1932) found an analogous time lag in his examination of boys' rule-conforming behavior and rule consciousness in the game of marbles. Furthermore, justice reasoning can be highly context-sensitive, as the moral atmosphere research in the prison and school interventions indicates. People typically move among various contexts in their lives (varieties of domestic, civic, correctional, academic, political, interpersonal, judicial, religious, commercial contexts), and their reasoning and judgments adapt as they move. There are a variety not only of cultural and subcultural regions of the world but also of contexts of action and reasoning within those regions. Therefore, we should expect decalage. That is, we should not be surprised at bimodal and trimodal distributions of stage-scorable responses in which no set of responses grouped by stage reaches 66 percent of total responses. Additionally, in many cases, mature moral reasoning requires a context-sensitive balancing of partiality and impartiality, of benevolence or care and justice (Kohlberg, Boyd, and Levine, 1990; Gilligan and Attanucci, 1988; Gilligan, Rogers, and Brown, 1990). Even as impartial justice is sometimes morally necessary, it is sometimes morally inadequate.

Kohlberg seems to have resisted most, and to the end, the idea that the importance of Stages 4–6 might be culturally relative. He assumed, as I have argued, that complex social institutions *are* lacking where they are absent, or that the reasoning structures that require participation in such institutions for their development are lacking where absent—or at least that it is conceivable that such reasoning structures could become necessary in some counterfactual circumstances. To avoid this assumption, Kohlberg would have had to concede that what counts as moral maturity may vary with culture or moral atmosphere. I suggest that it is worth considering to what extent his final understanding of respect for persons (Kohlberg, Boyd, and Levine, 1990), in which justice and benevolence are co-integral constituents of morally mature reasoning, in fact amounts to this concession.

Further, the way we construe morally problematic situations plays a (in some sense at least) "structurally basic" role in how we respond in those situations. However, we do not bring our construals reflectively online in every case (such that we would explicitly frame our responses for ourselves in their terms). We reflect explicitly only when we find ourselves at an impasse, in a dilemma, when by reflection we hope to gain our bearings. Sometimes we reflect not very articulately even then. In many moral situations in which we act, we do not reflectively describe our actions to ourselves. Nor, because of the time lag, are the construals we do articulate for ourselves and/or others necessarily accurate accounts of the structural bases of our responses. We may be *more* morally mature than we are able to show by the rationales we explicitly articulate. We also may on occasion be *less* mature than we indicate by the construals we verbalize, since (because of the moral-atmosphere sensitivity of moral reasoning) we can articulate stage-sequentially advanced rationales without judging them applicable in every case. One might think, for example, that were circumstances to fall out in one particular way, the situation should be construed in Stage 6 terms—though on one's reckoning circumstances may almost never actually fall out that way. We can articulate rationales for judgments and actions that fit hypothetical scenarios in ways they do not fit the actual scenarios to which researchers may mistakenly suppose respondents believe them to be relevantly similar. We can also simply lie.

In these respects the MJI and structural stage model do not by themselves provide us with a reliable (let alone comprehensive) account of the morality of people in their everyday lives. But it is important to remember that for Kohlberg the most vital tasks are not those of description but those of construction, construction of the practice of just, democratic community. In Kohlberg's work, the purpose of an accurate philosophical and psychological description of morality is subordinate to and a means toward the end of fostering justice. The structural stage model was to enable us to understand how to do justice and address injustice without arbitrarily imposing our personal or group agendas on others. In concentrating on the shortcomings of the structural stage model, we have not yet attended sufficiently to the constructive endeavors most directly related to the ultimate aim of Kohlberg's project. These endeavors can be adequately evaluated, as Kohlberg found, only in practice. If we are to give the Kohlbergian project its due, then, we will find ourselves following Kohlberg to the construction and practice of democratic community. And this will lead us to one of the most important and enduring lessons of Kohlberg's project. Namely, comprehensive and reliable research in moral development inevitably brings experimenter and subject into active moral engagement in community with each other, and it is in such engagement within communities of justice and not finally in theory that the problem of relativism is fully addressed.

Works Cited

Adler, Jonathan E. 1989. Particularity, Gilligan, and the two-levels view: A reply. *Ethics*, 99: 149–56.

Anscombe, G. E. M. 1958. Modern moral philosophy. *Philosophy*, 33: 1–19.

Baier, Kurt. 1965. *The Moral Point of View: A Rational Basis of Ethics*, rev. ed. New York: Random House.

Bardige, Betty, Janie Victoria Ward, Carol Gilligan, Jill McLean Taylor, and Gina Cohen. 1988. Moral concerns and considerations of urban youth. In Gilligan, Ward, and Taylor, 1988, pp. 159–73.

Baumrind, D. 1986. Sex differences in moral reasoning: Response to Walker's conclusion that there are none. *Child Development*, 57: 511–21.

Benhabib, Seyla. 1987. The generalized and the concrete other: The Kohlberg-Gilligan controversy and moral theory. In Eva Feder Kittay and Diana T. Meyers, eds., *Women and Moral Theory*. Savage, Md.: Rowman and Littlefield.

Berkowitz, Marvin W., and Fritz Oser, eds. 1985. *Moral Education: Theory and Application*. Hillsdale, N.J.: Lawrence Erlbaum.

Blasi, Augusto. 1980. Bridging moral cognition and moral action: A critical review of the literature. *Psychological Bulletin*, 88: 1–45.

Blatt, Moshe. 1969. The effects of classroom discussion programs upon children's level of moral development. Ph.D. dissertation, University of Chicago.

Blatt, Moshe, and Lawrence Kohlberg. 1975. The effects of classroom moral discussion upon children's level of moral judgment. *Journal of Moral Education*, 4: 129–61.

Blum, Lawrence. 1988. Gilligan and Kohlberg: Implications for moral theory. *Ethics* 98: 472–91.

Boyd, Dwight. 1980. The Rawls connection. In B. Munsey, ed., *Moral Development, Moral Education, and Kohlberg*. Birmingham, Ala.: Religious Education Press.

Brandt, Richard. 1961. *Value and Obligation: Systematic Readings in Ethics*. New York: Harcourt.

Brown, Lyn Mikel, and Carol Gilligan. 1991. Listening for voice in narratives of relationship. *New Directions for Child Development*, 54: 43–62.

———. 1992. *Meeting at the Crossroads: Women's Psychology and Girls' Development*. New York: Ballantine.

Brown, Lyn Mikel, Elizabeth Debold, Mark Tappan, and Carol Gilligan. 1991.

Reading narratives of conflict and choice for self and moral voices: A relational method. In Kurtines and Gewirtz, 1991, vol. 2.

Colby, Anne. 1978. Evolution of a moral-developmental theory. In Damon, 1978.

Colby, Anne, and Lawrence Kohlberg. 1987a. *The Measurement of Moral Judgment*. Vol. 1: *Theoretical Foundations and Research Validation*. New York: Cambridge University Press.

———. 1987b. *The Measurement of Moral Judgment*. Vol. 2: *Standard Issue Scoring Manual*. New York: Cambridge University Press.

Colby, Anne, Lawrence Kohlberg, John Gibbs, and M. Lieberman. 1983. *A Longitudinal Study of Moral Judgment*. Monographs of the Society for Research in Child Development, 48 (1–2, serial no. 200).

Damon, William, ed. 1978. *Moral Development. New Directions for Child Development* Vol. 1, no. 2. San Francisco: Jossey-Bass.

Durkheim, Emile. 1961. *Moral Education: A Study in the Theory and Application of the Sociology of Education*. New York: The Free Press.

Dworkin, Ronald. 1976. The original position. In N. Daniels, ed., *Reading Rawls*. New York: Basic Books.

Edwards, Carolyn Pope. 1974. The effect of experience on moral development: Results from Kenya. Doctoral dissertation, Harvard University.

———. 1975. Societal complexity and moral development: A Kenyan study. *Ethos*, 3: 505–27.

———. 1978. Social experience and moral judgment in East African young adults. *Journal of Genetic Psychology*, 133: 19–29.

———. 1981. The comparative study of the development of moral judgment and reasoning. In R. H. Munrow, R. L. Munroe, and B. B. Whiting, eds., *Handbook of Cross Cultural Human Development*. New York: Garland Press.

———. 1982. Moral development in comparative cultural perspective. In D. A. Wagner and H. W. Stevenson, eds., *Cultural Perspectives on Child Development*. New York: W. H. Freeman.

———. 1985. Another style of competence: The care-giving child. In A. Fogel and G. F. Melson, eds., *Origins of Nurturance*. New York: Lawrence Erlbaum.

———. 1986a. Cross-cultural research on Kohlberg's stages: The basis for consensus. In S. Modgil and C. Modgil, eds., *Lawrence Kohlberg: Consensus and Controversy*, pp. 419–30. Philadelphia: Falmer Press.

———. 1986b. Rationality, culture, and the construction of "ethical discourse": A comparative perspective. *Ethos*, 14: 318–39.

———. 1987. Culture and the construction of moral values: A comparative ethnography of moral encounters in two cultural settings. In Kagan and Lamb, 1987, pp. 123–51.

Edwards, C. P., and Beatrice Blyth Whiting. 1980. Differential socialization of girls and boys in light of cross-cultural research. *New Directions for Child Development,* 8: 45–57.

Flanagan, Owen. 1982a. Virtue, sex, and gender: Some philosophical reflections on the moral psychology debate. *Ethics,* 93: 499–512.

———. 1982b. A reply to Lawrence Kohlberg. *Ethics,* 93: 529–32.

———. 1984. *The Science of the Mind.* Cambridge, Mass.: MIT Press/Bradford Books.

———. 1991. *Varieties of Moral Personality: Ethics and Psychological Realism.* Cambridge, Mass.: Harvard University Press.

———. 1996. Ethics naturalized: Ethics as human ecology. In May, Friedman, and Clark, 1996, pp. 19–43.

Flanagan, Owen, and Jonathan Adler. 1983. Impartiality and particularity. *Social Research,* 50: 576–96.

Flanagan, Owen, and Kathryn Jackson. 1987. Justice, care, and gender: The Kohlberg-Gilligan debate revisited. *Ethics,* 97: 622–37.

Foot, Philippa. 1958. Moral arguments. *Mind,* 67. Reprinted in Philippa Foot, *Virtues and Vices.* Berkely: University of California Press, 1978.

———. 1958–59. Moral beliefs. *Proceedings of the Aristotelian Society,* 59: 83–104.

———. 1961. Goodness and choice. *Proceedings of the Aristotelian Society,* Supplement.

Fowler, James, John Snarey, and Karen DeNicola. 1988. *Remembrances of Lawrence Kohlberg: A compilation of the presentations given at the Service of Remembrance for Lawrence Kohlberg at Memorial Church, Harvard University, on May 20, 1987.* Atlanta: Center for Research in Faith and Moral Development, Emory University.

Frankena, William K. 1973. *Ethics,* 2nd ed. Englewood Cliffs, Prentice-Hall.

Friedman, Marilyn. 1987. Care and context in moral reasoning. In Kittay and Meyers, 1987, pp. 190–204.

Gadamer, Hans-Georg. 1986. *The Idea of the Good in Platonic-Aristotelian Philosophy.* P. Christopher Smith, trans. New Haven: Yale University Press.

Galston, William A. 1982a. Moral personality and liberal theory: John Rawls' Dewey Lectures. *Political Theory,* 10: 492–519.

———. 1982b. Defending liberalism. *American Political Science Review,* 76: 621–29.

———. 1989. Pluralism and social unity. *Ethics,* 99: 711–26.

———. 1991. *Liberal Purposes: Goods, virtues, and diversity in the liberal state.* New York: Cambridge University Press.

Geach, Peter T. 1956. Good and evil. *Analysis,* 17: 33–42.

———. 1969. The moral law and the law of God. In *God and the Soul.* New York: Schocken Books.

Gibbs, John C. 1977. Kohlberg's stages of moral development: A constructive critique. *Harvard Educational Review,* 47: 43–61.

———. 1979. Kohlberg's moral stage theory: A Piagetian revision. *Human Development,* 22: 89–112.

———. 1991. Toward an integration of Kohlberg's and Hoffman's theories of morality. In Kurtines & Gewirtz, 1991, vol. 1.

Gilligan, Carol. 1977. In a different voice: Women's conceptions of the self and of morality. *Harvard Educational Review,* 47: 481–517.

———. 1982. *In a Different Voice: Psychological Theory and Women's Development.* Cambridge, Mass.: Harvard University Press.

———. 1987. Moral orientation and moral development. In Kittay and Meyers, 1987.

———. 1988a. Remapping the moral domain: New images of self in relationship. In Gilligan, Ward, and Taylor, 1988.

———. 1988b. Adolescent development reconsidered. In Gilligan, Ward, and Taylor, 1988.

Gilligan, Carol, and Jane Attanucci. 1988. Two moral orientations. In Gilligan, Ward, and Taylor, 1988, pp. 73–86.

Gilligan, Carol, and Mary F. Belenky. 1980. A naturalistic study of abortion decisions. In R. Selman and R. Yando, eds., *Clinical Developmental Psychology.* San Francisco: Jossey-Bass.

Gilligan, Carol, Lawrence Kohlberg, J. Lerner, and Mary Belenky. 1971. Moral reasoning about sexual dilemmas. Technical Report of the Commission on Obscenity and Pornography, vol. 1 (No. 52560010). Washington, D.C.: U.S. Government Printing Office.

Gilligan, Carol, and Lawrence Kohlberg. 1977 [1973]. From adolescence to adulthood: The recovery of reality in a postconventional world. Proceedings of the Piaget Society. Reprinted in M. Appeal and B. Preseissen, eds., *Topics in Cognitive Development.* New York: Plenum Press.

Gilligan, Carol, and John Michael Murphy. 1979. Development from adolescence to adulthood: The philosopher and the "dilemma of the fact." In D. Kuhn, ed., *Intellectual Development Beyond Childhood.* San Francisco: Jossey-Bass.

Gilligan, Carol, Nona P. Lyons, and Trudy J. Hanmer, eds. 1990. *Making Connections: The Relational Worlds of Adolescent Girls at Emma Willard School.* Cambridge, Mass.: Harvard University Press.

Gilligan, Carol, Annie Rogers, and Lyn Mikel Brown. 1990. Epilogue: Soundings into development. In Gilligan, Lyons, and Hanmer, 1990.

Gilligan, Carol, and Grant Wiggins. 1987. The origins of morality in early childhood relationships. In Kagan and Lamb, 1987.

Gilligan, Carol, Janie Victoria Ward, and Jill McLean Taylor, eds. 1988. *Mapping the Moral Domain: A Contribution of Women's Thinking to Psychological Theory and Education.* Cambridge, Mass.: Harvard University Press.

Haan, N. 1971. Activism as moral protest: Moral judgments of hypothetical dilemmas and an actual situation of civil disobedience. Manuscript. University of California, Berkeley.

Habermas, Jürgen. 1979. *Communication and the Evolution of Society.* T. McCarthy, trans. Boston: Beacon Press.

———. 1982. A universal ethic of communication and problems of ethical relativity and skepticism. Paper presented at the International Symposium on Moral Education. Fribourg University, Switzerland.

———. 1990a [1983]. *Moral Consciousness and Communicative Action.* Christian Lenhardt and Shierry Weber Nicholsen, trans. Cambridge, Massachusetts: MIT. Originally published in 1983 as *Moralbewusstsein und kommunikatives Handeln.* Frankfurt: Suhrkamp.

———. 1990b [1984]. Justice and solidarity: On the discussion concerning Stage 6. In Thomas E. Wren, ed., *The Moral Domain: Essays in the Ongoing Discussion between Philosophy and the Social Sciences.* Cambridge, Massachusetts: MIT. Originally presented at a conference convened by the Max Planck Institute in 1984 in Germany and published in 1986 in *Zur Bestimmung der Moral: Philosophische und sozialwissenschaftliche Beiträge zur Moralforschung.* Frankfurt: Suhrkamp.

———. 1993. *Justification and Application: Remarks on Discourse Ethics.* Ciaran P. Cronin, trans. Cambridge, Mass.: MIT.

Hare, Richard M. 1952. *The Language of Morals.* New York: Oxford University Press.

———. 1957. Geach: Good and evil. *Analysis,* 18: 103–12.

———. 1963. *Freedom and Reason.* New York: Oxford University Press.

Harkness, S., C. P. Edwards, and C. M. Super. 1981. Social roles and moral reasoning: A case study in a rural African community. *Developmental Psychology,* 17: 595–603.

Harman, Gilbert. 1977. *The Nature of Morality: An Introduction to Ethics.* New York: Oxford University Press.

Hartshorne, H., and M. A. May. 1928–30. *Studies in the Nature of Character.* Columbia University Teachers College. Vol. 1: *Studies in Deceit.* Vol. 2: *Studies in Service and Self-Control.* Vol. 3: *Studies in Organization of Character.* New York; Macmillan.

Helkama, K. 1979. The development of the attribution of responsibility: A critical survey of empirical research and a theoretical outline. *Research Reports of the Development of Social Psychology,* 3. University of Helsinki.

Hickey, J., and P. Scharf, 1980. *Toward a Just Correctional System.* San Francisco: Jossey-Bass.

Higgins, Ann. 1980. Research and measurement issues in moral education interventions. In Mosher, 1980.

———. 1989. The just community educational program: The development of moral role-taking as the expression of justice and care. In Mary Brabeck, ed. *Who Cares? Theory, Research, and Educational Implications of the Ethic of Care*. New York: Praeger.

———. 1991a. Lawrence Kohlberg: The vocation of a moral psychologist and educator. Part II. In W. M. Kurtines and J. Gewirtz, eds., *Handbook of Moral Behavior and Development*. Vol. 1: *Theory*. Hillsdale, N.J.: Lawrence Erlbaum Associates.

———. 1991b. The just community approach to moral education: Evolution of the idea and recent findings. In W. M. Kurtines and J. Gewirtz, eds., *Handbook of Moral Behavior and Development*. Vol. 3: *Application*. Hillsdale, N.J.: Lawrence Erlbaum Associates.

Higgins, A., Clark Power, and Lawrence Kohlberg. 1984. The relationship of moral atmosphere to judgments of responsibility. In W. Kurtines and J. Gewirtz, eds. *Morality, Moral Behavior, and Moral Development*. New York: Wiley.

Hobbes, Thomas. 1968 [1651]. *Leviathan*. New York: Penguin.

Holstein, C. B. 1972. The relation of children's moral judgment level to that of their parents and to communications patterns in the family. In R. C. Smart and M. S. Smart, eds., *Readings in Child Development and Relationships*. New York: Macmillan.

———. 1976. Development of moral judgment: A longitudinal study of males and females. *Child Development*, 47: 51–61.

Jennings, W., and L. Kohlberg. 1983. Effects of just community program on the moral level and institutional perceptions of youthful offenders. *Journal of Moral Education*, 12.

Johnston, D. Kay. 1988. Adolescents' solutions to dilemmas in fables: Two moral orientations—two problem-solving strategies. In Gilligan, Ward, and Taylor, 1988, pp. 49–86.

Kagan, Jerome, and Sharon Lamb. 1987. *The Emergence of Morality in Young Children*. Chicago: University of Chicago Press.

Kant, Immanuel. 1983 [1785]. *Grounding for the Metaphysics of Morals*. In *Immanuel Kant: Ethical Philosophy*. Indianapolis: Hackett. Originally published in 1785 as *Grundlegung zur Metaphysik der Sitten*.

Keeley, Joseph. 1969. *The China Lobby Man*. New Rochelle: Arlington House.

Kekes, John. 1990. *Facing Evil*. Princeton: Princeton University Press.

Kittay, Eva Feder, and Diana T. Meyers, eds. 1987. *Women and Moral Theory*. Savage, Md.: Rowman and Littlefield.

Kohlberg, Laurence [sic]. 1948. Beds for bananas: A first-hand story of the S. S. Redemption and what happened afterwards in Cyprus and in Palestine. *Menorah Journal*, 36: 285–399.

Kohlberg, Lawrence. 1958. The development of modes of moral thinking and choice in the years 10 to 16. Ph.D. dissertation, University of Chicago.

———. 1966a. Moral education in the schools. *School Review*, 74: 1–30.

———. 1966b. A cognitive-developmental analysis of children's sex-role concepts and attitudes. In E. Maccoby, ed., *The Development of Sex Differences*. Stanford: Stanford University Press.

———. 1970. Education for justice: A modern statement of the Platonic view. In T. Sizer, ed., *Moral Education: Five Lectures*. Cambridge, Mass.: Harvard University Press. Reprinted in Kohlberg, 1981.

———. 1971a. Stages of moral development as a basis for moral education. In C. M. Beck, B. S. Crittenden, and E. V. Sullivan, eds. *Moral Education: Interdisciplinary Approaches*. Toronto: University of Toronto Press.

———. 1971b. Cognitive-developmental theory and the practice of collective moral education. In Martin Wolins and Meir Gottesman, eds., *Group Care: The Educational Path of Youth Aliyah*. New York: Gordon and Breach.

———. 1971c. Indoctrination versus relativity in value education. *Zygon*, 6: 285–310. Reprinted in Kohlberg, 1981.

———. 1971d. From is to ought: How to commit the naturalistic fallacy and get away with it in the study of moral development. In T. Mischel, ed. *Cognitive Development and Epistemology*. New York: Academic Press. Reprinted in Kohlberg, 1981.

———. 1973a. Continuities in childhood and adult moral development revisited. In P. B. Battes and K. W. Schaie, eds., *Life-Span Developmental Psychology: Personality and Socialization*. New York: Academic Press.

———. 1973b. The contribution of developmental psychology to education— Examples from moral education. *Educational Psychologist*, 10: 2–14.

———. 1978. Revisions of the theory and practice of moral development. In Damon, 1978.

———. 1979. Justice as reversibility: The claim to moral adequacy of a highest stage of moral judgment. In P. Laslett and J. Fishkin, eds., *Philosophy, Politics, and Society*. Oxford: Blackwell. Reprinted in Kohlberg, 1981.

———. 1980a. Educating for a just society: An updated and revised statement. In Munsey, 1980.

———. 1980b. High school democracy and educating for a just society. In Mosher, 1980, pp. 20–57.

———. 1981. *The Philosophy of Moral Development, Essays on Moral Development*, vol. 1. San Francisco: Harper and Row.

———. 1982. A reply to Owen Flanagan and some comments on the Puka-Goodpaster exchange. *Ethics*, 92: 513–28.

———. 1984. *The Psychology of Moral Development, Essays on Moral Development*, vol. 2. San Francisco: Harper and Row.

———. 1985. The just community approach to moral education in theory and practice. In Berkowitz and Oser, 1985.

———. 1991. My personal search for universal morality. In Kuhmerker, 1991.

Kohlberg, L., Dwight Boyd, and Charles Levine. 1986. *Die wiederkehr von Stufe 6: Der moralische standpunkt der hochsten entwicklungsstufe* [The return of Stage 6: The moral standpoint of the highest developmental stage].

In W. Edelstein and G. Nunner-Winkler, eds., *Zur Bestimmung der Moral: Philosophische und sozialwissenschaftliche Beiträge zur Moralforschung.* Frankfurt: Suhrkamp.

——. 1990. The return of stage 6: Its principle and moral point of view. In Thomas Wren, ed., *The Moral Domain: Essays in the Ongoing Discussion between Philosophy and the Social Sciences.* Cambridge, Mass.: MIT Press.

Kohlberg, L., and Carol Gilligan. 1971. The adolescent as a philosopher: The discovery of the self in a post-conventional world. *Daedalus,* 100: 1051–86.

Kohlberg, L., Joseph Hickey, and Peter Scharf. 1972. The justice structure of the prison: A theory and intervention. *The Prison Journal,* 51: 3–14.

Kohlberg, L., and Ann Higgins. 1987. School democracy and social interaction. In W. M. Kurtines and J. Gewirtz, eds., *Moral Development Through Social Interaction.* New York: Wiley.

Kohlberg, L., Kelsey Kauffman, Peter Scharf, and Joseph Hickey. 1975. The just community approach to corrections: A theory. *Journal of Moral Education,* 4: 243–60.

Kohlberg, L., and L. Kramer. 1969. Continuities and discontinuities in childhood and adult moral development. *Human Development,* 12: 93–120.

Kohlberg, L., Charles Levine, and Alexandra Hewer. 1983. Moral stages: A current formulation and a response to critics. *Contributions to Human Development,* 10. Basel: S. Karger. Reprinted in Kohlberg, 1984.

Kohlberg, L., and Rochelle Mayer. 1972. Development as the aim of education. *Harvard Educational Review,* 42: 449–96.

Kohlberg, L., and Clark Power. 1981. Moral development, religious thinking, and the question of a seventh stage. *Zygon,* 16. Reprinted in Kohlberg, 1981.

Kohlberg, L., and Elliot Turiel. 1971. Moral development and moral education. In Gerald S. Lesser, ed. *Psychology and Educational Practice.* Glenview, Ill.: Scott, Foresman.

Kohlberg, L., Elsa Wasserman, and N. Richardson. 1975. Published in 1978 as *Die Gerechte Schul-Kooperative: Ihre Theorie und das Experiment der Cambridge Cluster School.* In G. Portel, ed., *Socialisation und Moral: Neuere Ansatze zur Moralishen Entwicklung und Erziehung.* Wienheim, Basel: Beltz Verlag.

Kuhmerker, Lisa, ed. 1991. *The Kohlberg Legacy for the Helping Professions.* Birmingham: R.E.P. Books.

Kurtines, William M., and Jacob L. Gewirtz. 1991. *Handbook of Moral Behavior.* Vol. 1: *Theory.* Vol. 2: *Research.* Vol. 3: *Application.* Hillsdale, N.J.: Lawrence Erlbaum.

Lapsley, Daniel K. 1996. *Moral Psychology.* Madison, Wisconsin: Brown and Benchmark.

Loevinger, J., and R. Wessler. 1970. *Measuring Ego Development 1: Construction and Use of a Sentence Completion Test.* San Francisco: Jossey-Bass.

Lyons, Nona Plessner. 1982. *Conceptions of Self and Morality and Modes of Moral Choice: Identifying Justice and Care in Judgments of Actual Moral Dilemmas.* Doctoral dissertation, Harvard University, Cambridge, Mass.

———. 1983. Two perspectives: On self, relationships, and morality. *Harvard Educational Review,* 53: 125–45. Reprinted in Kittay and Meyers, 1987.

———. 1990. Listening to voices we have not heard: Emma Willard girls' ideas about self, relationships, and morality. In Gilligan, Lyons, and Hanmer, 1990, pp. 30–73.

MacIntyre, Alasdair C. 1959. Hume is "on" and "ought." Philosophical Review. Reprinted in W. D. Hudson, ed., *The Is-Ought Question,* London: Macmillan, 1969.

———. 1979. How moral education came to find its place in the schools. *Ethics and Moral Education: A Working Paper.* National Humanities Center.

———. 1981. *After Virtue: A study in moral theory.* Notre Dame: University of Notre Dame Press.

———. 1988. *Whose Justice? Which Rationality?* Notre Dame: University of Notre Dame Press.

May, Larry, Marilyn Friedman, and Andy Clark, eds. 1996. *Mind and Morals: Essays on Cognitive Science and Ethics.* Cambridge, Mass.: MIT.

Mead, George Herbert. 1934. *Mind, Self, and Society.* Chicago: University of Chicago Press.

Mosher, Ralph, ed. 1980. *Moral Education: A First Generation of Research and Development.* New York: Praeger.

Munsey, Brenda. 1980. Cognitive developmental theory and moral development: Metaethical issues. In B. Munsey, ed., *Moral Development, Moral Education, and Kohlberg.* Birmingham, Ala.: Religious Education Press.

Murdoch, Iris. 1964. The idea of perfection. *Yale Review.* Reprinted in Iris Murdoch, *The Sovereignty of the Good.* Boston: Routledge, 1985 [1970].

Murphy, J. M., and C. Gilligan. 1980. Moral development in late adolescence and adulthood: A critique and reconstruction of Kohlberg's theory. *Human Development,* 23: 77–104.

Nagel, Thomas. 1986. *The View from Nowhere.* New York: Oxford University Press.

Nissan, M., and L. Kohlberg. 1982. Universality and cross-cultural variation in moral development: A longitudinal and cross-sectional study in Turkey. *Child Development,* 53: 865–76.

Peters, Richard S. 1971. Moral development: A plea for pluralism. In T. Mischel, ed., *Cognitive Development and Epistemology.* New York: Academic Press.

Phillips, D., and J. Nicolayev. 1978. Kohlbergian moral development: A progressing or degenerating research program. *Educational Theory,* 28: 286–301.

Piaget, Jean. 1960. The general problem of the psychological development of the child. In J. M. Tanner and B. Inhelder, eds., *Discussions on Child Development: A Consideration of the Biological, Psychological, and Cultural Approaches to the Understanding of Human Development and Behavior,* vol. 4. New York: International Universities Press.

———. 1932. *The Moral Judgment of the Child.* Marjorie Gabain, trans. New York: The Free Press.

Plato. *Euthyphro, Laches, Meno, Republic, Symposium,* and *Laws.* In Edith Hamilton and Huntington Cairns, eds., *Plato: The Collected Dialogues.* Princeton: Princeton University Press.

Power, F. Clark. 1979. The moral atmosphere of a just community high school: A four year longitudinal study. Doctoral dissertation, Harvard University.

———. 1985. Democratic moral education in the large public high school. In Berkowitz and Oser, 1985.

———. 1988a. From moral judgment to moral atmosphere: The sociological turn in Kohlbergian research. *Counseling and Values,* 32: 172–78.

———. 1988b. The just community approach to moral education. *Journal of Moral Education,* 17: 195–208.

Power, F. Clark, Ann Higgins, and Lawrence Kohlberg. 1989. *Lawrence Kohlberg's Approach to Moral Education.* New York: Columbia University Press.

Power, Clark, Ann Higgins, and Lawrence Kohlberg. 1989. The habit of the common life: Building character through democratic community schools. In Nucci, ed., 1989.

Power, Clark, and Joseph Reimer. 1978. Moral atmosphere: An educational bridge between moral judgment and action. In Damon, 1978.

Puka, William. 1982. An interdisciplinary treatment of Kohlberg. *Ethics,* 92: 468–90.

———. 1990. The majesty and mystery of Kohlberg's Stage 6. In T. Wren, ed., *The Moral Domain,* pp. 182–223. Cambridge, Mass.: MIT.

———. 1991a. Toward the redevelopment of Kohlberg's theory: Preserving essential structure, removing controversial content. In W. Kurtines and J. Gewirtz, *Handbook of Moral Behavior and Development,* vol. 1: *Theory,* pp. 373–93.

———. 1991b. Interpretive experiments: Probing the care-justice debate in moral development. *Human Development,* 34: 61–80.

Rawls, John. 1955. Two concepts of rules. *Philosophical Review,* 64: 3–32.

———. 1958. Justice as fairness. *Philosophical Review,* 67:

———. 1971. *A Theory of Justice.* Cambridge, Mass.: Harvard University Press.

———. 1980. Kantian constructivism in moral theory: The Dewey lectures 1980. *The Journal of Philosophy,* 77: 515–72.

———. 1985. Justice as fairness: Political not metaphysical. *Philosophy and Public Affairs,* 14: 223–51.

———. 1987. The idea of an overlapping consensus. *Oxford Journal of Legal Studies,* 7: 1–25.

———. 1988. The priority of right and ideas of the good. *Philosophy and Public Affairs,* 17: 251–76.

———. 1993. *Political Liberalism.* New York: Columbia University Press.

Reed, Donald R. C. 1986. Socratic moral education: Kohlberg and Plato. Doctoral dissertation, Vanderbilt University.

Reimer, Joseph. 1977. A study in the moral development of kibbutz adolescents. Doctoral dissertation, Harvard University.

———. 1981. Moral education: The just community approach. *Phi Delta Kappan,* March: pp. 485–87.

Reimer, Joseph, and Clark Power. 1980. Educating for democratic community: Some unresolved dilemmas. In Mosher, 1980.

Rest, James. 1968. Developmental hierarchy in preference and comprehension of moral judgment. Doctoral dissertation, University of Chicago.

———. 1979. *Development in Judging Moral Issues.* Minneapolis: University of Minnesota Press.

———. 1983. Morality. In J. H. Flavell and E. Markman, eds., *Manual of Child Psychology,* 4th ed., vol. 3: *Cognitive Development.* New York: Wiley.

———. 1984. Major component processes in the production of moral behavior. In W. Kurtines and J. Gewirtz, eds., *Morality, Moral Behavior, and Moral Development.* New York: Wiley.

———. 1986. *Moral Development: Advances in Research and Theory.* New York: Praeger.

———. 1988. The legacy of Lawrence Kohlberg. *Counseling and Values,* 32: 156–62.

Rorty, Richard. 1989. *Contingency, Irony, and Solidarity.* New York: Cambridge University Press.

Sandel, Michael. 1982. *Liberalism and the Limits of Justice.* New York: Cambridge University Press.

Scharf, Peter. 1973. Moral atmosphere and intervention in the prison. Doctoral dissertation, Harvard University.

Schkolnick, Lisa. 1992. Kohlberg's dilemma. Unpublished biography written for course work at the Harvard University Law School and Graduate Department of Psychology.

Selman, Robert L. 1980. *The Growth of Interpersonal Understanding: Developmental and Clinical Analyses.* New York: Academic Press.

Selman, Robert L., and A. P. Demorest. 1986. Putting thoughts and feelings into perspective: A developmental view on how children deal with interpersonal disequilibrium. In S. Modgil and C. Modgil, eds., *Lawrence Kohlberg: Consensus and Controversy,* pp. 93–128. London: Taylor and Francis.

Shweder, Richard A. 1982a. Beyond self-constructed knowledge: The study of culture and morality. *Merrill-Palmer Quarterly* 28: 41–69.

———. 1982b. Liberalism as destiny: Review of Lawrence Kohlberg's *The Philosophy of Moral Development. Contemporary Psychology,* 27: 421–24.

———. 1982c. On savages and other children: Review of C. R. Hallpike's *The Foundations of Primitive Thought. American Anthropologist,* 84: 354–66.

———. 1986. Divergent rationalities. In D. W. Fiske and R. A. Shweder, eds., *Metatheory in Social Science.* Chicago: University of Chicago Press.

———. 1990. In defense of moral realism: A reply to Gabennesch. *Child Development,* 61: 2060–67.

———. 1991. *Thinking Through Cultures: Expeditions in Cultural Psychology.* Cambridge, Mass.: Harvard University Press.

———. 1993. "Why do men barbecue?" and other postmodern ironies of growing up in the decade of ethnicity. *Daedalus,* 122: 279–308.

———. 1994. Are moral intuitions self-evident truths? Review of J. Wilson's *The Moral Sense. Criminal Justice Ethics,* 13: 24–31.

Shweder, R. A., and Edmund J. Bourne. 1982. Does the concept of the person vary cross-culturally? In A. J. Marsella and G. M. White, eds., 1982, *Cultural Conceptions of Mental Health and Therapy.* Notwell, Mass.: Kluwer: Reprinted in Shweder, 1991.

Shweder, R. A., and Jonathan Haidt. 1993. The future of moral psychology: Truth, intuition, and the pluralist way. *Psychological Science,* 4: 360–65.

Shweder, R. A., Lene Arnett Jensen, and William M. Goldstein. 1995. Who sleeps by whom revisited: A method for extracting the moral goods implicit in Practice. *New Directions for Child Development,* 67: 21–39.

Shweder, R. A., Manamohan Mahapatra, and Joan G. Miller. 1987. Culture and moral development. In Kagan and Lamb, 1987, pp. 1–83.

Shweder, R. A., and Joan G. Miller. 1985. The social construction of the person: How is it possible? In K. J. Gergen and K. E. Davis, eds. *The Social Construction of the Person.* Springer-Verlag. Reprinted in Shweder, 1991.

Shweder, R. A., and Nancy C. Much. 1987. Determinations of meaning: Discourse and moral socialization. In W. M. Kurtines and J. Gewirtz, eds., 1987, *Moral Development Through Social Interaction.* Wiley. Reprinted in Shweder, 1991.

Shweder, R. A., N. C. Much, M. Mahapatra, and Lawrence Park. In press. The "big three" of morality (autonomy, community, divinity), and the "big three" explanations of suffering. Forthcoming in A. Brandt and P. Rozin, eds., *Morality and Health.* Stanford: Stanford University Press.

Shweder, R. A., and Maria A. Sullivan. 1993. Cultural psychology: Who needs it? *Annual Review of Psychology,* 44: 497–523.

Shweder, R. A., E. Turiel, and N. C. Much. 1981. The moral intuitions of the child. In J. H. Flavell and L. Ross, eds., *Social Cognitive Development: Frontiers and Possible Futures.* New York: Cambridge University Press.

Simpson, E. L. 1974. Moral development research: A case study of scientific cultural bias. *Human Development,* 17: 81–106.

Snarey, John. 1985. The cross-cultural universality of social-moral development: A critical review of Kohlbergian research. *Psychological Bulletin,* 97: 202–32.

Snarey, John, and Kurt Keljo. 1991. In a *Gemeinschaft* voice: The cross-cultural expansion of moral development theory. In Kurtines and Gewirtz, 1991, vol. 1, pp. 395–424.

Snarey, John, Joseph Reimer, and Lawrence Kohlberg. 1985. The development of socio-moral reasoning among kibbutz adolescents: A longitudinal cross-cultural study. *Developmental Psychology,* 20: 3–17.

Stevenson, Charles Leslie. 1945. *Ethics and Language.* New Haven: Yale University Press.

———. 1965. *Facts and Values: Studies in Ethical Analysis.* New Haven: Yale University Press.

Sullivan, E. 1977. A study of Kohlberg's structural theory of moral development: A critique. *Human Development,* 20: 352–76.

Sullivan, William. 1986. *Reconstructing Public Philosophy.* Berkeley: University of California Press.

Turiel, Elliot. 1966. An experimental test of the sequentiality of developmental stages in the child's moral judgment. *Journal of Personality and Social Psychology,* 3: 611–18.

———. 1973. A comparative analysis of moral knowledge and moral judgment in males and females. Manuscript, Harvard University.

———. 1983. *The Development of Social Knowledge: Morality and Convention.* New York: Cambridge University Press.

Turiel, E., C. P. Edwards, and L. Kohlberg. 1978. Moral development in Turkish children, adolescents, and young adults. *Journal of Cross-Cultural Psychology,* 9: 75–85.

Turiel, E., Melanie Killen, and Charles C. Helwig. 1987. Morality: Its structure, functions, and vagaries. In Kagan and Lamb, 1987, pp. 155–243.

Von Wright, G. H. 1960. The Gifford Lectures. Reprinted in G. H. von Wright (1963), *The Varieties of Goodness.* Atlantic Highlands, N.J.: Humanities Press.

Walker, Lawrence. 1984. Sex differences in the development of moral reasoning: A critical review. *Child Development,* 55: 677–91.

———. 1986. Sex differences in the development of moral reasoning: A rejoinder to Baumrind. *Child Development,* 57: 522–26.

———. 1989. A longitudinal study of moral reasoning. *Child Development,* 60: 157–66.

———. 1991. Sex differences in moral reasoning. In Kurtines and Gewirtz, vol. 2, pp. 333–64.

Walker, L., B. de Vries, and S. D. Trevethan. 1987. Moral stages and moral orientations in real-life and hypothetical dilemmas. *Child Development,* 58: 842–58.

Wasserman, Elsa. 1976. Implementing Kohlberg's "just community concept" in an alternative high school. *Social Education,* 40: 203–7.

——. 1980. An alternative high school based on Kohlberg's just community approach to education. In Mosher, 1980.

Wasserman, E., and Andrew Garrod. 1983. Application of Kohlberg's theory to curricula and democratic schools. *Educational Analysis,* 5: 17–36.

White, Sheldon. 1991. Personal communication.

Whiting, B. B., and C. P. Edwards. 1988. *Children of Different Worlds: The Formation of Social Behavior.* Cambridge, Mass.: Harvard University Press.

Winch, Peter. 1959–60. Nature and convention. In P. Winch, 1972, *Ethics and Action,* pp. 50–72. London: Routledge.

Youniss, James. 1980. *Parents and Peers in Social Development: A Sullivan-Piaget Perspective.* Chicago: University of Chicago Press.

Index

abortion, 36, 88, 90, 112, 114–15, 229, 230, 247
adaptation, 74, 78, 89, 107, 135–36, 138, 141–42, 150, 156–57, 194, 214, 234, 244, 248
adequacy, 84, 86, 98, 107, 114, 124, 129, 130, 136–39, 144–50, 158–60, 232, 238
Adler, Jonathan E., 120
anomaly, 9, 13, 76, 78, 80, 83, 231
Anscombe, G. E. M., 86, 111, 115, 201
anthropology, 19, 25, 96, 197–200, 222
Antirelativism, 41, 197
Aristotle, 111, 125, 174, 176
assessment of moral development, 2, 79, 153, 184
Athens, 10–11, 102, 189, 219
attachment, 14, 64, 87, 128, 134, 197–98, 228, 233, 244, 245, 253
Attanucci, Jane, 233–34, 236–37
authoritarianism, 14, 161
authority, 4, 15, 50–51, 79, 121, 138, 171, 180, 205, 210
autonomy, 22, 50–51, 54, 56, 59, 79, 80–81, 92, 108, 135, 180, 195, 205–6, 210, 214, 218, 251–53, 257

bag of virtues, 17, 37, 120, 174, 175–80
Baier, Kurt, 118, 145
Baldwin, James Mark, 12, 15, 48, 73, 135
behaviorism, 108, 111, 210
Belenky, Mary Field, 93
Bennett, William, 174
biologically normal, 74, 125, 134
Blatt, Moshe, 12, 173, 180–83, 185, 200–201
Bloom, Allan, 133
Bobbitt, Lorena, 123
Bovet, Lucien, 48
Boyd, Dwight, 129, 212, 247, 250–55

Brandt, Richard, 116
breakdown of community, 147–48, 206
Brown, Lyn Mikel, 239–40, 252–53

care, 14, 31–34, 63–64, 83, 85, 87, 99–100, 109, 114, 148, 151, 158–59, 197, 199, 209–19, 224–58
  care orientation, 100, 235–36, 245–47, 250
  care voice, 226–28, 233–35, 240, 248–49, 255
cave (Plato's), 171
character, 6, 14, 15, 29, 38, 55, 119, 125, 165, 174–75, 177–80, 219, 238
character education partnership, 174
Cheshire Reformatory, 95, 182–83
Chicago, University of, 6, 10, 12–13, 15, 48, 133, 180, 200, 205
childhood, 3, 6, 46, 51, 97, 132–34
children, 2, 3, 5, 12, 22–24, 30, 35, 36, 47, 49–51, 57, 59, 90, 103, 105, 131, 139, 148, 151–52, 154, 158–59, 166, 171, 173, 175, 195, 196, 210, 212, 213
cluster school, 12, 95, 165, 183–91, 196, 204, 206, 212, 214, 232, 239
codification, 50, 52
cognitivism, 107–10
cognitive-developmental theory, 48, 51, 74, 107, 139, 143, 155, 156, 164, 179, 182, 184, 221, 223–25, 255, 257
cognitive-moral development, 37, 83, 86, 109, 130, 135, 144, 224, 235
Colby, Anne, 60, 232, 242
collectivism, 37, 182–84, 202, 256
  collective identity, 203–5, 218, 241
  collective responsibility, 195, 197, 202–3, 206, 209, 218
communication, 54, 199, 216